Women in the Qur'an, Traditions, and Interpretation

Women in the Qur'an, Traditions, and Interpretation

BARBARA FREYER STOWASSER

New York   Oxford
OXFORD UNIVERSITY PRESS
1994

Oxford University Press

Oxford   New York   Toronto
Delhi   Bombay   Calcutta   Madras   Karachi
Kuala Lumpur   Singapore   Hong Kong   Tokyo
Nairobi   Dar es Salaam   Cape Town
Melbourne   Auckland   Madrid

and associated companies in
Berlin   Ibadan

Copyright © 1994 by Barbara Freyer Stowasser

Published by Oxford University Press, Inc.
200 Madison Avenue, New York New York 10016

Oxford is a registered trademark of Oxford University Press, Inc.

Library of Congress Cataloging-in-Publication Data
Stowasser, Barbara Freyer, 1935–
Women in the Qur'an, traditions, and interpretation /
Barbara Freyer Stowasser.
p.   cm.   Includes bibliographical references and index.
ISBN 0-19-508480-2
1. Women in the Koran.   2. Koran—Biography.
3. Women in Islam.
I. Title.   BP134.W6S76   1994
297'.1228—dc20   94-3968

The calligraphy of the text of Sura 66,
vs. 11-12 on the book jacket is the work of Mohamed Zakariya

2 4 6 8 9 7 5 3 1

Printed in the United States of America
on acid-free paper

For my friends and colleagues
Hans-Wolfgang Liepmann,
Thomas P. McTighe,
Amin Bonnah,
and Richard Dorn

And God sets forth,
As an example
To the Believers,
The wife of Pharaoh . . .
And Mary, the daughter of Imran . . .
Qur'an, Sura 66, vs. 11–12

Preface

My interest in women in Islam is long-standing and has taken some circuitous routes in its scholarly expression. Work on women's issues in the Qur'anic text and its interpretations began more than a decade ago, first as an exercise in medieval scripturalism. The project and its implications and approaches were vitalized during a sabbatical from my university in 1985 when a Fulbright-Hays Training Grant and a Social Science Research Council Fellowship provided opportunity and means to interview scholars of the faculties of theology at Ankara University, Istanbul University, the University of Jordan in Amman, and al-Azhar University in Cairo, as well as religious officials and lay religious thinkers and leaders in Turkey, Jordan, Syria, Egypt, and Saudi Arabia. During these and later travels to the Middle East, I was shown much hospitality and support by old and new friends, including many from among the American diplomatic corps then serving in these countries.

I am grateful for the support of Georgetown University, especially that of Rev. J. Donald Freeze, S.J., (former) provost and academic vice president; Dr. James Alatis, dean of the School of Languages and Linguistics; Dr. Richard Schwartz, dean of the Graduate School; Dr. Gerald Mara, associate dean of the Graduate School; and Dr. Peter Krogh, dean of the School of Foreign Service. From among my colleagues, I extend special thanks to Dr. Karin Ryding, Dr. Irfan Shahid, Dr. Solomon Sara, S.J., Dr. Bassam Frangieh, Ms. Amira el-Zein, Ms. Zeinab Taha, Dr. Amira al-Azhari Sonbol, and Ms. Brenda Bickett, Georgetown University Arabic materials librarian. My students—who during the past decade have shared, debated, and challenged my research data—deserve special recognition. Some of them have acted as research assistants and/or personally engaged critics; here, special thanks go to Mr. John Gerald; Ms. Michele Durocher; Mr. Ramsen Betfarhad; Mr. David Mehall, who checked and formated this book's footnotes and prepared its glossary and bibliography; and Mr. Joseph Ayoub, who prepared the index. From among the many friends who have supported me during the larger research project on women in Islam and also the preparation of the present volume, special thanks go to

Dr. Laraine Mansfield; Dr. Peter Bechtold; Ms. Anne O'Leary (presently director of the American Cultural Center, Alexandria, Egypt); and also Dr. Michael Albin (Library of Congress), who was instrumental in the purchasing and shipping of classical Islamic sources in, and out of, Egypt in 1985.

I am particularly grateful to three colleagues in the field of Arab/Islamic studies: Dr. John L. Esposito, Dr. Afaf Lutfi al-Sayyid Marsot, and Dr. Yvonne Y. Haddad, all of whom read and commented on the whole or parts of this manuscript. I have benefited greatly from their constructive comments. Nevertheless, I alone bear responsibility for this book's contents.

The four friends and colleagues to whom I am dedicating this book have in many ways contributed most toward its completion; it was their support and energy that have kept me and this project afloat. Even though the present volume is not the whole story on women in Islam, I hope that it gives a credible introduction to the many dimensions of the role of the female in Islamic faith, law, and imagination. Many thanks to them and to all others who have helped me in this enterprise.

Washington, D.C.   B. F. S.
June 1993

Contents

Women in the Qur'an,
Traditions, and
Interpretation

Introduction

This book is a study in religious texts. It forms part of a larger research project on Women in Qur'an and Interpretation, which has occupied the past decade of my life. During the years of assembling the Qur'anic data and their medieval and modern interpretations, my attention was initially focused on the Qur'anic laws regarding women's social rights and obligations. The Qur'anic "lessons" (of warning and guidance) as embodied in the stories of female figures in sacred history were to be the introductory chapter to a work that was to deal with such items as women's citizenship and family roles. At some point, however, the present book began to write itself. Perhaps this was because many of the protagonists in Qur'anic sacred history were, at least initially, so familiar to me, a Lutheran Christian. Perhaps it also had to do with the fact that, while some literature of sociopolitical and legal orientation on the Muslim woman's Islamic rights and obligations was already available in Western analyses, the Qur'an's female characters had not been systematically explored. Yet, the hundreds of contemporary religious books, booklets, and pamphlets on "women's issues in Islam" that I have purchased in the Middle East present much of their teaching by reference to the models of the sacred past. Certainly the Prophet's wives, recognized early on as sources of *sunna* ("model behavior" in the terms of Islamic law), here function prominently as models for emulation. Therefore, the Islamic images of the Prophet's wives, both past and present, have been explored in the second part of this book. But the women associated with the (pre-Muhammadan) prophets from Adam to Jesus are also a living part of the contemporary Islamic religious worldview, and their lessons have remained powerful teaching devices for the community of the faithful. Following these figures' stories through the Qur'an and its medieval and modern exegesis has brought a rich harvest.

The insights garnered on this exploration are, firstly, a clearer understanding that the Qur'anic tales about the women of the sacred past are profoundly Islamic as to nature, setting, theme, theological doctrine, moral teaching, and the like. These Qur'anic narratives belong firmly to their specific Qur'anic context; they "tell themselves and bear a larger cosmic message at the same time."[1] Secondly, research on these narratives' exegetic development provided a clearer grasp of the historical importance of Bible-related traditions to Islamic scriptural commentary, especially in its initial stages, but also revealed the essentially Islamic focus and character of Muslim interpretation. By extension, thirdly, the exegetic texts proved a valuable record of the scholarly debate on sociopolitical questions, since religious thinkers past and present strive to "apply" the Qur'an's women narratives in these terms, thereby providing a number of scripture-based but differing understandings of women's status in family and society (which now include, most often by way of their rejection, such items as women's extradomestic work and political participation). It would be incorrect to label such readings of scripture as "innovations," however, because to the faithful interpreter they were and are merely the scripture's extensions, "a better disclosure of what was already there."[2] Therefore, fourthly, neither the formal *tafsir*—past and present—nor Qur'an-based literature in other forms could be classified as "interpretation" in the sense of analytical and/or unengaged inquiry. All (or most) Muslim writings quoted in this book are "extensions of scripture . . . part of its productivity . . . hence, [i.e. in the modern sense of scriptural criticism] themselves in need of interpretation."[3] Consequently, the fifth insight had to do with the larger question of "religious ideas" in two meanings of this term: ideas as ("revealed and transmitted") religious truths, and ideas as interpretations of these truths by the faithful (often taken as mores). While the Muslim authorities presented in this book clearly believed and believe that religious ideas (qua doctrines and norms) shape social reality from above, the observer who stands outside their domain takes into consideration that religious ideas are linked with social reality in mutually affective relationships, shaping it and being shaped by it in turn. Clifford Geertz has defined religion as "a cultural system of symbols"[4] in which "religious patterns" (made up of clusters of such symbols) are "frames of perception, symbolic screens through which experience is interpreted" while also being "guides for action, blueprints for conduct."[5] The importance of religion consists in "its capacity to serve, for an individual or for a group, as a source of general, yet distinctive, conceptions of the world, the self, and the relations between them. . . . Religious concepts spread beyond their specifically metaphysical contexts to provide a framework of general ideas [or paradigms] in terms of which a wide range of experience—intellectual, emotional, moral—can be given meaningful form."[6] One such paradigm of faith is the "lessons" the Qur'an imparts to the believers by way of narratives and legislation on its female characters. Comparison of its contemporary and modern formulations with those of the Middle Ages leads to the discovery of differences which demonstrate how Islamic selfperception has been conditioned by the historical situation.

The Modern Debate

The postcolonialist Muslim debate on the structure, functions, and goals of Islam in the contemporary world is a complex debate whose many participants formulate contradictory assessments and plans for action, often in tones of mutual animosity. What unites their voices is a shared vision of Islam's contemporary situation as one of crisis, and also the conviction that Islam is an important—for many the most important or even the only legitimate—force of solidarity and cohesion in today's world, and one that is now called upon to overcome the traumatic experience of Western colonialism and its legacy. Islam must combat the wrenching impact of alien forces whose influence in economic, political, and cultural permutations continues to prevail. For many religious thinkers, the goal to strengthen Islam through internal renewal (*tajdid*) is linked with the desire not to "suffer" modernity but actively accept and foster modernization, and to do so in a religious context that is in harmony with the indigenous culture. This, in turn, to many requires reenforcement as well as reformulation of the Qur'an's divinely legislated spiritual, political, social, and economic moral values, since it is only when contemporary Muslims heed the call for equality, equity, and justice—as proclaimed and exemplified in Qur'an and Sunna—that they can alleviate the harmful effects of Westernization and ensure that the Islamic world will once again be made whole.

The inner-Islamic debate on indigenous values and modernity has historical roots that reach back to the nineteenth century and beyond. New, though, is the sense of urgency that derives from the magnitude of economic, political, sociodemographic, and cultural problems in societies where traditional structures are neither solid nor unquestioned any longer, and whose problems must now be played out in a world that has shrunk to domestic dimensions. Also new are some formulations of the issues, as is the case with, for example, definitions of legitimate government and political participation and reprepresentation. In the debate on moral society, women's issues have consistently played a major role. With the beginning of the modern age and increasingly so at present, they symbolize main aspects of the Islamic struggle for the maintenance of indigenous values and "cultural authenticity." Women's questions, then, have been indicators of direction and are a parameter of the greater search for Islam's identity and role in the modern world.

Those involved in the contemporary inner-Islamic debate can be grouped into three broad categories. The *modernists* distinguish the pristine faith and way of life of the Prophet and his first community from later manifestations, which resulted from the internationalization of Islam, that is, its expansion outside of Arabia's borders, and a host of ultimately damaging acculturation processes. To derive the living value system as it was practiced in its sacred origins, modernists require *ijtihad*, individual interpretation of scripture—and also the need of legal reform (perceived as separation of the true *shari'a* from its medieval juridic formulation, the *fiqh*). In his call for the moral rebirth of Islamic society, the modernist Egyptian theologian and jurist Muhammad Abduh (d. 1905) identified women's liberation from male oppression (the latter sanctioned in the polygamy and divorce laws of medieval *fiqh* formulation) as an essential precondition for the building of a virtuous society. Abduh and his followers emphasized women's full human dignity as well as importance for the Islamic weal. In this book, modernism is represented by Muhammad Abduh's Qur'anic exegesis (known as *Tafsir al-Manar*), given form during a lecture course at al-Azhar University and first published in the monthly review *al-Manar*, which was then edited by Abduh's friend and disciple Rashid Rida (d. 1935). Abduh's commentary, which ended with Sura 4:125, was transcribed and augmented by Rida, and when Abduh died, Rida continued the *Tafsir* until Sura 12:25.[7] In addition, a number of later works by lay modernist thinkers have here also been consulted, in which women's Islamic right to sociopolitical equality with men is expressed in progressively more inclusive and absolute terms.

The *conservatives* or *traditionalists* view Islam as an inherited, balanced system of faith and action based on, and sanctioned by, scripture and its interpretation through the verifying authority of community consensus. Conservatism takes a defensive stand against modernity, which it perceives in terms of Westernization and, hence, cultural contamination. Emphasis is on the need to preserve the stable structures of past tradition, which, concerning women, stipulate female legal inequality with men as enshrined in (classical) Islamic law. Until fairly recently, modern conservatism continued to evoke the medieval theme of women's innate physical and mental deficiency as proof of the justice of their paradigm. Since the 1960s, the "deficiencies aspect" has given way to an emphasis on women's equality with men in the spiritual and cultural sense, which emphasis, however, continues to pit woman's emotionality (prime quality of the good mother) against man's rationality (prime quality of the head of household and its provider), and thereby also gives justice to the old tradition of excluding women from political participation. The conservative sources presented in what follows include works by professional theologians, especially from among the faculty of al-Azhar University, and also some by lay religious thinkers and writers.

The *fundamentalists* are scripturalist activists who see themselves as the conscience of the Islamic way of life, soldiers in Islam's battle against the forces of darkness without and within, whose ambitions parallel, in no small part, those of America's Puritan tradition and Europe's Radical Reformation. Fundamentalists insist on the literal interpretation of scripture and translate the sacred text directly into contemporary thought and action; thereby, they often bypass and disregard the work of centuries of theological-legal experts. Adverse both to diversity in local customs and also the acculturationist encrustations of the past, fundamentalists aim to formulate the true Qur'anic message in, and for, the *modern world*. This involves their rejection of past and present customary adaptations, and centers their paradigm on the Qur'anic text by means of *ijtihad* (individual scripturalist interpretation) in rejection of the conservative *'ulama'*-formulated community consensus. And in doing so, stand in political opposition and incur the wrath of the established authority in almost all Muslim nations. The fundamentalist scripture-based platform for the sociomoral reconstruction of Islam centers on issues of social equality, economic justice, and political legitimacy. In their struggle to Islamicize (infuse Islamic values into) presently immoral and corrupt, to them often "Western", structures and practices, fundamentalists recognize women as soldiers in a popular battle for communal righteousness. In her traditional role as loving wife and nurturing mother, the woman fights a holy war for the sake of Islamic values where her conduct, domesticity, and dress are vital for the survival of the Islamic way of life. Religion, morality, and culture stand and fall with her. The fundamentalist voice in what follows is mainly that of the Muslim Brother Sayyid Qutb (hanged by Nasser in 1966), whose writings continue to be influential with a wide spectrum of contemporary fundamentalist groups. Even though Qutb's Qur'anic exegesis, entitled *Fi zilal al-Qur'an,* is more "traditional" than are his later writings,[8] the fundamentalist worldview can clearly be discerned.

The following chapters will show how each of the three groups—modernists, conservatives, and fundamentalists—has understood the Qur'an's female images and models in different ways, and always in accordance with their own larger worldview and sociopolitical agenda. The interpretations thus symbolize larger ideas, while also contributing to their formation.

Medieval Sources and Approaches

In medieval religious scholarship, the variety of views expressed on the import of the Qur'an's female images and models derives largely from dogmatic differences, not sociopolitical concerns. Islam's position in the premodern, precolonialist world—and the role of women in its societies—was largely unchallenged. Its world was initially marked by territorial expansion, economic growth, and cultural preeminence in which the civil and legal formulations of Arab Islam were exported to, and also profoundly influenced by, the conquered neighboring cultures. Excepting the Christian crusaders (eleventh through thirteenth centuries) and the pagan Mongols (thirteenth century), later medieval conquests of the heartlands of Islam were accomplished by those converted powers who had adopted its spiritual and legal/social conventions. In spite of political control and exploitation by foreign (nonindigenous) Muslim dynasties, life proceeded along traditional cultural paths regardless of changes in government, that is, rulers, their soldiers, and their tax collectors. The position of women in law and society formed part of the traditional structures and coherences that firmly underlay the medieval Muslim worldview and provided for its transregional solidarities. By the time of the classical Qur'anic exegetes and historians presented in this book (ninth to fourteenth century), Islamic tradition and law had formulated a theological-legal paradigm that enshrined cultural assumptions about gender, women, and institutionalized structures governing male-female relations which mirrored the social reality and practices of the postconquest, acculturated Islamic world.[9] Once formulated, the paradigm largely prevailed because of the absence of large-scale external—or internal—challenges or pressures to change it. After women had been sucessfully excluded from institutionalized participation in public life and (at least the upper-class ones among them) had been segregated and secluded (in the privacy of rich men's harems), this state of affairs continued to underlie the theological-legal interpretation of the Qur'anic teachings on women. The system, in turn, was continually reinforced by theological-legal sanction of its justice and morality. This is why the medieval exegetic sources presented in what follows, while differing in methodology and intellectual outlook and agenda, largely agree on issues related to a woman's place in moral society and, hence, also a woman's "nature." For the medieval theologians, the Qur'an's female images and models both symbolized essential aspects of the Islamic order as they knew it, and also aided them in its preservation.

The medieval interpretations presented here range from traditionist (Hadith-based) to rationalist, legend minded to legal minded, consensus oriented to (in some measure) consensus critical.

The traditionalist Abu Ja'far Muhammad ibn Jarir al-Tabari (d. 923) authored a traditionist Qur'anic exegesis, *Jami' al-bayan 'an ta'wil ay al-Qur'an* (or *fi tafsir al-Qur'an*), and a traditionist History of the world, *Tarikh al-rusul wal-muluk*; in both he included records of hadith authentication (*isnads*) but also added lexical and grammatical explanations as well as his own scholarly comments, criticism, and valuation of the materials.

In contrast to this and other traditionist approaches in scriptural exegesis, the Qur'an commentary entitled *al-Kashshaf 'an haqa'iq al-tanzil* by the grammarian and theologian Abu l-Qasim Mahmud ibn Umar al-Zamakhshari (d. 1144) represents the rationalist approach of the Mu'tazila. (The latter school of thought, which had flourished in Iraq under Abbasid sponsorship in the early ninth century, had survived in small pockets in, especially, Northern and Western Iran.) Mu'tazilite rationalist theology argued ethical and metaphysical principles, especially the principles of God's Unity and Justice, and their implications, with the strictest logic. Mu'tazilite theology was speculative, intellectualist, and strictly Qur'anic; thus, the Mu'tazilites were neither philosophers nor freethinkers or liberals, but theologians in the strictest sense of the word. Their rationalist approach to scripture profoundly affected the course of Islamic scholastic theology (*kalam*) but not the medieval view on gender relations and women's "nature," because these issues were not part of Mu'tazilite dogmatic interest.

Mainstream (orthodox) opposition to Mu'tazilite theology was thereafter formulated by al-Ash'ari (d. 935) and his school, a school that came to dominate Sunni theology until modern times.[10] Ash'arism's greatest representative among the medieval Qur'anic exegetes was Abu Abdallah Muhammad ibn Umar ibn al-Husayn al-Razi, known as Fakhr al-Din al-Razi (d. 1209). In his enormous commentary on the Qur'an, *al-Tafsir al-kabir* (also known as *Mafatih al-ghayb*), he brilliantly fused the principles of (Qur'an-based) Ash'arism with those of *falsafa*, Islamic heir to Greek philosophy.

Abdallah ibn Umar al-Baydawi's (d. 1286?) Qur'anic interpretation *Anwar al-tanzil wa-asrar al-ta'wil* is a concise recapitulation of the gist of previous exegetic works, especially those of Zamakhshari and Razi. Because he briefly states the main issues of a Qur'anic passage and their generally accepted interpretation, Baydawi's commentary, although not original in the sense of its predecessors and sources, has achieved great popularity as a "*tafsir* reference book."

Of the works of Abu l-Fida Isma'il ibn Umar Ibn Kathir (d. 1373), the following considers his *Qisas al-anbiya'*, a two-volume work that represents the first two tomes of his universal history entitled *al-Bidaya wal-nihaya*, and also his Qur'anic commentary entitled *al-Qur'an al-'azim*. Ibn Kathir, although a Shafiite, was disciple and friend of the Hanbalite authority Ibn Taymiyya (d. 1328). Antirationalist, traditionalist, and Hadith oriented, Ibn Kathir nevertheless chose his traditions carefully. The ongoing popularity of his *Tafsir* has surely derived from the conservative tenor of his work.[11]

Of the other medieval sources presented in what follows, mention must be made of al-Kisa'i, author of a *Qisas al-anbiya'* work. The identity of the compiler of this work is unknown; his person and lifetime (twelfth century or earlier) have been subjects of debate.[12]

Among Hadith collections, this book has relied on the *Sahih* by the most respected among all Sunni Hadith collectors, Abu Abdallah Muhammad ibn Isma'il al-Bukhari (d. 869); more extensive use was made of the work by the biographer/historian/Hadith collector and critic Abu Abdallah Muhammad Ibn Sa'd (d. 845) entitled *Kitab al-tabaqat al-kabir*, of which the eighth volume ("On the Women") presents much information on the Prophet's wives.

This book on female figures in Qur'anic narrative and legislation, and their interpretations, is a study in scripturalist literature and its symbols. It hopes to achieve two major goals. First among them is to fully tell the tales themselves and report on the "lessons" and laws revealed about, and for, the women of Islamic sacred history. By following Sunni Islamic exegesis through the Middle Ages to the modern and contemporary periods, this book also intends to show the importance of the female symbol in the Islamic formulation of selfidentity, a matter vastly different in the classical period from what it became in the nineteenth and twentieth centuries. This could only be achieved through rigorous research of the primary sources. This book's main merit may lie in the disclosure of many Arabic-Islamic texts, old and new, to a Western audience. All Qur'anic and most interpretational quotations here used are based on the author's own translations of the texts. The transliteration system has been greatly simplified. It makes no use of word-external case markers, nor does it distinguish between word-internal long or short vowels. No consonants foreign to English are transscribed except for the glottal stop (*hamza*) and the voiced pharengeal fricative (*'ayn*), which are both represented here by the same symbol ('). Of these two consonants, only the *'ayn* is represented word-initially, except in proper names. Proper names and nouns are capitalized, as is the first word of Arabic book and article titles.

I

Women in Sacred History

1

The Qur'an and God's Prophets

The Qur'an, God's Word revealed to the Prophet Muhammad, teaches the believers the doctrine of its own nature. Firstly, the Arabic Qur'an is truly and literally God's Word as revealed *verbatim*[1] (word for word) and *seriatim* (in a continuous series over time)[2] to God's Prophet Muhammad, Seal of the prophets,[3] through a heavenly messenger, Gabriel.[4] Secondly, the Qur'an, Sacred Word of God, is the faithful copy of a text contained in a preexistent heavenly tablet (*lawh mahfuz*),[5] God's heavenly Scripture (*al-kitab*).[6] Thirdly, the Qur'an is God's final message to the world, a guidance for humankind.[7] Fourthly, the Qur'an followed and confirmed other, earlier revelations that, likewise taken from God's heavenly Scripture, were sent to the various peoples of history.[8] These earlier revelations, however, were incomplete.[9] In addition, the earlier monotheistic communities (mainly Jews and Christians)[10] had corrupted[11] their prophets' revelations (Torah and Evangel), so that the versions of scripture as preserved by their communities bore the traits of their falsifications.[12] The Qur'an was sent down to correct all that had thus been corrupted,[13] and also to complete God's message to the world. The Qur'an, then, is both God's original and eternal Scripture and also His last, perfect and unchangeable revelation to humankind.[14]

The Qur'an teaches that the Eternal and Everlasting God created, and continues to create, mortal man. The first human was a natural creation, fashioned from matter; he was also a special creation without equal in that God breathed into him (of) His own spirit. Jealous of man's nature, rank, and knowledge, Satan rebelled and made himself man's avowed enemy. He instigated the first act of human disobedience against God, which led to man's and woman's temporary banishment to earth. On earth, Satan has continued to work against the human by deceit and cunning, so that the human has had to wage an unceasing moral struggle between good and evil, for which his individual balance sheet will be drawn up on the Last Day.

The course of collective human history has likewise been determined by collective moral stances in that societies and civilizations have risen and endured, or declined and disappeared, according to the quality of their collective moral choices. History, like Scripture, provides clear "signs" and lessons of God's sovereignty and His intervention in human development.[15] Qur'anic history, the history recorded in the Qur'an, is the specific record of human success or failure to recognize and heed *God's sunna* (God's unalterable law, or practice, for mankind)[16] as revealed to and implemented by His messengers and prophets. In its very essence, the authority of God's prophets supercedes the authority of manmade laws and practices, ancestral traditions, "the custom of the ancients" (*sunnat al-awwalin*).[17] When during the course of history a prophet is met with disobedience, rejection, threats, and ridicule, then his rejecting people are doomed to perdition. *God's sunna* means the inevitable punishment of such disobedience, be it immediately, during the course of history, or at the end of human time.[18]

The institution of prophethood, then, is absolutely essential for humankind. Since man can only gain knowledge of God and guidance in His way through divine revelation, fulfillment of man's purpose on earth depends on the messages God reveals to whom He chooses for His spokesmen and historical agents.[19] Exegesis therefore places the beginning of prophethood in Adam, whom God "chose" (20:122; 3:33), "guided" (2:38; 20:122–123), and "taught" (2:31–33, 37).

The Qur'an does not clearly state the number of God's messengers, nor does it specify the chronological order of prophetic succession from Adam to Muhammad.[20] The Qur'an indicates, however, that God chose Adam, Noah, the family of Abraham, and the family of Amram (Imran), "descendants one of the other," as bearers of His revelation to mankind in family succession (3:33–34). Several prophetic lists are provided in the Qur'anic text. Chronologically—by order of Qur'anic revelation to the Prophet Muhammad—the earliest of these may be 26:10–189, dated into the Middle Meccan period of Muhammad's prophethood[21], which mentions Moses (Musa), Aaron (Harun), Abraham (Ibrahim), Noah (Nuh), Hud, Salih, Lot (Lut), and Shu'ayb.[22] Sura 19:1–58, also of the Middle Meccan period, mentions Zacharia (Zakariyya), his son John (Yahya), Jesus (Isa), Abraham, Isaac (Ishaq), Jacob (Ya'qub), Moses, Aaron, Ishmael (Isma'il), Idris, and Moses. The longest prophetic lists are found in 21:48–91 (Middle Meccan) and 6:83–86 (Late Meccan). In the former occur the names of Moses, Aaron, Abraham, Lot, Isaac, Jacob, Noah, David (Da'ud), Solomon (Sulayman), Job (Ayyub), Ishmael, Idris, Dhu l-Kifl, Jonah (Yunus, also *dhu al-nun*, "the man of the fish"), Zacharia, John, Mary (Maryam), and Jesus. In the latter are mentioned Abraham, Isaac, Jacob, "and before them

Noah," David, Solomon, Job, Joseph (Yusuf), Moses, Aaron, Zacharia, John, Jesus, Elijah (Ilyas), Ishmael, Elisha (al-Yasa'), Jonah, and Lot.[23] Sura 2:136 (Early Medinan) mentions Abraham, Ishmael, Isaac, Jacob and "the Tribes" (*al-asbat*, most likely the twelve sons of Jacob) as those to whom a message had been sent down; thereafter Moses and Jesus. This list is repeated in 3:84 (Medinan). Sura 3:33–34 (Medinan) mentions Adam, Noah, Abraham's family, and the family of Amram (Imran).[24] Sura 57:26–28 (likewise Medinan) anchors the prophetic succession in Noah, followed by Abraham, then prophets in their line, including the prophets Jesus and Muhammad. Sura 4:163–164 (Medinan) begins with Noah, followed by the prophets Abraham, Ishmael, Isaac, Jacob, the Tribes, Jesus, Job, Jonah, Aaron, Solomon, David, and Moses. Sura 33:7 (Medinan) gives the names of the prophets with whom God had made a solemn covenant as: Noah, Abraham, Moses, Jesus, and Muhammad.[25] For the Muslim theologian Fazlur Rahman, the most "systematic" accounts of chronology of the major prophets are found in Suras 11 (vs. 25ff) and 7 (vs. 59ff), both late Meccan Suras, in which Noah, Hud, and Salih precede Abraham and Lot, while Shu'ayb precedes Moses. Rahman points out that Arab prophetology, then, is independent of the Biblical tradition in that "except for Noah, the Arabian prophets (Hud and Salih) are more ancient than the entire Biblical tradition."[26] Early Islamic scholarship later arranged the Qur'anic prophets in chronological sequence largely corresponding to their Biblical order.

The Qur'an teaches the full humanity of all of God's prophets. It refutes as erroneous that a messenger from God would be an angel (17:94; 11:31; 41:14; 6:8–9), asserting that God's messengers are humans (21:7–8; 17:94–96; 14:11; 12:109; 7:35).[27] These eat and go about the market places (25:20), and they have wives and children (13:38). As a rule, the prophets' task is difficult, because they are mocked (15:11; 43:7; 36:30), treated as impostors (67:9; 50:12–14; 15:80; 10:39; 38:14; 23:44), and said to be possessed (51:52); they are opposed (65:8) and persecuted, even killed (3:183; 2:61 and 91; 3:21, 112, 181; 4:155). Yet it is they who come with authority delegated from God (59:6), and God expects that His messengers will be obeyed (4:64). In proof of their mission, God's prophets are given the *bayyina* ("clear evidentiary signs," or "indisputable evidence"), both in the message itself (20:133; 2:209; 6:157; 29:49) and also in the power to work miracles (17:101; 7:73; 3:184; 35:25; 16:44). Such miracles are also called *ayat* ("signs") (40:78; 21:5; 6:109, 124; 17:59), and the power to work them is bestowed by God when and how He sees fit (14:11; 29:50; 6:109).

God's prophets, then, are humans divinely chosen but most often rejected by their people. Prophets must suffer and persevere until a community forms under their leadership that accepts prophetic authority and message and, in the end, defeats the rejectors. In terms of mission and personal struggle, figures such as Noah, Abraham, Moses, Jesus, and many others are thus "prefigurations" of Muhammad. Muslim and also non-Muslim scholarship has understood the pre-Muhammadan prophetic figures of sacred history in this meaning. In a recent Western analysis of Sura 26, for instance, the prophets Moses, Abraham, Noah, Hud, Salih, Lot, and Shu'ayb have been termed "typo-

logical prefigurements" that valorized and validated Muhammad's mission
. . . and whose roles Muhammad, as their "anti-type," ultimately heightened
and fulfilled.[28] Salvation history per se has been seen as symbol "within a body
of symbols that provide a framework for religious self-understanding," where
(again in reference to Sura 26) prophetic figures "furnish exempla within the
contemporary enunciation of the text."[29]

Muslim exegesis, of course, views sacred history and the prophetic figures that constitute it from a different, "insider's" vantage point.[30] The notions
that Muhammad was prefigured in the prophets who preceded him and, especially, that Muhammad fulfilled his predecessors' roles are important elements
in the Muslim exegetic paradigm. That paradigm's touchstone, however, lies
in Muslim belief in the historical reality, that is, the historicity of the Qur'an's
prophetic events.

The Qur'an as History—Tarikh (History), Tafsir (Exegesis), Qisas al-Anbiya' (Tales of the Prophets), and a Modern Muslim Interpretation

In the Qur'an, God's prophets as successive bearers of His communication to
mankind are the main actors in human history, pivots in the development of
humankind. For the classical Muslim religious scholars and their modern conservative descendants, the events of Qur'anic history were, and are, factual
history. Thus, the prophetic events as recorded in the Qur'an must underlie a
historian's true reconstruction of the past.[31] "The monotheistic environment
of the Near East provided a powerful model for the idea that history must be
written as beginning with the creation of the world. In Islam, the tradition
continued, and history was presented as a continuum stretching seamlessly from
the six days of creation to contemporary times."[32] Tabari's (d. 923) *Tarikh
al-rusul wal-muluk* ("History of Prophets and Kings") thus begins with accounts
of the creation followed by the history of the Qur'anic prophets, patriarchs,
and "other rulers of old," to move on to the events of the rise of Islam and
later Islamic history into the author's own time.[33] Traditionist (tradition-based)
Qur'an exegesis, being both primary material source for the early chapters of
such medieval world histories and also an independent genre of scholarship
with its own agenda and dynamics[34], likewise gives abundant detail on exactly
where, and exactly when, God's prophets lived and struggled; where Adam
and his wife arrived on earth after their banishment, where and how Noah's
boat was built, precisely how many years, centuries, or generations separated
these and other prophets, and so forth.[35] Here again the clearest example of
interconnectedness of history writing and Qur'anic exegesis is provided in
Tabari, who authored the world history quoted above and also a voluminous
tafsir.[36]

In addition to these two learned literary genres—world histories or universal chronologies on the one hand, and *tafsir* works on the other—there also
existed a popular storytelling tradition of prophetic legends that was instruc-
tional and moralistic as much as it was entertaining. It appertained to the *qussas*

("narrators"), freelance preachers and popular theologians whose audiences were the illiterate masses within the mosques and without, and from it was developed the popular literary genre of *qisas al-anbiya'* ("tales of the prophets"). Some *qisas* works, however, were put together by establishment theologians, for example Ibn Kathir (d. 1373), whose two-volume *Qisas al-anbiya'* actually represents the first two volumes of his standard world history, *al-Bidaya wal-nihaya.*[37] Since some professional religious scholars, then, pursued more than one approach, the lines between world history, Qur'an exegesis proper, and *qisas al-anbiya'* works were not always clearly drawn. More important for the present discussion, however, is that the three genres equally proclaimed the historicity of Qur'anic figures and events, albeit with varying degrees of exegetic detail.[38] Bible-related tradition was there to use, especially when pitting the truth of the monotheistic tradition against the error of other religious communities.[39]

Together with this—or, rather, *within* this—fundamental acknowledgement of the historicity of the Qur'anic prophetic events, traditionist interpretation has also consistently understood the Qur'anic history materials in terms both of doctrinal teaching and legal (sociopolitical) paradigm.[40] Theological definitions of righteousness and sin, ethical individualism, free will, predestination, and the like are frequently elaborated in relation to these materials, as is the Islamic dogma on Judaism and Christianity and their relation to Islam. In addition, the exegetic search for social applicability of the tenets enshrined in the Qur'an's historical tales has likewise been persistent, especially in relation to Qur'anic women figures, as is shown below.

The classical understanding of Qur'anic prophetic history as a sequence of events defined by actual time and place was modified in the nineteenth century by the Egyptian theologian and legal authority Muhammad Abduh (d. 1905) and his modernist school. For Abduh and his disciples, Qur'anic history remains "factual" (in the meaning that its factuality is not overtly denied). Perhaps more importantly, however, Qur'anic history is also mainly understood as history of divine paradigms, lessons, examples, admonitions, "signs."[41] This shift in modernist exegesis derived from a number of factors, some of which had been prefigured in the medieval rationalist exegesis of, especially, al-Razi (d. 1209), Abduh's preferred classical source.[42]

Abduh's modernist rationalism amplified both Razi's medieval mistrust of traditional exegetic lore and also Razi's search for the spiritual and paradigmatic message and meaning of the Qur'anic tales. In his interpretation of the Adam and Eve story, for instance, Abduh contends that the story's purpose is to serve as an example of admonition and guidance; the story serves to define human nature and man's God-willed mission on earth.[43] Furthermore, the story is also understood as parable for mankind's historical development from innocence to greed and strife, to be followed, "God willing," by a better future in an age of reason and reflection.[44] Abduh goes so far as to say that this story has nothing to do with history, because history does not concern religion. Indeed, the very faultiness of the Biblical creation story as reported in The Book of Genesis lies in its claim to be history, where modern science has proved it to be wrong.[45] Simultaneously, however, Abduh appears to maintain the validity of this story as an historical document when he suggests that, perhaps, Adam and his wife were the ancestors of some nations but not of mankind as a whole, because "unlike the Torah as presently taught by the Jews, the Qur'an does not indicate that all of humanity descended from Adam, and, indeed, there are many races and nations on earth who have never heard of Adam or Eve."[46] Ultimately, Abduh declares that this matter is *mubham* ("implicit," "metaphorical") and should be left at that. Those who believe that Adam is the father of humankind, then, should go on in this belief.[47] This example may serve to show the complexity of Abduh's exegesis. Even though he consistently emphasizes the teaching-and-guidance function of Qur'anic story materials by searching for their aspect of *'ibra* ("example," "lesson," "warning"), Abduh does not disclaim that the historical elements in the Qur'an are true.[48]

Later modernist rationalist scholars of Islam have continued to read the Qur'anic prophetic accounts primarily as paradigmatic lessons on man's duty to make moral choices and build the righteous society.[49] Such interpretations lack the search for specific chronological or topographical coordinates, the implication being that a certain "ageless" quality is part of the Qur'anic stories' essence. At the same time, however, the Qur'anic events here still remain securely *within* pre-Muhammadan factual history in that all earlier Qur'anic prophets, in divinely ordained sequence, preceded Muhammad in whom their task historically found its completion. The modernist Muslim scholar Fazlur Rahman sums up the paradigmatic function of the historic tales and also their chronological/historical nature when he says "(the) task of preventing the rot, or curing it once it had set in, was the function of each community instituted by every Messenger; through Muhammad it devolved upon the Muslim community, which is charged with 'being witness upon mankind' and 'calling to goodness and prohibiting evil.'"[50]

It was precisely the dual problematic of the chronological attribution of the Qur'an's historical narratives and their paradigmatic function in the development of the Islamic message that was tackled by the Egyptian scholar Muhammad Ahmad Khalafallah in his *al-Fann al-qasasi fi al-Qur'an* ("The Art of Storytelling in the Qur'an"), originally that author's dissertation as submitted at Fu'ad University (now Cairo University) in 1947.[51] Khalafallah's thesis was mentored by Shaykh Amin al-Khuli. By the mid-1940s, the latter had introduced some new, Western-inspired courses and projects in literary criticism at Fu'ad University; he had also decided to work toward a new methodology of Qur'anic interpretation that was to utilize the disciplines of philology, psychology, and sociology, and of which Khalafallah's dissertation was an example.[52] Fu'ad University rejected Khalafallah's thesis, largely under pressure from the Azhar; furthermore, however, the "case" was popularized and kept alive by the Egyptian press, and it continued to engage Egyptian public opinion for several years.[53] The reasons for the condemnation of this piece by professional theologians and the conservative reading public alike were manifold. In part, they had to do with Khalafallah's assertion that the Qur'anic story materials were "literary pieces" that, by divine purpose, design, and style, required a different "reading" from that accorded the Qur'anic legislative verses. More importantly, Khalafallah maintained that the Qur'anic narratives were not "historical documents," even though he strongly asserted his belief that the Qur'an was the revealed word of God.[54] The divine purpose in their revelation was not to provide historical fact but principles of direction and guidance to mankind in general and, most especially, the Prophet Muhammad and his first community. Indeed, the stories were specifically sent to sustain Islam in its nascent stage,[55] to console and encourage the Prophet in his struggles against his foes and to put fear into the hearts of his opponents.[56]

The stories, says Khalafallah, were cast by God in affective language and in dramatic (*tamthili*) style.[57] He differentiates between "literary truth" (*haqiqiyya adabiyya*) and "rational truth" (*haqiqiyya 'aqliyya*)[58]; "artistic truth" (*sidq fanni*) and "rational truth" (*sidq 'aqli*);[59] "psychological logic" (*mantiq nafsi*) and "rational logic" (*mantiq 'aqli*);[60] "literary understanding" (*fahm adabi*) and "literalist understanding" (*fahm harfi*)[61]—all in order to establish that the Qur'anic revelation utilizes two different modes of divine teaching that the believer is called upon to approach and understand accordingly. According to Khalafallah, the Qur'an is cast in language that follows seventh century Arabian rules of rhetorical discourse, the divine purpose being that the Qur'an's message be fully effective in the temporal setting of nascent Islam.[62] Even legends and parables "pre-existent in the environment," that is, legends then already familiar to the Meccan pagans and their Jewish and Christian contemporaries,[63] may or could have been employed in the revelation, because God had endowed these "legends" with a new meaning and purpose. It is such narratives' new meaning and purpose, and not the factual "historical ideas" conveyed in the revelations per se, that according to Khalafallah here constitute the Qur'an's miraculous and inimitable nature (*i'jaz*);[64] this, however, also necessitates that one read the Qur'anic stories correctly as a "religious text," and not as an "historical text."

To substantiate his theory that the Qur'anic story materials "preach a lesson" rather than impart historical facts, and that "the lesson" was, historically, first directed at the Prophet Muhammad and his early community, Khalafallah subjects the materials in question to a literary-critical analysis that considers such items as: the lack of Qur'anic topographical and chronological detail provided in the lives of the prophets; the lack of the prophets' "individualization" by way of personal character traits; the fact that the Qur'an groups prophetic stories of similar "intent" without consideration of chronological sequence; the fact that "identical speech" is recorded for a number of Qur'anic prophets, while some other prophets' words and stories are related more than once and in different versions; also the fact that some prophets are dealt with in much greater detail than others.[65] He notes that the "idols" mentioned in relation to Noah are identical to the idols recognized in pagan Mecca during Muhammad's time.[66] In addition, he notes that the Qur'anic women figures remain unidentified by name[67] or physical characteristics and merely represent a number of roles, all of which were consistent with the societal norms recognized for women in the early Islamic environment."[68]

The sharp rejection that this book received by Azhar shaykhs and the con-

servative reading public in Egypt some forty years ago, then, was based on far
more than general discomfort at a new and admittedly Western-inspired literary-critical approach to the Qur'anic story materials. The main thrust of the
criticism was specifically directed at Khalafallah's reading of the Qur'anic history materials in terms that meshed (perhaps all too well) with the historical
setting and sociocultural environment of Muhammad's early prophetic career.
Because Khalafallah's reading placed the Qur'anic revelations squarely into the
historical parameters of the early Muslim community, he was perceived as questioning not only the factuality of Qur'anic prophetic history but also the eternal nature of the Qur'anic revelation (the latter accusation most vigorously
refuted by Khalafallah, in this book and elsewhere).[69] In its reaction to Khalafallah's thesis, then, Islamic conservatism reaffirmed the tenet that the Qur'an
is (among many other things) an historical source—even if it is not primarily
a book of history.[70]

Women Figures in the Qur'an: History and Mimesis

All of God's prophets and messengers, from Adam to Muhammad, were men.
Muslim consensus has established that God's blueprint for women's work in
realizing His will on earth did not include the prophethood. Some dissenting
voices were raised, however, which attributed "prophethood" (though not
"messengerhood") to several Qur'anic women figures; these will be reviewed
in the chapter on Mary (Chapter 7).

   In telling the history of God's chosen agents on earth, the Qur'an speaks
of a number of women associated with one or the other of the prophets of
God. The Qur'an relates these women's stories with varying degrees of detail
and complexity. Some figures are little more than names, or are subjects of
small vignettes, while others are drawn in larger size, depth, and detail. In
their entirety, the women's stories present a rich collection of sacred history
and paradigmatic example for Muslim contemplation and guidance.

   For the classical Muslim scholars and their modern traditionalist descendants, the women of sacred Qur'anic history, like the prophetic figures with
whom they are associated, belong into that realm of past factual events that
marked humankind's evolution toward God's final message in human time,
and of which the Prophet Muhammad received knowledge by way of revelation. While it takes the women of the Qur'an-recorded past for historical figures, this tenet does not attach importance to the fact that the figures' "chronological sequence" is not a primary Qur'anic concern. Such sequencing is
provided in some medieval universal histories and also the *qisas al-anbiya'*, "tales
of the prophets," collections. Under the acknowledged influence of religious
authorities familiar with the Bible and Bible-related lore, this literature arranged
the Qur'anic figures in a chronological order that largely reflected the Biblical one.[71]

   Even the most literalist interpreters past and present, however, have also
recognized the symbolic dimension of the Qur'anic message on the women
figures of the sacred past. It is the Qur'an itself that establishes some of the

women as "examples." In 66:10–12, four such are given, two of warning ("examples to the unbelievers": the wives of Noah and Lot) and two for emulation ("examples to the believers": Pharaoh's wife and Mary the mother of Jesus). Other figures likewise serve as examplars of sin and righteousness, weakness and strength, vice and virtue. In the female protagonists, sin is exemplified as rebellion against God, unbelief, and also disobedience toward the husband if he be righteous. Virtue is faith to the point of martyrdom, obedience to God, "purity," and obedience to the husband if he be righteous; it also is modesty, bashfulness, and motherly love. In scripture and exegesis, the female examplars of sacred history can thus be said to function as images (metaphorical extensions) of what was and is "historical reality."[72]

When drawing upon these scripturalist images for the teaching of lessons, however, Islamic exegesis past and present has extended their symbolic range to accomodate different "readings," that is, mental associations arising from the interpreter's specific worldview. Thus, the Qur'ans female exemplars (though to varying degrees) came to serve as "models," symbolic entities representing past human experience but also called upon to shape present and future human reality; their symbolic function was and is that of "models of" and also "models for" the Islamic way of life.[73] Therefore, the specific content and meaning of Qur'anic "images" and "models" have varied with the interpreters' culturally determined formulations over time. Meaning to reflect, but also to enforce, their societies' prevailing values, Islamic scripturalist scholars have molded the images of the women figures in the Qur'an to provide both cultural self-understanding and also direction[74] in ways that often changed the images' Qur'anic nature and role, that is, their first didactic import. Classical Islamic interpretation of the notion of "woman's nature" as exemplified in Adam's wife, for instance, represents an example of cultural adaptation of the Qur'anic theme of female ethical responsibility and freedom. Here as elsewhere, the "shift in understanding" was achieved by way of adaptation of Bible-related lore (isra'iliyyat). Even beyond Eve, women's spiritual freedom and moral responsibility are prominent Qur'anic themes that appear in the revelations both symbolically (personified in sacred history) and also in the form of community-directed legislation. Many of the Qur'an's women's stories bear the lesson that a woman's faith and righteousness depend on her own will and decision, and that neither association with a godly man nor a sinner decides a woman's commitment to God. Medieval Islamic exegesis, however, viewing women's innate nature as weak but also dangerous to the established moral order, largely excluded the Qur'anic theme of female spiritual freedom and moral responsibility in favor of the exegetic maxim that "woman is (i.e., should be) man's follower in all things." Here as elsewhere, modern interpretation has shown a marked difference from the classical in formulation and application of the Qur'anic "examples."

The stories the Qur'an tells of women in sacred history are richer, however, than Muslim theological and legal exegesis could contain, and these have reverberated, beyond the codes born of normative scholarly endeavor, in popular pious imagination and the arts. This is most clearly the case with those rich Qur'anic parables of human nature—tales of desire, and love, and the striving for political power—that teach of the clash of human ambition with God's plan. Exegesis has here woven colorful tapestries around the Qur'anic protagonists. Furthermore, some of the Qur'anic women figures have become the heroines of medieval epics and also medieval and modern folk tales and romances. Especially in the latter, their Qur'anic personae are developed beyond the realm of pious legend or Sufi teaching into figures of fiction in love and adventure stories. While Qur'an-related epics, romances, and popular tales go beyond scope and purpose of this book, some of the story materials recorded in *tafsir* and *qisas al-anbiya'* works will be considered.

The following chapters present the Qur'anic revelations on the women of sacred history, followed by an introduction to their exegesis. Several approaches have here been pursued in order to show that the interrelationship of scripturalist "images" and Muslim selfperception has occurred in a variety of modes. On the figures of Eve, Zulaykha (the Aziz's, or "Potiphar's," wife), and Mary the mother of Jesus, the interpretations are taken from a series of major Sunni Qur'an commentaries, that is, the *tafasir* of the traditionalist Tabari (d. 923); the Mu'tazilite rationalist Zamakhshari (d. 1144) and the Ash'arite rationalist Razi (d. 1209); the traditionalists Baydawi (d. 1286?) and Ibn Kathir (d. 1373); the modernists Muhammad Abduh (d. 1905) and Rashid Rida (d. 1935); and the fundamentalist Sayyid Qutb (d. 1966). Furthermore, some modern Qur'an- and Hadith-related literature by theologians and lay writers has been considered as well. In the chapters on Eve and the Aziz's wife, this approach shows the changes in Muslim perceptions of women's nature, status, and appropriate societal roles over time. (In the case of Mary mother of Jesus, exegesis is more purely concerned with problems of theological dogma, not women's questions. Thus the chapter on Mary primarily presents the evolution of her story as well as some related theological issues in medieval and modern interpretation). Exegesis on the remaining Qur'anic women figures is documented mainly by way of *qisas al-anbiya'* materials. Serving to solve some scripturalist issues but also to nourish and give form to pious imagination, these materials were part of medieval Islamic religious culture, and their echo continues to sound in modern inspirational tales and literature for the pious.

In introducing the format and material-based themes of the following chapters, it is worthy of note that, on women's issues, not only the "pious tales" of the *qisas al-anbiya'* but also the medieval works of Qur'anic exegesis and world history of scholarly provenance have consistently and widely relied on Bible-related traditions.[75] In a seminal article on the *isra'iliyyat* (Bible-related traditions), Gordon Newby has stipulated that such traditions, important in early Muslim Qur'anic commentary and sacred history writing, lost stature and formative function in Islamic selfdefinition when the early Abbasid jurists, and among them especially al-Shafi'i (d. 820), developed the theoretical framework for the formulation of Islamic law. Inasmuch as the latter established the Prophet Muhammad's *sunna* (exemplary behavior) as a source of law second only to the Qur'an, all other inspirational models (such as those contained in the *isra'iliyyat*) failed to meet the criteria of the new, and stricter, religious principles, and thus the *isra'iliyyat* "fell out of favor and were relegated to the entertainment genre of the *qisas al-anbiya'*."[76] In medieval establishment exegetic literature on the Qur'anic women figures, however, this "falling out of favor" of *isra'iliyyat* cannot be discerned. To a large part, this must be related to the fact that medieval Islamic society was patriarchal to a far higher degree than had been the early Islamic community in Mecca and Medina, first recipient of the Qur'an's revelations. Even though the Islamic conquests had established Islam's message in the conquered territories outside of the Arabian Peninsula where it largely superceded the older, antecedent religions (mainly Zoroastrianism in Iran and Orthodox Christianity in the Byzantine provinces), indigenous culture, customs, and institutions in these areas, in turn, left their imprint on the emerging medieval Islamic civilization, including much that had to do with women's status questions. The medieval establishment theologians who then and thereafter interpreted God's revealed word for their contemporaries were, themselves, urbanized and acculturated spokesmen of and for their societies' values. While formulating normative interpretations of the Qur'an's women parables in accordance with existing social norms and values, these scholars' consensus, of need, embraced and canonized preexisting traditions in scripturalist language.

In Islamic exegetic literature, the Bible-related traditions continued to impart to the faithful hagiographic detail on the women figures of Islam's sacred history, which included illustration and clarification of points of Islamic doctrine and even ritual. At the same time, they helped to enforce some of the sociopolitical values underlying the medieval Islamic worldview. Thus, Bible-related traditions, including their symbolic images of the female's defective nature, were seemlessly integrated into an Islamic framework. The following chapters document that the theme of "woman's weakness" with its paradoxical twin, "woman as threat to the male and society," dominated the Islamic scripture-based paradigm on gender throughout the medieval period, and that *isra'iliyyat* played a major part in its formulation. What, then, of the negative reaction that *isra'iliyyat* traditions received on the part of medieval religious scholarship (beginning with the rise of the Abbasid age), which prompted formulation of new criteria for traditionist authenticity, with the goal to eliminate *isra'iliyyat* from the Islamic corpus? In his work on the Abraham-Ishmael legends in Islamic exegesis, Reuven Firestone, noting the pervasive and enduring role of "Israelite tales" on Biblical characters in Islamic religious literature as a whole, has correctly drawn a distinction between these materials as a literary genre and the specific term "*isra'iliyyat*," a derogatory label first documented in the ninth century which applied only to traditions considered inauthentic (by way of chain of transmission) or, much more importantly, which were in opposition to Islamic doctrine (or even an author's point of view).[77] The bulk of Bible-related traditions, "which were in keeping with Islamic sensibilites, were not affected."[78] The modern age, which in the Arab world had its first stirrings in the eighteenth century and broke in full force during the nineteenth, required a different scripturalist canon on women. As the images of female spiritual, mental, and physical defectiveness were being replaced by those of female nurturing strength and the female's importance in the struggle for cultural survival, the old Bible-related legends ceased to be meaningful. It is, therefore, in nineteenth-century modernist exegesis that we find a full-scale rejection of *isra'iliyyat* traditions. The following chapters document that, in their search for new paradigms on gender issues, contemporary Islamic modernism and fundamentalism have both continued and even intensified this rejective stance. Here, the semantic range of the term *isra'iliyyat* has also expanded considerably. In keeping with the modernist and fundamentalist focus on the Qur'anic text (and concomitant de-emphasis of Hadith as a whole), *isra'iliyyat* has come to mean any kind of medieval "lore," from the phantastic, scurrilous, or merely legendary to the paradigmatic no longer in tune with modern doctrine. The moderns' use of the term *isra'iliyyat* perpetuates the medieval meaning of "stamp-of-disapproval," but it is also made to apply to a far wider range of traditions. Inasmuch as conservative/traditionalist thought is by nature anchored in past conventions, Bible-related traditions of gender images have survived in conservative exegesis into the twentieth century. But even here, the pressures of a changed world have begun to affect changes in the nature of the conservative message on women's role in Islam, and the usefulness of *isra'iliyyat* within that message.

In what follows, the focus is on Islamic scripturalism, not antecedent Jewish and Christian parallels. Therefore, references to the Bible and Bible-related sources have been de-emphasized. Some Biblical references have been provided for each of the Qur'anic women figures. For plot-and-motif parallels of Islamic traditions with earlier texts, the reader may wish to consult such works as Louis Ginzberg, *The Legends of the Jews*;[79] Katherine Pfisterer Darr, *Far More Precious Than Jewels: Perspectives on Biblical Women*;[80] Marina Warner, *Alone Of All Her Sex: The Myth and the Cult of the Virgin Mary*;[81] Gail Paterson Corrington, *Her Image of Salvation: Female Saviors and Formative Christianity*;[82] and others.

2

The Chapter of Eve

The Wife of the Prophet Adam in the Qur'an

The Qur'an speaks of Adam and his wife[1] in several Suras. In each instance, the story is a rounded narrative endowed with a specific focus that differs from one version to the other. The Qur'an does not mention Adam's wife by name, nor does it indicate how she was created.[2] Of the five Qur'anic accounts relating to Adam, the woman appears in three; in all three, the emphasis of the narrative lies with the disobedience of the human toward God, and the Forbidden Tree and/or Satan's guile are prominent features of the story. By contrast, the remaining two accounts that do not mention the woman focus on Iblis (Satan) and Iblis' disobedience and rebellion.

Taken together, the Qur'anic accounts of the events involving the creation of Adam and the rebellion of Iblis indicate that God created Adam from clay, or from sounding clay, from mud moulded into shape (15:26; 38:71); God fashioned Adam with His hands (38:75)[3] in due proportion and breathed into him of His spirit (*ruh*) (15:29; 38:72). Thus, while created from matter, Adam's nature included a divine breath, a spark, which God granted to the human beyond all other creatures. This higher nature conferred dignity and also obligation. The Qur'an states this by saying that God's purpose in Adam's creation was to make him God's vicegerent (*khalifa*)[4] on earth (2:30). He endowed Adam with creative knowledge concerning the natures of things by teaching him "the names, all of them" (2:31), so that Adam's knowledge was above that of the angels (2:32–33); and God commanded the angels to prostrate themselves before Adam. Only Iblis[5] refused to acknowledge the human's superiority, and instead asserted his own. He rebelled against God's command, was arrogant (and became Satan) (20:116; 15:30–33; 38:73–76; 7:11–12; 2:34). For this disobedience, God cursed and banished Iblis but gave him respite until the Day of Judgment, until which time Iblis vowed to tempt and assault all humankind except for those strong enough to withstand him, that is, God's devoted servants (15:34–43; 38:77–85; 7:13–18, 26–27). These accounts center on man and Satan, telling both their histories and defining their innate natures. Satan is shown to have started his career together with Adam, as Adam's coeval;[6] thus his role is essentially linked with man, his nature is brought out by antagonism against man, he is an "anti-man" force. Satan's very rebellion against God needed man to express itself, and it is perpetuated through history in Satan's labors to seduce and tempt man away from morality to sin.

It is only in the second half of the Qur'anic story, which tells of human disobedience to God and man's banishment from the Garden, that the woman appears. Adam's wife is first mentioned as Adam's partner in God's injunction to "dwell in the Garden and eat freely of its bountiful fruit," but "not to approach this Tree" (7:19, 2:35). Sura 20 relates that it was Adam to whom God addressed the warning that Iblis was his and his wife's enemy; if he let Iblis get the two of them ejected from the Garden, he (Adam) would be landed in misery (or, come to toil) (20:117). It was also to Adam that Satan then whispered his temptation concerning "the Tree of eternal life, and an everlasting kingdom" (20:120), and it was Adam who "disobeyed his Lord, and went astray" (20:121). By contrast, Sura 7 mentions the woman's participation in the acts of disobedience and repentance: "Satan whispered to them twain, in order to reveal to them their private parts, and said: 'Your Lord only forbade you this Tree lest you be angels, or of eternal life.' And he swore to them: 'I am indeed your sincere adviser.' And he caused their fall with deception" (7:20–22). When Adam and his wife ate of the Tree, they perceived their private parts (or, "shame," *saw'at*) and began to sew together leaves from the Garden to cover themselves (20:121, 7:22). Thus did Iblis cause their expulsion from the Garden (2:36), so they would live on earth for a time in mutual enmity (20:123, 7:24, 2:36). According to Sura 20, God "chose" Adam and forgave him and guided him (20:122), and whoever follows God's guidance will not lose his way nor fall into misery (or, toil) (20:123). According to Sura 7, both man and woman asked for God's forgiveness and mercy, saying that they had wronged themselves (or, committed an outrage against their own natures) (7:23), and God bestowed (on mankind) the garment of righteousness (7:26). Sura 2 here adds that Adam received from his Lord "words" (of inspiration) and God forgave him (2:37) and promised freedom from fear and grief to all humans who heed His guidance (2:38).

Since each of these Qur'anic narratives varies from the others as to focus, sequencing of events, and the involvement of the woman, a brief analysis of each account in chronological order may be useful. As indicated above, the main textual body of the accounts is found in Suras 2:30–39, 7:11–27, 15:26–43, 20:115–124, and 38:71–85. Nöldeke[7] places the Suras in the following chronological order: Suras 20, 15, and 38 revealed in the Middle Meccan period, Sura 7 in the Late Meccan period, and Sura 2 in (early) Medina. In Sura 20 (the earliest account), God's warning, Satan's temptation, and God's forgiveness are all directed at Adam, even though both man and woman eat of the Forbidden Tree and are expelled from the Garden. Suras 15 and 38 (both Middle Meccan) speak of Adam's creation and Iblis' rebellion, banishment, and curse. Man's disobedience toward God is not part of the narrative, and the woman is not mentioned. In Sura 7 (the latest of these narratives revealed in Mecca), both male and female are tempted and tricked by Iblis, both succumb, repent, and are banished. The final version of the story in Sura 2, revealed in Medina, emphasizes that the purpose of Adam's creation was as God's "vicegerent" on earth and tells of Adam's God-given higher knowledge. God's ordinance to stay away from the Tree is here addressed to both Adam and his wife; there is, however, no temptation or seduction scene, merely the statement that it was Satan who caused the couple's "slip" and expulsion. The narrative then makes mention of the "words" Adam received from his Lord and of God's forgiveness for Adam, both expressed in a single verse that is inserted between two divine commands of expulsion. The account ends with God's promise of guidance for all and His pledge that "whoever follows My guidance shall have no fear, nor shall they grieve" (2:38).

The dynamics of the narrative procede from a focus on Adam (Sura 20) to one involving both Adam and his wife (Sura 7); the final version of the story, however, transcends both by way of introducing the additional notions of man's vicegerency on earth, higher knowledge, God-given inspiration ("words")[8] and the promise of (spiritual) well-being of all humans who heed God's guidance. Thus, as the drama is related in various, dynamically evolving plots, the woman gradually appears as participant in the events of rebellion, repentance, and banishment; but the gender question remains a mere detail that bears no importance for the drama, and in the end the main theme has shifted away from it altogether to the issue of mankind's purpose on earth and the ways of God's guidance. The latter theme, central to the Qur'anic message, is expanded upon in 33:72–73, a later Medinan revelation that speaks of a primeval covenant between God and the human in terms of "the Trust" (*al-amana*), which God offered "to the heavens and the earth, and the mountains, but they refused the burden, and were afraid of it. But the human undertook to bear it. He was indeed wanton (or, unfair to himself), and foolhardy.[9] So that God punish the male and female hypocrites, and the male and female unbelievers, but forgive the male and female believers" (33:72–73). The Qur'an, then, declares that humans, male and female, are free and equal agents called upon to wage the battle of righteousness against Satan. Adam's and his wife's "slip" (or "error," *zalla*) did not result in a lasting defect of human primordial nature. Cast out to live on earth for a time (7:24, 2:36), the banishment did not include the burden of the curse of original sin. Man and woman may be weak and lagging, proud and ungrateful, but the Qur'an judges neither as lost to forgiveness as long as they continue to believe in God.

The Wife of the Prophet Adam in Islamic Interpretation

Classical Muslim interpretation of the Qur'anic story of the rebellion of Adam and his wife[10] against their Lord departs from the scripturalist referent in numerous ways. Extraneous detail transmitted in Hadith form and frequently originating in the Bible and Bible-related sources not only fleshes out the story but drastically changes it, especially with regard to the woman's role. In that the first woman stands for her sex, she is a religious symbol that serves as model "of" as well as "for" the value structure of the community of its formulation. Medieval interpretation of woman's origin and nature denies female rationality and female moral responsibility. This signifies both a social base of gender inequality and also the existence of structures (such as a clerical institution with legislative or juridic powers) bent on its preservation. The Hadith materials on women's inferior nature were accepted and propagated by the consensus ('*ijma*') of the learned doctors of law and theology until eighteenth-century premodern reformists began to question their authoritative status. Since the nineteenth century, Islamic modernists have denied the authenticity and doctrinal validity of what they viewed as medieval extraneous interpretative "lore," while re-emphasizing the Qur'anic notion of the female's full personhood and moral responsibility. New social realities as well as modernist desire to "renew" and "strengthen" Islam by way of effecting social reform in Islamic terms are now exemplified in the modernist exegesis of the first woman's Qur'anic story.

When al-Tabari (d. 923) wrote his great Hadith-based Qur'an commentary in the late ninth and early tenth centuries,[11] many traditions on the story of Adam and his wife were in circulation, which the Muslim scholars—as Tabari repeatedly acknowledges—"had learned from the people of the Torah."[12] While he quotes large numbers of these traditions, Tabari remains cautious as to these traditions' reliability; frequently he indicates mental reservations with the phrase *wa-llahu a'lam* ("God knows best"), or by expressing his hope that (his sources such as) Ibn 'Abbas and Wahb ibn Munabbih, "God willing," are right, or by opining that their accounts represent interpretations "within the realm of possibility" (I:532).[13]

According to Tabari and all other traditionist commentators, the first human was called "Adam" because when God desired to create him, He sent the angel of death to earth who scooped up good ground and bad, of red, white, and black color, from various parts of the earth's surface (*adim*). Therefore, Adam's progeny differed morally as well as physically, and therefore Adam was named Adam (I:480–482).[14] Tabari then quotes numerous traditions to elucidate the purpose for which the woman was created. "After Iblis had refused to prostrate himself before Adam, and had been cursed and expelled from the Garden, Adam was made to dwell there. But he felt lonely without a mate 'in whom he could find rest' (cf. Qur'an 7:189, 30:21). Then God cast a slumber over him, took a rib from his left side, soldered its place with flesh (while Adam continued to sleep) and from the rib created his wife Hawwa' in the form of a woman, so that Adam would find rest in her. When Adam awoke, he saw her at his side and said—according to what they allege, and God knows best—'my flesh, my blood, my wife,' and he found rest in her" (I:514).

Another cluster of traditions quoted by Tabari concerns itself with the woman's name, Hawwa'. This name appears only in the Hadith, not in the Qur'an; and its meaning is likewise defined in relation to the woman's creation from the man's body: "When Adam awoke, behold! there was a woman sitting by his head. He asked: who are you? She said: Woman. He said: Why were you created? She said: So you will find rest in me. Then the angels, desirous to know the extent of Adam's knowledge [of the names of all things] asked: What is her name, Adam? He answered: Hawwa'. The angels said: Why was she named Hawwa'? He said: Because she was created from a living (*hayy*) thing." (I:513).[15] Most of the traditions in Tabari place the woman's creation into the period of Adam's stay in the Garden, while some maintain that she was created before (I:514).

After some speculation on the species of the Tree (whether it was spikenard (i.e., "head of grain," "ear of corn": *sunbula*),[16] olive, wheat, vine, fig, or the Tree of eternal life) (I:517–521), Tabari turns to the question of Adam's and Hawwa's temptation by Satan. He quotes traditions that repeat the Qur'anic information that Satan tempted both the man and the woman with the promise of eternal life, which the Tree would provide (I:528–529), or that Satan tricked Adam into believing him because he swore by God's name to be their sincere adviser (XII:353–354). Most of the traditions brought together by Tabari, however, blame the woman, as it was the majority opinion of theological experts by Tabari's time that it was only through the woman's weakness and guile that Satan could bring about Adam's downfall. The traditions show some variation as to specific details of the event. It is said that Satan entered the Garden, from which he had previously been expelled, in the belly (or the mouth, fangs, jaw) of a snake. At that time, the snake was a four-legged, splendid riding animal resembling the Bactrian camel; some say that it wore clothes; it was also the only animal willing to heed Satan's request for transportation into the Garden (I:525,530). Once inside, Iblis emerged from the snake, took a piece from the Tree, and approached Hawwa' with the words: "Look at this Tree! How good it smells, how good it tastes, how nice its color is!" Hawwa' succumbed, then went to Adam and addressed him with Satan's very words; and Adam ate (I:525–527). Other traditions report that Hawwa' commanded her husband to eat (I:528), or that she urged him on by saying: "I have just eaten of it, and it has not harmed me" (I:527). Else, sexual desire or intoxication are made to explain the absence of Adam's rational powers at this critical moment: Satan made Hawwa' appear attractive to Adam, and when he wanted her for his desire, she refused to obey unless he first ate of the Tree (I:529), or: she gave him wine, and when he was drunk and his rational faculties had left him, she led him to the Tree and he ate (I:530).

As soon as Adam had eaten, the couple's genitals became visible to them both, and they began to sew leaves together to cover themselves. The traditions report that it had been Iblis' main goal to make the couple aware of their genitals. He knew that they had sexual organs because he had read the angels' books, while Adam had not been aware of his or Hawwa's private parts (I:527) since he and she were clothed in *al-zufr* ("fingernails," i.e., "white, sheer and thick skin")[17] (I:527, XII:354); or else in finery (I:530); or in light (XII:347, 352,355). Here, however, it was Adam and not Hawwa' who was overcome with shame. Tabari reports that "Adam resembled a tall, smooth-trunked palm tree and had much hair on his head, and when he had made 'the mistake' . . . he fled; a tree stood in his way and caught him, and he said to it: let me go! But it said: I am not about to do so! Then his Lord called him: Adam, are you fleeing from me? He answered: No, but I am ashamed of you" (XII:352–354).

God then put His curse on the woman and on the snake, but He did not curse the man, only the earth from which he had been created. The traditions report that God cursed "the earth from which you (Adam) were created, so that its fruits will turn to thorns" (I:526), and that he banished Adam to a life of want and work, "where he learned to forge iron, ploughed, planted, irrigated, harvested, threshed, winnowed, ground to flour, kneaded dough, baked, and ate" (XII:353).[18] God's curse on the woman, however, was *ad personam* and more severe; it involved the constitution and mental abilities, indeed the very personhood of Hawwa' and her daughters for all time to come. Because Hawwa' had tempted God's servant and had made the Tree bleed when she picked its fruit, she was condemned to bleed once a month, to carry and deliver her children against her will, and to be often close to death at delivery (I:526,531, XII:356). God also made the woman foolish and stupid, while He had created her wise and intelligent. "Were it not for the calamity that afflicted Hawwa', the women of this world would not menstruate, would be wise, and would bear their children with ease" (I:529). The snake in whose belly Iblis had entered the Garden was cursed to slither (naked) on its belly, to eat dust, and to be the eternal enemy of man, stinging his heel and having its head crushed by him whenever they would meet (I:526,530–531, XII:356,358), wherefore the Prophet commanded the Muslims to "kill the snake wherever you find it" (I:538). On the question of the humans' repentance after their disobedience, some traditions quoted by Tabari indicate that both the man and the woman acknowledged their sin and asked God's forgiveness and mercy, but a larger number of reports specify that the prayer for forgiveness and God's promise of eternal life involved Adam alone (XII:356ff).

By Tabari's time, the Qur'anic story had undergone a fundamental reinterpretation. The woman—in the Qur'an a participant in human error, repentance, and God's challenge to recover human pristine innate nature (*fitra*) through struggle for righteousness on earth—had become Satan's tool and was seen as afflicted with the curse of moral, mental, and physical deficiency. Conversely the man, in the Qur'an her partner and spokesman, now alone embodied the human conscience, was aware of his error, and repented; free of God's curse, he was forgiven.

Later classical exegetes continued to use many of the Hadith materials found in Tabari's Tafsir. Scholarly consensus (*'ijma'*) supported the tenet of the woman's responsibility for Adam's fall, even though many interpreters continued to follow Tabari's example in registering mental reservations concerning the traditions' Islamic authenticity. On the whole, differences in interpretation found in the various works of the later Middle Ages resulted from selection of some traditions over others to make a specific point, as the story was put to some new uses in the theological debate. This, however, did not affect the dogmatic paradigm as a whole.

The Mu'tazilite Qur'an interpreter Zamakhshari (d. 1144),[19] expanding on Tabari's notion that "genitals" (*saw'at*) and "evil" (*su'*) are derived from the same Arabic root and thus semantically related, places great weight on the appearance of the first couple's nakedness as a sign of their sin, because "the uncovering of one's genitals is a terrible thing, condemned by natural disposition and reckoned repulsive by natural comprehension" (II:74). Sound nature, then, shrinks from such behavior, which Zamakhshari further proves with a tradition from the Prophet's wife A'isha that "I did not see his, nor did he see mine" (II:75). This emphatic condemnation of nudity (even in the marital setting), while recorded in Hadith and earlier Tafsir, is an important concern of medieval religious teaching and appears frequently in the later Tafsir and elsewhere. Perhaps this is an indication that sexual mores in the later Islamic Middle Ages were considered "loose" and in need of vigilant clerical control.

On the whole, however, Zamakhshari at first glance appears not very interested in Hawwa's role in humankind's primeval error, because, being a Mu'tazilite, he regards Adam's and Hawwa's sin as "minor"; it involved disobedience, not apostasy, and thus (in Mu'tazilite understanding, which emphasizes God's *justice*), "God *had* to forgive it."[20] Consequently Zamakhshari attributes the first couples' repentance to their "exaggerated righteousness" and says that they acted "in the manner of saints and the righteous who regard minor sins as major, but enormous good deeds as minor" (II:76). This reading of the story, however, is a scholastic one; its purpose is to support the Mu'tazilite definition of "sin," not to exonerate Hawwa'. Indeed, to Zamakhshari Hawwa' remains as guilty as she first appeared to the early traditionists. Zamakhshari establishes this by quoting a tradition[21] according to which the angels surrounded Adam on his deathbed. Then, when Hawwa' circled around them to reach her husband, Adam commanded her to leave the Lord's angels alone, since what had happened to him had only happened because of her. Indeed, her culpability was such that the angels did not permit her to participate in washing, embalming, and burying Adam's body (II:76).

The great Qur'anic commentary of Fakhr al-Din Razi (d. 1209)[22] is generally regarded as the most brilliant Ash'arite defense against Mu'tazilite exegesis.[23] While Razi, in his interpretation of the story of Adam and Eve, continues to include much of the Hadith material also found in Tabari, Razi's scholastic inquiry is on the whole concerned with questions that go beyond the immediate story, such as whether the Garden was on earth or in heaven (III:3–4), whether Adam's sin was major or minor (III:11,14), whether Adam's sin occurred before or after his call to prophethood (III:5), that is, whether Adam's prophethood began before or after his expulsion from the Garden (II:177), and so on. Even so, Razi's commentary continues to provide many instructive glimpses at medieval theological thought on women's nature and status. For example, when Razi encounters a doctrinal problem in God's command to the angels to "prostrate themselves before Adam," a mere mortal, Razi has recourse to the Prophetic hadith: "If I were to order anyone to prostrate himself before another but God, I would command the woman to prostrate herself before her husband because of the magnitude of his rights over her" (which hadith leads Razi to conclude that the angels' prostration was to glorify Adam, not to worship him) (II:213). When Razi ponders the question whether Hawwa' was created in the Garden or before the couple's sojourn there, he quotes a tradition from Ibn Abbas that shows the continued popularity of some of the colorful detail with which the story had been embroidered: "God sent an army of angels who carried Adam and Hawwa' on a golden bed, as kings are carried. Their garments were of light. Each wore a golden crown adorned with a wreath of precious stones and pearls; Adam wore a girdle studded with pearls and jewels, until he was made to enter the Garden." (Although this tradition indicates that Hawwa' was created before entrance into the Garden, Razi settles the question of the date of her creation with the remark that "God knows best") (III:2).

As a scholastic theologian (*mutakallim*) whose main frame of reference is the Qur'anic text, Razi at times questions the consensus of the doctors of law and theology, rethinks the Hadith in terms of inner-Qur'anic logic and rationalist dogma, and measures traditional lore against the categories of Islamic law. For example, Razi reports that "the consensus of the leaders of the Community has identified Adam's wife as Hawwa', created from one of Adam's ribs, but the Qur'anic text does not specify this" (III:2). Nevertheless, even Razi finds occasion to quote the widely circulated and still popular *woman-as-rib* hadith, which reflects Hawwa's origin in Adam and also means to describe female nature. The hadith, found in Bukhari and other canonical Hadith collections, indicates on the authority of the Prophet that "the woman was created from a crooked rib. If you set out to straighten her, you will break her, and if you leave her alone while there is crookedness in her, you will enjoy her" (IX:161). When Razi contends that the traditions blaming Adam's lapse on Hawwa's wine that besotted his senses "are not farfetched," he does so "because Adam was permitted to partake of all things (in the Garden) except for that Tree" (III:12).

The real issue in this temptation story for Razi, however, is neither the woman nor the wine but concerns the problematic of free will as opposed to predestination. To Razi, the chain of disobedience leading from Iblis to Adam must originate somewhere in God's intention (III:16), and the trouble with Iblis, says Razi, is that he argues for predestination in his own case while explaining (i.e., explaining away) his seduction of the human "in the manner of the free-will party"[24] (XIV:37). Logically, Razi concludes that Iblis must have seduced Adam directly, without the woman's interference (XIV:46–48). This interpretation, however, has a scholastic/theological purpose. In providing it, Razi is uninterested in "salvaging" the woman's role in this drama. Indeed, when he critiques established lore for the sake of logical argument,

Razi's attitude toward the woman is merely what it is toward the snake. If Satan had wished to do so, he says, Satan could have transformed himself into a snake. Furthermore, the snake that reportedly smuggled Satan into the Garden could not have been punished in any case, because as an animal it was neither mentally nor legally competent to merit punishment. (Therefore, Razi opts for those traditions, which indicate that Adam and Hawwa' were within hearing distance of Iblis at one of the Garden gates, so Satan could whisper his temptations to them directly [III:15, XIV:46].)

With all of its rationalism and Qur'an-centeredness, then, Razi's exegesis reflects the legal and social realities of his age. To give a further example, Razi finds proof of male authority over the woman and woman's exclusion from activities outside of her house in the Qur'anic accounts of the first couple's repentance and punishment. Razi emphasizes the fact that Adam repented "while the woman was his follower" (III:26). The punishment of Adam's earthly "toil" (Sura 20:117), firstly, was not really a punishment, because toil enjoined on a person is a means of atonement as well as a source of recompense for a man (III:17); secondly, the burden of "toil" was imposed on Adam alone because a man must also toil for his wife whose guardian he is; and, thirdly, "toil" implies the fatigue of the quest after sustenance, which is incumbent on the man, not the woman (XXIII:125).

The Qur'anic Tafsir of al-Baydawi (d. 1286?),[25] one of the more concise and also the most popular of medieval Qur'anic interpretations, includes some bits and pieces of information generally derived from his predecessors but given greater prominence since Baydawi excluded so much else. For example, Baydawi identifies "the Garden" as an abode of perpetuity, either identical with Paradise or located somewhere in Palestine or in Iran between Kerman and Fars (I:52). Furthermore, like Zamakhshari, he identifies the very *purpose* of Satan's whispering to Adam and Hawwa' as Satan's desire to harm them by causing them to reveal their private parts, "because the uncovering of one's genitals, be it in solitude or in the presence of the spouse, is reprehensible and naturally improper; indeed, this is the first evil which man obtained from Satan" (I:321–322).

The Tafsir of the fourteenth century historian, theologian, and Qur'an interpreter Ibn Kathir (d.1373)[26] reflects the fact that this author was also proficient and productive in the *qisas al-anbiya'* genre. In both his exegesis proper and the "Tales of the Prophets," part of his Universal History, Ibn Kathir records mental reservations toward the reliability of esoteric legendary information generally derived from *isra'iliyyat* but continues to include such information in both of these works. Many of his traditions, however, are also marked by a more pronounced "Islam-centrism." Thus, in his relatively brief Tafsir, Ibn Kathir has room for traditions such as that Adam's sojourn in the Garden lasted the equivalent of the time period between "afternoon prayer" and "sunset prayer" (else it lasted one hour of celestial time, equivalent to 130 years of earthly time); or that it began and ended on a "Friday," which was also the day of Adam's creation (I:80).[27] Ibn Kathir furthermore specifies the places in which Adam, Hawwa', Iblis, and the snake found themselves after they had been cast out of the Garden: Adam, together with the Black Stone (of the Ka'ba) and a handful of leaves from the Garden, came down in India, Hawwa' in Jidda, or he in Safa and she in Marwa; Iblis fell to a place not far from Basra, and the snake arrived in Isfahan! (I:80)[28]

It was ultimately irrelevant, however, whether individual exegetes doubted the authenticity of some of the Hadith materials that they used in their interpretations (or even whether one or the other omitted some materials because of such doubts). Once the Hadith had "recorded" the woman's guilt in humanity's primeval tragedy, the basic tenor of the Hawwa' story remained constant. It served as scripturalist proof of woman's lower moral, mental, and physical nature, and the consensus of the learned doctors of Islam supported and perpetuated this teaching as a doctrine of the faith.

The onslaught of modernity challenged this state of affairs and changed the interpretation of the Qur'anic story of Adam and his wife beyond recognition. The Egyptian theologian and jurist Muhammad Abduh (d. 1905), Islamic modernism's most important early representative in the Arab world, combined professional expertise in Islamic theology and law with an awareness of Western modernity and Western scientific theories. To Abduh, Islam was eminently compatible with modernization.[29] His main goal was to "renew" Muslim morality and reform the traditional social structures of his day and particularly his region, Egypt, by way of a return to the pristine and dynamic faith and morality of Islam's first generations. Reformation of Muslim society in that moral mold would bring about an Islamic modernism both indigenous and also righteous, internally dynamic and externally powerful.

Although familiar with the classical Tafsir literature to which he frequently refers, Abduh approaches the Qur'anic text here under consideration in his own exegesis[30] in new ways. He pays attention to time and place of the revelations ("occasions of revelation"), emphasizes the literal meaning of the Qur'anic verses as well as their context, and largely de-emphasizes the Hadith, most particularly its *isra'iliyyat*. By way of an interpretation "purified of foreign lore," Abduh seeks to rediscover the original meaning of the Qur'an, which shaped the faith and ethics of the "righteous forefathers" (*al-salaf al-salih*), that is, the members of the first Muslim community, in order to recapture a sense of their morality for infusion into his own society. Here, Abduh places great importance on the notions of woman's full humanity and equality with the man before God, both because they are Qur'anic in origin and also because they are, in his opinion, indispensible in shaping a truly moral society.

Consequently, Abduh opines that the story of Hawwa's creation from Adam's rib, which has no foundation in the Qur'anic text, represents the interference of "unreliable foreign materials." Adam's story in the Qur'an, he says, is meant to serve as an example of admonition and guidance; its purpose is to define human nature as well as man's God-willed mission on earth. This story, then, has nothing to do with history, because history does not concern religion. The very faultiness of the Biblical creation story lies in its claim to be history, where (even) modern science has proved it to be wrong (I:279–280). Much of the Qur'anic story is *mutashabih*, that is, it belongs to the "implicit" verses of the Qur'an.[31] Adam here signifies the human species, but the latter also includes his wife, "because the woman is constituted and prepared for all human concerns just as is the man" (I:281). God's command to both to "dwell in the Garden and eat freely" signifies His command of creation as well as His inspiration of what is good. Conversely, the forbidden Tree signifies man's God-given knowledge of what is evil. God, then, gave the human the power of discernment, after He had created him with an original nature (*fitra*) that inclines toward the good and deviates only under Satan's evil inspiration. The exodus from the Garden is a parable for the hardship the human encounters when he permits his original nature to go astray (I:281–283). Human capacity for repentance and God's willingness to forgive, however, indicate that human nature is not flawed, and that God's guidance restores and liberates the human. This refutes the Christian doctrine that man was lost until saved by Jesus; according to Abduh, this Christian doctrine runs counter to human original nature as well as to established prophetic tradition (I:283). Abduh then links the Islamic belief in humankind's perfectability with his own conviction that "the Muslim society" of his era can and will be reformed in a moral mold. The Adam story, "this parable for the history of mankind," teaches that mankind began in innocence, went on to an age of greed, strife, and suffering, and will in the future—God willing—reach the age of repentance and guidance, or reason and reflection (I:283–284). This will occur when the human realizes that his freedom is not the freedom of beasts, but that true freedom is possible only within the Law, which alone brings serenity and full enjoyment of the goods of this world (I:286).

In the mid-1940s, almost two generations after Abduh, the Egyptian Azharite theologian al-Maraghi published his great Tafsir[32] which, though bearing the imprint of some of Abduh's reformist ideas, continues to utilize much of the traditionist detail that Abduh had discarded. Concerning Hawwa', al-Maraghi writes that "Satan had kindled the fires of Adam's instinctual desire to discover the unknown and want the forbidden . . . to the point where Adam had no strength of will left to resist his wife" (VIII:120). For this interpretation, al-Maraghi finds his proof in a tradition from the Prophet's companion Abu Hurayra: "Were it not for Hawwa', no woman would deceive her husband." It was Hawwa', al-Maraghi says, who suggested that Adam should eat of the Tree, since "the woman was created to suggest to the man what *she* desires, and be it by means of deceiving him" (VIII:120).

By al-Maraghi's time, lay thinkers had long begun to add their voices to the ongoing religious debate on the nature and social role of women. Even though lay "interpretations" on women's issues were made in forms other than formal Qur'an exegesis, their authors continued to appeal to Qur'an and Hadith as scripturalist bases of truth finding. In this manner, they used the story of Hawwa' in new ways to reflect a variety of ideological, in some cases also personal, perspectives.

The best-known work of this genre in the 1950s was penned by the misogynist Egyptian writer and intellectual Mahmud Abbas al-Aqqad, who had fallen out of love with Western culture by the time that he published *al-Mar'a fi l-Qur'an* ("Woman in the Qur'an"). With al-Aqqad, as with some others, a defensive pride in Islam went hand-in-hand with a penchant for Western-inspired psychosocial analysis loosely anchored in Qur'an and Hadith. Aqqad celebrates the woman's unique, unprecedented rights in Islam when he says that "the Qur'an elevated her from abasement to the position of a human being, free from Satan's impurities and the degradation of animals . . . and provided her with the greatest legal right by lifting from her the curse of original sin. . . ."[33] At the same time (and within the same book) Aqqad understands the story of Adam and Hawwa' psychologically within the framework of a pseudo-Darwinian survival-of-the-species theory. He points out that the story is of Biblical, not Qur'anic, origin. Referring to the Hadith, he stipulates that "the Story of the Tree" symbolizes every female trait, such as women's desire for the forbidden, inquisitiveness, ignorance, coyness, impatience, and weakness.[34] Female will, a mixture of obstinacy and seductiveness, is negative, while male will, based on strength and decisiveness, is positive. Woman's power over the male derives from male sexual desire and habit, weaknesses much like man's addiction to wine and tobacco. Woman's strongest suit is her power of hypocrisy; she was trained to hide her feelings, because, like all weaklings, she must cajole and flatter the strong. In some ways, both sexes deceive themselves as well as each other, because their desire "to find rest"[35] in each other necessarily involves deception.[36] To preserve the strength of the species, the man was given the power to coerce the woman into submission. The children in this case descend from a strong father and a seductive, beautiful mother. Had the woman been given the power of coercion, she would be capable of defeating the weakest males only, and the species would fade away. As it is, women derive pleasure from male coercion, just as they do from the pain of pregnancy and childbirth, while men rebel against pain.[37] Aqqad views the woman as the goalpost in a competitive race staged by the males. Like the goalpost, metaphor of passivity, the woman is unable to decide on the winner; she also remains the target only so long as the male spirit of competition survives. Yet, according to Aqqad, the female will always remain that target because she is part of all the motivations that can possibly underlie a man's actions, fueled as these may be by a quest for power, or survival, or pleasure, or by deep-seated sexual complexes. "Thus grows the second fruit on that Tree."[38]

Even in the eyes of conservatives comfortable with and supportive of traditionist (and traditionalist) notions of women's inferior nature, Aqqad's work with its mixture of misogyny and aspects of Western survival-of-the-species theory remained an oddity, although a widely read one. Furthermore, Aqqad's book was published at a time when pressures of social change (and often also the pressure of governmental policies) had forced even conservative Muslims to verbalize that an essential human equality of man and woman lay at the core of the Qur'anic paradigm and would henceforth be counted as distinguishing mark of righteous Islamic society. By the 1960s, many were critical not only of Aqqad's work but also of all traditional accounts of the "story of the fall" and, especially, Hawwa's role as Satan's tool. This criticism, argued on the basis of the Qur'anic text, involved the rejection of Torah-inspired traditions as "alien"; in its emphasis on the Qur'anic doctrine of male and female individual moral responsibility, this conservative criticsm clearly meant to strike a blow against male oppression of women, albeit within the traditional system of the sexes' functional segregation.[39]

Contemporary conservative voices continue to emphasize the equality of the sexes in Islam but stipulate this equality ever more urgently on the divinely decreed, immutable, and complete differences of their natures. God, they say, created the sexes as mutually complementary halves. To the man He gave decisive will, power of reason, and physical strength. The woman He created sensitive, emotional, supportive, and caring. Since this doctrine of the sexes' psychological and physical difference lacks a clear scripturalist referent, contemporary conservatives once again make use of the Hadith, and here the *woman-as-rib* tradition reappears, but now it emerges in a new context and underlies a new purpose:

> The Prophet said about the women that "they were created from a crooked rib; the most crooked part is its top portion, and if you were to straighten it, you would break it (the breaking signifying divorce); so enjoy her as crooked as she is." He was not blaming the woman when he said this, but was defining women's natural disposition and the preponderance of emotions over rationality, with which God has distinguished them, unlike the male in whom rationality surpasses the emotions. Neither man nor woman are inferior one to the other. The "crookedness" in the hadith does not imply any corruption or imperfection in woman's nature, because it is this crookedness of hers that enables her to perform her task, which is to deal with children who need strong compassion and sympathy, not rationality. The words "the most crooked portion of the rib is its uppermost part" signify the compassion which the woman feels for her child and the supremacy of her emotion over her rational mind. On this basis, her "crookedness" has become a laudatory attribute for the woman, because this "crookedness" is in reality woman's "straightest" qualification for her task.[40]

Contemporary conservatives find scripturalist support for related arguments in the Qur'anic account of the Adam and Hawwa' story of Sura 20, which deals only with Adam, as outlined above. In particular, it is Sura 20:117[41] that is understood as God's mandate to the man to toil in the world at large and His command that the woman remain at home, to be a wife and mother. "God warned Adam (alone) of Iblis' enmity and said that he would come to toil . . . as God meant for Adam to expend all of his energies in life (outside of the home) . . . and then return to the woman (in the home) to find rest in her[42] . . . because she was created to provide him with that tenderness which caresses away all of his troubles, so he can resume life's struggle more energetically thereafter."[43] The story of Adam and Hawwa', then, now teaches that the woman was created for wifehood and motherhood and can only fulfill these God-ordained functions, achieve rank and honor, and realize her full potential if she stays away from the "toil" of the job market (imposed upon Adam), which would divert her energies to her own detriment and that of her family and Muslim society as a whole.

Contemporary fundamentalists speak even more forcefully of woman's equality than do these contemporary "reformed" conservatives. To the fundamentalists, the Muslim woman now is a warrior of the faith; she is a soldier in the war against Satan and all corrupting influences that come in his name. Thus in his exegesis of the Qur'anic story of Adam and Hawwa', Sayyid Qutb (d. 1966),[44] for instance, has eliminated all classical Hadith materials. In the language and with the symbols of gnosticism, he speaks solely of the war the Muslim must wage for God's covenant against Satan's temptation, for faith against unbelief, for truth against the lie, for right guidance against error, "a confrontation in which the human himself is both battleground and warrior" (I:61). Here, the male and the female believer are equally qualified to shoulder the responsibility; both are called to battle and are equally rewarded for their struggle in the way of God.

In its contemporary struggle for the survival of traditional Muslim socio-moral structures, mainstream Islamic religious thought has begun to do away with a theological paradigm that had informed classical Islamic religious thinking for more than a thousand years. In faith, dignity, and moral responsibility, male and female Muslims are now increasingly hailed as equals. Mode and arena of their struggle for righteousness, however, are seen as different by God's command. Traditional societal divisions and, especially, the exclusion of women from the public sphere thereby remain fully valid. Indeed, conservatives and also fundamentalists both brand as subversive the demand that the principle of absolute gender equality be applied in the social, political, and economic areas. Such demands, they say, are merely rooted in Western secular (hence immoral) ideology, which aims to destroy the Islamic order.

3

The Women of Noah, Lot, and Abraham

The consorts of the prophets Noah, Lot, and Abraham represent various dimensions of the female in the history of God's sacred interaction with humankind. These women's scripturalist images span the specter from wickedness to righteousness, betrayal to loyalty, idolatry to faith.

The Wives of Noah and Lot

In scripture and interpretation, the wives of Noah and Lot are examples of rebelliousness against God and His chosen spokesmen. They acted falsely toward their husbands, both righteous servants of God; these prophets, in turn, then did not (could not?) help them in the final reckoning before God, and the two sinners were condemned to hell. The Qur'anic "lesson of warning" on the wives of Noah and Lot appears in Sura 66:10 where, by inner-Qur'anic context, it belongs together with the Sura as a whole. The main theme of Sura 66 is female rebellion in a prophet's household and its punishment.[1] The first five verses of Sura 66 deal with a specific crisis in the Prophet Muhammad's household. These verses mention: The release of the Prophet from some past (voluntary?) restrictions in dealing with his wives; the duty to expiate (hasty?) oaths; the wife who "betrayed the secret"; warning to two women (of the household) who conspired against the Prophet; threat of divorce of all of the Prophet's wives; and enumeration of wifely virtues.[2] Verses six and seven of Sura 66 speak of the certainty of hell, a warning to the believers and a divinely ordained requital for the unbelievers. In 66:8 the believers are called upon to repent so that God forgive their bad deeds and admit them to paradise on the day when the Prophet and those who believe will not be humiliated. Sura 66:9 calls upon the Prophet to stand steadfast against unbelievers and hypocrites. In 66:10, the wives of Noah and Lot are then established as examples of how God punishes sinful conduct on the part of consorts of righteous prophets.

The wives of Noah and Lot, then, appear in 66:10 as symbolic prefigurations of acts of betrayal by the Prophet's own, and their stories exemplify the seriousness of such betrayal, which leads to eternal punishment in hell. Islamic exegesis has shown some awareness of the links between these "warning examples" and Muhammad's wives (although in a reverse mode) by emphasizing that the "treachery" of Lot's wife against her husband did not include adultery, because God's revelation of Sura 24:1–26, vouchsafed to clear the reputation of Muhammad's wife A'isha after "the affair of the slander"[3] established that "no wife of a prophet has ever been adulterous."[4] As indicated above, however, thrust and purpose of Islamic exegesis have been to approach the Qur'anic revelation synchronically in another sense. Centering on the scripture's symbolic images—its eternally valid "lessons"—for temporal application, the wives of Noah and Lot have thus been recognized as models of, and for, the human condition. Here they have come to represent the tenet of free will, that is, individual human freedom of choice and concomitant responsibility in matters of morality and faith. Even a woman, and even a prophet's wife, is a free agent when she answers the essential question of the purpose of life. Thereafter, she will gain her eternal reward according to the quality of this, her most fundamental, decision.

The Wife of the Prophet Noah (Nuh) in the Qur'an

The Qur'anic revelations on Noah[5] are of the Middle and Late Meccan periods. These indicate that when Noah had complained to his Lord that his people had disobeyed, and plotted, and called for the continuing worship of their gods,[6] he asked God to remove all unbelievers from the earth lest they breed new generations of sinners and unbelievers (71:5–24, 26–27). Noah then prayed for forgiveness for himself, his parents, all those entering his house in faith, and all believing men and women (71:28). God inspired Noah to construct "the ship" (*al-fulk*) under His guidance (11:37–39). Then He commanded him to take on board "pairs of every species, male and female, and your family, except those of them against whom the pronouncement (*al-qawl*) has already gone forth" (23:27; 11:40). Noah was also commanded to save "the believers who, however, were few in number" (11:40). God forbade Noah to plead with Him for the sinners not included in this group who were to drown (23:27). God opened the gates of heaven with water pouring forth and caused the earth to gush forth springs, and the waters met according to a preordained command (54:11–12). The sinners were drowned and made to enter the Fire, and found none to help them (beyond God) (71:25). The late Medinan revelation of 66:10, presented above, then establishes Noah's wife as "an example to the unbelievers" because of her *khiyana* ("faithlessness," "disloyalty," "falsehood,"

"treachery") toward her righteous husband who, though God's prophet, was
of no avail to her when God condemned her to hell.

The Wife of the Prophet Noah in Islamic Exegesis

Exegesis identifies Noah's wife as Waligha, or Wa'ila. Her scripturalist twin,
Lot's wife, is Waliha, but the names are sometimes reversed.[7] The Qur'an does
not state how Noah's wife died. Most interpreters surmise that her death occured
during the deluge. Like Lot's wife, she is said to have been left behind to die
a violent death while the righteous husband saved himself and his believing
followers. This interpretation, then, is Qur'an based in that the joint condemnation of the wives of Noah and Lot of Sura 66:10 is extended to include
similarities in their fate.

In their "tales of the prophets," Ibn Kathir[8] and al-Kisa'i,[9] however, report
that Noah's wife was among the women taken aboard the ship "which is what
the Torah says."[10] This tradition was potentially problematic within the Islamic
context; but Ibn Kathir tries to account for both the Qur'anic condemnation
of Noah's wife and also the validity of the Torah-derived hadith by wonder-
ing if, perhaps, the woman had been saved on the ship and fell into unbelief
thereafter.[11] This example, and many others presented above and in what follows, indicate that medieval religious scholarship continued not only to rely
on the older, Bible-related traditions but also attempted to integrate those
materials into the Islamic framework as much as possible.

Contemporary pious literature now is more concerned with the precise
nature of this woman's Qur'an-proclaimed sinfulness, in order to better elucidate her "lesson." A contemporary primer on women in the Qur'an, for example, tells of Noah's wife's devotion to the idols in the Sun Temple, her zeal in
keeping her female neighbors away from Noah's preaching, and her derisive-
ness toward her husband. Her treachery, then, is shown as threefold: disbelief
in God, the attempt to thwart her husband's mission, and a wife's betrayal of
her duties toward her husband.[12] Contemporary conservative Muslim women's
literature also uses the story of Noah's wife to prove that Islam—that is,
indigenous true monotheism[13]—gives the woman complete freedom in
the matter of her faith. Once she has chosen, she becomes responsible for
her choice; in the case of Noah's wife, that meant death as well as eternal
damnation.[14]

The Wife of the Prophet Lot in the Qur'an

As in the case of Noah's wife, the Qur'anic revelation on the sin and divine
condemnation of the wife of Lot[15] (66:10) is of late Medinan provenance. By
contrast, the history of Lot's career as preacher, warner, and prophet among
the Sodomites, his flight to safety, and the unbelievers' destruction is related
in a number of revelations from the Early Meccan, Middle Meccan, and Late
Meccan periods.[16]

The Qur'an instructs that Lot and his believing followers lived among a sinful people whose lives were filled with acts of lewdness, sexual perversion, intoxication, wickedness, and crime (26:165–166; 15:67–71; 27:54–55; 11:77–80; 29:28–31). Lot attempted to save the sinners from their evil ways (26:160; 15:68–71; 27:54–55; 29:28–29) but encountered only hostility from them (26:167; 27:56; 29:29). God's angelic messengers visited Lot to warn him and his family of God's impending punishment. The men of the city then had evil designs on Lot's guests; to protect his guests, Lot offered his country-men his own daughters (11:77–80), but they refused and sought to lure the guests away, until God blinded their eyes (54:37). The angels commanded Lot to save himself, his household, and his followers by fleeing in the dark of night (15:63–66; 11:81; 29:33). He should be at the rear of the party to prevent any from looking back, except his wife, who would suffer the unbelievers' fate (15:65; 11:81). When God's command was issued and the mighty blast and shower of brimstone, hard as baked clay, descended on the city (26:173; 15:73–75; 27:58; 11:82–83), "an old woman" was not among those who were saved. She lagged behind and died together with the other sinners (37:133–135; 15:58–60; 27:57; 29:32–33; cf. 51:32–37; 54:33–39). The Medinan revelation of 66:10 identifies this woman's sin as *khiyana* ("faithlessness," "dis-loyalty," "falsehood") toward her righteous husband, the prophet Lot. Because of it, her husband was then of no avail to her in God's reckoning, and she was condemned to hell.

The Wife of the Prophet Lot in Islamic Exegesis

Qur'an commentators have identified Lot's wife as Waliha.[17] Her *khiyana* ("dis-loyalty," "treachery," "faithlessness") established in Sura 66:10 is seen as three-fold: she did not believe in God; she undermined her husband's prophetic mission by informing the lewd inhabitants of the city when beautiful male guests had arrived to visit Lot, so that the curs could come rushing to accost them;[18] thus, she also betrayed her wifely duties toward her husband. Her signals to the sinful were to grind wheat during the day, and kindle a fire at night. When the angels arrived, she went out with a lighted lamp in her hand to inform the Sodomites of these guests' presence.[19]

The divine retribution that followed came as the uprooting of the city, or cities, of the Sodomites by way of Gabriel's wing. Buildings, people, animals, and fields were raised skyward until the angels in heaven could hear the earthly voices of roosters and dogs. Then all crashed back to earth upside down. Each of the hard stones that thereafter rained from heaven bore the name of the one for whom it was intended. Lot's wife may have been destroyed among her people. Others say that she left the city with her husband and daughters but turned around when she heard the city fall, and it was then that she was killed.[20] Ibn Kathir sees this story as proof of God's might in avenging sin. The story also proves that sodomy is an immoral act punishable by stoning.[21]

Contemporary religious literature emphasizes that Lot's wife was the instru-ment by which the Sodomites attempted to thwart Lot's mission, the Call (*da'wa*) of God's true religion. These unbelievers paid the traitoress of God's cause for her services, and she did her informing of what went on in her husband's household for material gain, "mere pieces of silver." Being part of Sodomite corruption, she then shared in their punishment.[22] All of this occurred by her own free will, because (in Islam) the woman is free to choose her spiritual path. Once she has chosen, she also becomes responsible for her choice.[23]

The Women of Abraham

In Sara, the wife of Abraham, and Hagar, his Egyptian concubine, the matriarchal aspect of the prophetic consort is redefined. After the deluge, which marked a new beginning in the history of God's creation of the world, Abraham and Sara, and Abraham and Hagar, embody the renewed presence of God's blessing in human history.[24] That the wife and concubine of Abraham were both strong and resourceful women, mothers of his progeny but separated from each other by jealousy and also legal and economic barriers that enabled one (Sara) to oppress and then exile the other (Hagar), would be powerful and complex scripturalist teaching in and of itself. What extends, further complicates, but also focuses their stories is the fact that Sara and Hagar became the founding matriarchs of different "tribes," that is, religions, where Sara and Isaac provide the Abrahamic lineage of Judaism while Hagar and Ishmael (through their descendant Muhammad) provide that of Islam. Yet both female figures conjoin in symbolizing the strength and courage of God's chosen agents, here in the role of matriarchs in God's sacred history.

Even though Abraham is a prophet of great prominence in the Qur'an, the revelations on his wife Sara are few, and they concern mainly God's promise of a child (after years of barrenness and in old age) by way of an angelic annunciation to which Sara reacts with incredulous laughter. Exegesis has added much information on Sara, which has shaped her image for the believers into a series of personae: the young monotheist who was her husband's first follower and helpmate; the beautiful young woman lusted after by a tyrant against whose advances God protected her; the barren wife who wished for a child of Abraham's (even when conceived by her handmaiden); the jealous wife who resented her handmaiden's motherhood and its fruit; and, finally, the matriarch who needed to ensure her own son's preeminence over his older half brother.

If Islamic exegesis has seen Sara as scripturalist prefiguration of or for a later sacred time, it has done so in terms of Sara's role as her husband's first follower and supporter, an image that links Sara with Muhammad's wife Khadija.[25] Mainly, however, the exegetic literature has celebrated Sara's motherhood for what it is, the continuation of the prophetic lineage into which belong most of the post-Abrahamic Qur'anic prophets and messengers. Only Ishmael, son of Hagar, and their descendant Muhammad are children of Abraham outside of Sara's line.

If the Qur'anic revelations on Sara are scant, they are almost nonexistent on Hagar. Indeed, it is only in Abraham's prayer to God of Qur'an 14:37 "to protect some of his offspring whom he has made to dwell in a barren valley by God's Sacred House [the Ka'ba], so that they establish prayer there. . . ." that Hagar's role as the righteous but exiled mother of Ishmael is said to have been acknowledged. Hagar's history is thus mainly constituted by Islamic tradition; but here she is a most powerful figure. Hagar began her adult life in bondage; as a young mother she suffered exile because of a wife's jealousy, fought to the best of her abilities for her child's survival in a waterless place, and was saved together with him by divine providence. Thereafter, she saw to her son's integration into the Arab environment of their exile. Finally, she herself and her history became symbolically intertwined with God's shrine in Mecca after Abraham and Ishmael had raised up the foundations of the Ka'ba and purified it for pilgrimage and for prayer (Qur'an 2:124–129).

The conflict between Sara and Hagar is fully part of this story. In some contemporary Western Jewish and/or feminist literature, this conflict is decried as the tragedy that befalls female rivals in a patriarchal household.[26] Islamic interpretation past and present has seen this drama not in a personal but a geneological and spiritual light; when two strong mothers clash over the position of their sons and lineage in the eyes of God, female domestic tensions are absorbed into the greater scheme of things. Thus, Islamic interpretation has not seen Hagar's expulsion from Abraham's household at Sara's hands as an occurrence of female oppression but as part of the divine plan to reestablish God's true sanctuary and its pure rituals in the wilds of a barren valley far away. In her suffering for this cause, Hagar had to endure the distress and danger that have typically marked the careers of God's chosen historical agents. Like God's prophets, Hagar persevered, and thus her name and memory came to be part of Islam's sacred history and ritual.

Because of the fact that Sara-Isaac and Hagar-Ishmael represent the "bifurcation" of the legacy of Abraham, their images have been widely explored in, especially, Jewish scripturalist literature. Even where some of the newer Jewish writings with a feminist bend have decried Sara's oppressive relationship with Hagar,[27] however, that question has here also been debated from within the doctrinal parameters of an established faith. In the Bible, God's covenant is concluded with Isaac, and Ishmael is rejected. In Islam, Ishmael is loved, recognized, and protected by his father. According to Islamic tradition, Abraham even "chose" a fitting wife for Ishmael by the patriarchal counsel to divorce an unfitting (rude and inhospitable) wife and retain another (gracious and hospitable one)[28] to ensure the impeccable lineage that would later bring forth the Prophet Muhammad. The question of legitimate succession to Abraham has likewise been central to the question of identity of the (willing) sacrificial victim whom Abraham offered up to God but whom God redeemed. Medieval Islamic exegesis was divided on whether Isaac or Ishmael was that chosen victim, for reasons that have been ascribed to the enduring influence of the Biblical on the Islamic tradition, until the latter more forcefully differentiated itself from antecedent influences.[29] When, during sabbatical stays in Turkey, Jordan, Egypt, Syria, and Saudi Arabia in 1985, I asked hundreds of lay Muslims to identify the son of Abraham divinely chosen for God's sacrifice, the answer was that it had been Ishmael, and Sara's oppression of Hagar in Abraham's household was attributed to "Jewish envy of Islam."

The Islamic traditions quoted in what follows do not aspire to do more than give a glimpse of the traditionist literature on Sara and Hagar, and on Hagar's role in Muslim selfperception. A full analysis of the medieval Islamic tradition can be found in Firestone's work on the Abraham-Ishmael legends in Islamic exegesis.[30]

The Wife of the Prophet Abraham (Ibrahim) in the Qur'an

Of the women of Abraham's[31] household, the Qur'an mentions only his old and barren wife who appears in the context of the annunciation of the birth of Isaac (Ishaq). On their way to the Prophet Lot, God's angelic messengers entered into Abraham's presence "as his honored guests." Abraham brought out a roasted calf for their meal. Not knowing who they were, he began to feel afraid when they did not eat. They calmed his fears and gave him glad tidings of a son "endowed with knowledge." But Abraham's wife struck her face and shouted that she was barren and old (51:24–29).[32] A later revelation (11:69–72)[33] informs that God's messengers calmed Abraham's fears by saying that they had been sent against Lot's people, and they told Abraham's wife who was standing there, laughing, that she would give birth to Isaac. She was incredulous because she and Abraham were very old. The messengers, however, affirmed that this was by God's decree, grace, and blessings (51:30; 11:73).

The Wife of the Prophet Abraham in Islamic Exegesis

Exegesis has identified Abraham's wife as Sara, or Sarra ("She who gladdens"). She is said to have been Abraham's first cousin, daughter of his paternal uncle Haran; or his niece, daughter of his brother Haran; some say that she was the daughter of king Haran, the ruler of Haran or Harran, the star-worshipping community through which Abraham passed on his way from Mesopotamia to Palestine.[34] Sara became Abraham's first follower. It was she and then Lot—Abraham's paternal cousin, or his nephew (i.e., according to some, Sara's brother)—who first believed in Abraham's prophetic mission.[35] When Palestine suffered a drought, Abraham and Sara migrated to Egypt, where they entered the realm of the tyrant Pharaoh, known for his taste for women. Sara was exceedingly beautiful; her beauty was second only to that of Eve.[36] In selfprotection, to escape death at the hands of the Pharaoh, or because he meant it "in a religious sense," Abraham identified Sara as his sister.[37] Pharaoh then sent for her, but when he meant to assault her he fell under a spell, or his hand shrivelled up,[38] until she asked God to release him.[39] Else, Abraham at home and Sara in the Pharaoh's presence spent the time in prayer for God's protection; or God "removed the curtain of distance" between Abraham's house and the Pharaoh's palace and made the walls transparent as thin, clear glass, so that Abraham could witness God's protection of Sara. The Pharaoh thought her "a satan, not a human";[40] and he gave her an Egyptian slave girl named

Hagar.[41]This story has survived in the oral storytelling tradition to the present day. Knappert, for example, reports the (unattributed) legend that Abraham tried to smuggle Sara into Egypt in a large suitcase. The customs officer at the border insisted on opening it, saw the beautiful woman, and reported her arrival to the king.[42] Abraham then watched them sitting on a sofa together in the king's "inner chamber," because the castle walls had become transparent. When the king's hand had shrivelled up, Abraham presented himself as a physician and cured the hand for the price of the woman. The king was pleased and gave him not only Sara but also the slave girl Hagar.[43]

The heavenly visitors who came to Abraham's house on their way to Lot's people were the angels Gabriel, Michael, and Israfil (perhaps also Izra'il, angel of childbirth and death). At their good tidings of the birth of a son, Sara cried and struck her face "as women do when they are astonished," and she and Abraham rejoiced and laughed, because they had ceased to hope for a child since Abraham was one hundred years old and Sara was ninety.[44] Thus Sara bore Isaac. She conceived him in the night in which Lot's people were destroyed, and she was delivered of the child on a Friday night, the Ashura.[45] The child's forehead shone with a strong light and he fell from his mother's womb to earth in prostration to God, raising his hands to proclaim His Unity.[46] While Sara and Abraham were still alive, Isaac's son Jacob (Ya'qub) was born; he succeeded his father and grandfather in the prophetic line. It was Jacob who built the *Masjid al-aqsa* in Jerusalem, forty years after Abraham and Ishmael had built the Ka'ba in Mecca.[47] Sara died at the age of 127 in Hebron in the land of Kanaan. Abraham buried her in a cave he had purchased for four hundred *mithqal* from Afrun ibn Sakhr of the Bani Hayth. Many years later, Abraham was buried in the same cave.[48]

Contemporary inspirational women's literature repeats the medieval traditions on Sara's beauty and her God-given release from Pharaoh's evil designs. What is especially emphasized now, however, is the fact that Sara was the first to believe in her husband's mission, together with his cousin, or nephew, Lot.[49] In this manner, the story of Sara and Abraham is now mainly presented as paradigmatic antecedent to the history of Khadija and Muhammad, since it was Muhammad's wife Khadija who first believed in the Prophet's mission together with his first cousin, later also son-in-law, Ali ibn Abi Talib.

Hagar, the Concubine of the Prophet Abraham

The Qur'an does not relate details of the story of Abraham's concubine Hagar,[50] the slave woman from Egypt and mother of Abraham's older son Ishmael with whom Abraham (re)built the Ka'ba. Exegesis has recognized the Qur'anic referent to Hagar's role in Abraham's reconstitution of mankind's primeval monotheism and its rituals in Qur'an 14:37, Abraham's prayer to God: "Oh our Lord, I have settled some of my offspring in a barren valley at your Sacred House, oh Lord, so that they establish the prayer. So make the hearts of (some) people incline toward them and provide them with fruit. Perhaps they will give thanks." Even though the detail of Hagar's hagiography, then, is based on Islamic tradition, not Qur'anic revelation, Hagar's importance is very great. Participant in Abraham's mission to re-establish true monotheism on earth, she is also the ancestress of Abraham's true heirs, the Muslims—since it was her descendant, the Prophet Muhammad, who restored Abraham's religion after the world had once again fallen away from the true faith and proper worship of God. Muhammad's early biographer Ibn Ishaq (d. 767) calls Hagar "the mother of the Arabs."[51] Celebrated in a specific ritual of the pilgrimage, "the running (sa'y),"[52] Hagar is one of the pillars of Islamic consciousness.

Traditions report that the handmaiden Hagar was given to Sara for a servant by the Pharaoh of Egypt.[53] This was long before the birth of Isaac, when Abraham had no children. Sara, knowing herself to be barren, suggested to Abraham "that he sleep with this slave-girl of hers, so perhaps God would give Sara a son from Hagar."[54] After Hagar had conceived, she became haughty toward her mistress, while Sara grew increasingly jealous. In her jealousy, Sara vowed to cut "three limbs" of Hagar's; so Abraham ordered Hagar to pierce her ears and have herself circumcised. "These customs," therefore, "began with Hagar."[55] Frightened by Sara's jealousy and harshness, for which her own haughty behavior was partially responsible, Hagar fled into the wilderness where an angel appeared who commanded her to return to the household. The angel assured Hagar that the child in her womb was a male, to be named Ishmael, through whom God would work much good and who would come to own the lands of his brothers. The angel's words were fulfilled with Ishmael's descendant Muhammad the Prophet "through whom the Arabs gained predominance and possession of all lands West and East, while God provided them with useful knowledge and righteous works unlike any other community before, because (their) Prophet was honored above all other prophets."[56]

Ishmael was born thirteen years before Isaac. His birth made Sara ever more jealous and she asked Abraham to take Hagar away. He removed the young mother and her suckling infant to the place where he later (re)built the Ka'ba. "When he left the two of them there and turned his back on them, Hagar clung to his robes and said: Abraham, where are you going, leaving us here without the means to stay alive? He did not answer. When she insisted, he would still not answer. So she said: Did God command you to do this? He said: Yes. Then Hagar said: He will not let us perish."[57] Abraham rode off until he was hidden from their view. Then he faced the Ka'ba[58] and prayed: "Oh Lord, I have made some of my offspring settle in an unfruitful valley by your Holy House, oh Lord, so that they establish the prayer. Therefore make the hearts of some people inclined toward them and provide them with fruits. Perhaps they will give thanks" (Qur'an 14:37). When the waterskin was empty, Hagar and Ishmael became very thirsty. She saw the child squirm and went away because she could not bear to look at him. Seven times she ran toward the hill of Safa and then the hill of Marwa in search of help. (The Qur'an in 2:158 speaks of Safa and Marwa as *sha'a'ir*, "rites" [or, "cultic symbols"] of God, which the pilgrim on major pilgrimage [*hajj*] or minor pilgrimage ['*umra*] may circumambulate.)[59] Hagar then found herself face to face with the angel Gabriel, who scraped the dust with his heel, or his wing, until the spring of "primordial water,"[60] the well of Zamzam, gushed forth.[61] Hagar then built a dam to contain the water lest it flow away, and she drank and gave her child to drink. A caravan approached and saw birds hovering over the spot, which told them that there was water there. Hagar permitted them to dwell in this place and to drink of the well, since it was a gift from God.[62] Later, Hagar married Ishmael to a woman of this tribe, the Jurhum, who taught him Arabic.[63] When Hagar had died, she was buried in al-Hijr, the crescent-shaped tomb adjacent to the Ka'ba and within the area of its *tawaf* ("circumambulation"). When Ishmael died at age 137, he was buried in the same place.[64]

Abraham and Ishmael (re)built the Ka'ba. In the Qur'an, the Ka'ba is called the Holy House (5:100), the Ancient House (22:29,33), the first place of worship founded on earth (3:96). Qur'an 3:97 teaches that "in it are clear signs. [It is] the place [or: station] of Abraham; whosoever enters it is safe. Humans owe God the pilgrimage to the House—those who can afford [find a possible way to] it. . . ." Qur'an 2:124–129 then speaks of Abraham's and Ishmael's connection to this Holy House. According to 2:124, Abraham was tried by his Lord with "words" (*kalimat*) which he (He?) fulfilled; Abraham was made an *imam* ("example") for the humans; God's covenant would include Abraham's progeny but not the sinful. In 2:125, God reminds humankind that He had established the House as a place of refuge and security for humankind, so they would make the place of Abraham (*maqam Ibrahim*) a place for prayer, since God had commissioned Abraham and Ishmael to purify His House for the worshippers. And when (2:127) Abraham raised the foundations, with Ishmael, (he/they) prayed that God would accept this service from them. And they prayed (2:128) that God would make the two of them submit to His will ("Muslims"), and of their progeny a submitting ("Muslim") community, and (2:129) send among their progeny an apostle of their own, who would recite unto them God's signs, and teach them the scripture, and wisdom, and purify them. And Abraham was commanded to prescribe the pilgrimage (22:27ff).

Traditions are divided on whether Abraham and Ishmael built the first Ka'ba (at the holy site known to all prophets since Adam, but where no building had been before),[65] or whether they rebuilt the Ka'ba on the foundations first erected by Adam.[66] God guided Abraham to the site by inspiration; or God sent a Gale Wind with two wings and the head of a snake, which swept the house's first foundations bare, and Abraham and Ishmael dug into these until they had laid down the base.[67] Ishmael then got the stones and Abraham built, while both were praying with the words of Qur'an 2:127. When the building had reached Abraham's height, Ishmael placed the stone of *maqam Ibrahim* down for him and he continued his labor while standing on it until the stone showed the imprint of his feet.[68] The Black Stone was brought (and/or) inserted by the angel Gabriel. This stone in paradise had been a white jewel; when it fell to earth together with Adam, it became black from human sin. Gabriel had fetched it from India, or the Meccan mountain of Abu Qubays, where it had been kept since the flood.[69] Just as the Black Stone is material symbol of God's covenant with man, so also is the Ka'ba "the navel," center of the foundation of the world; it stands on the seventh earth in a direct line below

God's throne in seventh heaven, and as angels circumambulate God's throne so do humans circumambulate the Ka'ba.[70] Abraham and Ishmael were then guided to restore the rituals of worship in this holy place as first instituted through Adam. After a second period of corruption, these were later reinstituted in their correct form by Abraham's and Hagar's descendant, the Prophet Muhammad. No role has been recorded for Hagar in the building of the Ka'ba. Indeed, according to a number of traditions, the Ka'ba was built after Hagar's death. But as her tomb lies within the sacred precinct and her anguished "running" between Safa and Marwa is part of established pilgrimage ritual, Hagar's figure is central to the hajj experience.[71]

Islamic exegesis has traditionally been divided on whether Ishmael or Isaac was Abraham's intended sacrifice whom God ransomed with a white ram from paradise (Qur'an 37:102–107, where the son's name is not mentioned).[72] The bulk of al-Kisa'i's interpretation, for example, identifies the sacrifice as Isaac (in agreement with Genesis Chapter 22),[73] while Ibn Kathir[74] specifies that the sacrifice was Abraham's first-born son, Ishmael: "Those who claim differently are under the influence of *isra'iliyyat* lore . . . it is not even known whether Isaac travelled to Mecca as a small boy . . . the very fact that the Jews identify Abraham's sacrifice as their progenitor Isaac betrays their envy of the Arabs whose progenitor is Ishmael."[75] Such traditions are already found in the eighth-century *Sira* of Ibn Ishaq, where the obedience of Abraham and Ishmael is extended to include Hagar. Iblis, it is said, tempted all three separately to disobey God's command, but each chose to obey God.[76] Here, as in her acceptance to stay in the desert with her infant son, Hagar symbolizes faith. In her "ordeal," the "running" to save her child from death, she has also been seen as symbol of reason and resourcefulness.[77] This woman, then, is image of both the submitting and also the active aspects of being Muslim.

Among all of sacred history's female images, then, Hagar's may have been the most productive of ongoing change and interpretation in the Islamic imagination. Inasmuch as the palpable tensions embodied in the scripturalist tales on Sara and Hagar have to do with Islamic processes of acceptance of the Biblical heritage while also establishing Islam's own, the figures of Sara and Hagar symbolize Islam's selfdefinition as continuation, but also corrective completion, of the monotheistic tradition. During the early medieval period, the stories of Isaac's (Syrian) and Ishmael's (Meccan) role as Abraham's chosen sacrifice both appear to have existed side by side for a while; thus, these sons' mothers were then also more ambiguously ranked. With the ninth and tenth centuries, however, the Mecca-Ishmael-Hagar tradition rose in prominence[78] and, with it, Hagar's rank as one of Islam's most important female figures, a symbol of Islamic identity.

4

The Chapter of Zulaykha

Among the many female figures whom Qur'anic sacred history portrays for the faithful, the image of Joseph's mistress, wife of his Egyptian master, stands out by its complexity. In her story, the themes of female desire and cunning are woven together with those of love, repentance, honesty, and fidelity. As Qur'anic metaphor, this tale, then, embodies the worst and the best in woman's nature on the terrestrial plain. Of all the Qur'anic women's stories, it may be the richest and most penetrating in terms of female psychology.

In traditional scholarly exegesis, the character thereafter lost much of her human fullness because of exegetic emphasis on this woman's nature as symbol of the sexually aggressive, destabilizing, and dangerous nature of women as a whole. The love motif, on the other hand, was fully developed in the pious popular storytelling traditions past and present, and also underlay a number of famous and influential medieval romantic and mystic epics. In this literature, the protagonist symbolizes the enduring power of female selfless love and faithfulness, which (according to most of this literature) is rewarded with the bliss of reunion with the beloved.

The Aziz's Wife, the Women of Egypt, and the Prophet Joseph (*Yusuf*) in the Qur'an

Among the Qur'anic prophetic narratives only the story of Joseph[1] is told sequentially within a single Sura (Sura 12, of Late Meccan provenance), which also bears Joseph's name. The Qur'an describes it as "the best [or, most beau-

50

tiful] of narratives" (12:3). This chapter has long been the favorite of Qur'an reciters and their audiences, also the students and interpreters of the Qur'an. Indeed, Sura 12 may be the Qur'an's most-interpreted portion.[2] What follows are the verses that deal with Joseph's relations with the Aziz's[3] wife and the women of Egypt.

After Joseph had been betrayed by his jealous brothers and sold into captivity, he was purchased by an Egyptian notable who instructed his wife to treat Joseph with hospitality since he might bring them benefits or they might adopt him as a son.

(12:22) When Joseph had attained full manhood, God gave him power of judgment and knowledge. (23) And she in whose house he was sought to seduce him. She locked the doors and said: Come here. He said: God forbid! My master has received me well. The sinners will not prosper. (24) She wanted to involve herself with him [*hammat bihi*] and he wanted to involve himself with her [*hamma biha*], if he had not seen God's *burhan* ["proof," "evidence," "sign"]. So did We [interfere] in order to turn away from him evil and abomination, because he is [one] of our favored servants. (25) And they raced to the door, and she tore his shirt from behind. And they found her master at the door. She said: He who wants to do evil to your wife deserves only to be imprisoned, or a painful punishment. (26) He [Joseph] said: She sought to seduce me. And a witness from her family gave witness: If his shirt is torn from the front, she is telling the truth and he is one of the liars. (27) And if his shirt is torn from behind, then she lies and he is one of those who tell the truth. (28) So when he saw that his shirt was torn from behind, he said: Indeed, this is [a trick] of your [women's] cunning, and your cunning is, indeed, enormous. (29) Joseph, let it be! And you [woman], ask for forgiveness, you have been of those who commit a sin.

(30) And women in the city said: the Aziz's wife is seeking to seduce her slave. She is very much in love with him. We see her to be in clear error. (31) When she heard about their cunning, she sent to them and prepared for them a banquet. And she gave to each of them a knife. And she said [to Joseph]: Come out to them. And when they saw him, they found him grand [or, they extolled him, *akbarnahu*] and they cut their hands and said: God forbid. This is no human, this is but a noble angel. (32) She said: He is the one because of whom you blamed me. I sought to seduce him and he remained sinless. And if he does not do what I command, he will certainly be jailed and be of those who are lowly. (33) He said: My Lord, to be imprisoned is dearer to me than what they are calling me to do. Unless you turn their cunning away from me, I will feel desire for them and I will be among the fools [or, those lost in spiritual ignorance]. (34) And his Lord answered his prayer and turned their cunning away from him. He hears and knows all. (35) Then it occurred to them [the men] after they had seen the signs that he be imprisoned for a while.

(50) And the king said: Bring him to me. And when the messenger came to him [Joseph in prison], he said: Go back to your master and ask him how it is with the women who cut their hands. My master [or, my Lord] knows about their cunning. (51) He [the king] said to them [the women]: What happened to you when you sought to seduce Joseph? They said: God forbid,

we know of no evil against him. The Aziz's wife said: Now the truth has come to light. I sought to seduce him, and he is one of those who tell the truth. (52) This is so that he know that I did not betray him secretly and that God does not guide [to completion] the cunning of the treacherous. (53) I do not claim to be innocent [or, absolve myself from blame]. The *nafs* ["human soul"] commands evil as long as my Lord is not merciful. He is ready to forgive and compassionate.[4]

The Aziz's Wife, the Women of Egypt, and the Prophet Joseph in Islamic Interpretation

In the Qur'anic rendition of the story of Joseph and the women, the themes of female seductiveness and cunning figure with some prominence. Both appear in the Hadith as symbolized in the concept of *fitna* ("social anarchy," "social chaos," "temptation"),[5] which indicates that to be female is to be sexually aggressive and, hence, dangerous to social stability. According to tradition, God has instilled an irresistible attraction to women in man's soul, which works through the pleasure he experiences when he looks at her or deals with anything related to her. She resembles Satan in his irresistible power over the individual.[6]

In Tabari's (d. 923) traditionist exegesis, the woman of the Joseph story is referred to by her Qur'anic name, "the Aziz's wife;" al-Aziz is identified as a title ("the notable"), referring to the supervisor of Egypt's treasury, the noble Qitfir or Itfir at the court of the Egyptian king al-Rayyan ibn al-Walid of the Amalekites (XVI:17). When these events occurred, Joseph was eighteen years old, or twenty, or thirty-three. In any case, he had reached the age of full manhood which, according to Tabari, is the period "between eighteen and sixty," or "eighteen and forty." With the help of different hadiths, Tabari then provides a number of scenarios of seduction. When the Aziz's wife had begun to desire Joseph and wished to seduce him, she began to speak of his charms (the beauty of his face, his hair) and thereby awakened his desire for her. She gave Joseph her whole attention, inviting him to the pleasures that men desire in beautiful, fair, and wealthy women like her. And Joseph was young, and lustful as all men are. He turned toward her because of the *affection* she showed him. He did not fear her until he had begun to desire her and they were alone in the house together (XVI:33ff). Tabari then quotes a large number of traditions on what exactly happened between the two of them. Joseph unfastened the belt of his trousers and sat before her "as the circumciser sits"; she lay down for him and he sat between her legs; she lay down on her back and he sat between her legs and loosened his garment (or her garment); he dropped his pants to his buttocks; he sat with her as a man sits with his wife, etc. (XVI:35ff). What these scenarios have in common is that the action stops short of actual intercourse. Tabari uses the hadiths to elaborate on the legal-theological distinction between *natural appetite* and *desire* as opposed to *resolution* and *deed*, of which only the latter are punishable (XVI:38ff). Before Joseph had reached resolution and deed, God sent him the *burhan* ("sign") to strengthen his *'isma*

("state of sinlessness" of prophets). The "sign" was the specter of Joseph's father
Jacob anxiously biting his fingers and warning Joseph of the consequences of
what he was about to do. Else, Qur'anic verses appeared on the wall, or the
roof, of the chamber. Or Joseph saw the specter of the angel Gabriel, or of his
master the Aziz, or of the king. In any case, "Joseph was sore afraid and his
lust went out of him by the tips of his fingers" (XVI:34–49). The woman's
false accusation against Joseph is interpreted as an example of her sex's penchant for trickery and craftiness (XVI:50ff), but Tabari also places great emphasis on the woman's true love for Joseph (XVI:62ff). The women of Egypt were
openly critical of her behavior for moral and also social reasons.[7] Furthermore,
they were curious to see this young man. During the banquet, the women were
offered *utruj* (citrus fruit), *bazmaward* (cakes), and *'asal* (honey) to spread on
the tart fruit slices. Their reaction to Joseph's beauty was delight and praise:
akbarnahu is interpreted to mean "they found him grand," "they extolled and
praised him." Tabari here rejects the interpretation of *akbarna* as "they began
to menstruate," provided in a small number of his sources, as far-fetched and
unlikely (XVI:76–77).[8] The women merely cut their hands because of their
confusion at the young man's beauty (XVI:78). According to Tabari, Joseph's
ensuing imprisonment was a period of atonement. It was also a necessary
societal measure, since the beautiful Joseph had become a *fitna* ("source of social
chaos"), and such must be confined and concealed in order to protect the
smooth workings of society (XVI:133–146). Tabari's interpretation of these
segments of the twelfth Sura, then, is mainly psychological. He sees Joseph's
beauty as the main cause for the love and desire of one woman and the awe
and confusion of a group of women. While such is understandable as part of
human nature, it is nevertheless disturbing to the social order, and therefore
such *fitna* must be removed from the public eye. The element of Joseph's *'isma*,
"prophetic sinlessness," does not play an important role in this psychological
interpretation.

In al-Baydawi's (d. 1286?) exegesis, the elements of prophetic *'isma* and
female slyness are more clearly elaborated and juxtaposed; indeed, these two
concepts have now become the pivots around which the story moves. The
doctrine of Joseph's sinless nature leads Baydawi to interpret 12:24 (*hamma
biha*, "he wanted to involve himself with her") as a sign of Joseph's strength,
not weakness, "because he whose sexual passion is aroused and who refrains
from acting upon it deserves God's praise and recompense" (I:456–457). Conversely, Baydawi suggests that the Aziz's words in 12:28 ("your cunning is
enormous") apply to women in general terms; slyness is part of female innate
nature where it derives from and also produces evil. By nature, women's slyness is delicate. Their cunning works through men's sexual and emotional
pleasure. Men's *nafs* ("soul," "life energy," also "appetite," "desire") is forcefully
affected by such slyness which, in turn, has its grounding in Satan's whisper-
ings (I:458). The Aziz's wife's[9] desire for the young Joseph, then, is here not
seen in relation to the woman's love but derives from an essential flaw in female
nature. As for the "forty women" who attended the banquet, their reaction to
Joseph's beauty[10] was "violent sexual desire which brought on their men-

struation." Unlike Tabari, then, Baydawi does not reject the interpretation of *akbarna(hu)* (12:31) in the meaning of "they began to menstruate."[11] Indeed, the image has become a central part of the story, as Joseph's beauty, enhanced by the quality of sinlessness, calls forth female menstruation, the unclean aspect of women's nature. Baydawi adds that fear of female cunning filled Joseph's heart when he confronted the forty women with daggers in their hands whose fingers also began to drip with blood (I:459). The dark carnality of the female sex was threatening and also enticing. Baydawi points out that Joseph was aware and much afraid of the women's power to attract him. Carnal appetite against infallible morality, the body against the spirit, this is how Tabari's "love story" has been transformed in Baydawi's exegesis.

The exegesis of this story at the hands of the (Shi'i) Sufi authority al-Nisaburi (d.1328)[12] consists of two parts, a conventional *tafsir* and an esoteric Sufi *ta'wil*. In the former, Nisaburi further develops Baydawi's ideas, especially the juxtaposition of Joseph's holy, purified and prophetic self and the women's evil nature (V:99–100). The Aziz's wife, here called Zulaykha, is in part presented as a lover who does not want to hurt her beloved; the women as a group, however, are merely Satan's snares.[13] Their physical reaction (cut fingers and menstruation) is brought on by the light of prophethood they perceive in Joseph. His perfection instills despair, confusion, fear, and love (V:102). In the esoteric portion of his exegesis (*ta'wil*), Nisaburi identifies the woman Zulaykha as *al-dunya* ("the lower world," i.e., the world of matter and brute facticity, of the body and the senses) while Joseph is *al-qalb* ("the human heart in quest of God"). There is no inherent antagonism between the two in that Joseph's heart was grounded in her sphere, the earth of "being human," just as a tree needs to be rooted in the earth to bring forth its fruit. A true antagonism exists, however, between Joseph and the women of Egypt, whom Nisaburi identifies as the human qualities of brute physicality, predatoriness, "the satanic ways of the city of the body" (V:105–106).[14]

With the modern age, Islamic interpretation began to shift from the theme of women's inherently evil nature. In particular, it was the modernist and fundamentalist exegetes who began to read the story of "Joseph and the women" as a parable with communal rather than just gender-related meaning. An example of such new interpretation is found in the Qur'an commentary of the Egyptian ~~fundam~~entalist Sayyid Qutb (d. 1966), whose work will here suffice as an example. ~~For~~ Qutb, the main theme of the story is the struggle between religious righteousness and a corrupt society. Joseph is the righteous slave who never betrayed his moral nature. Even though he was young[15] and had grown to manhood in the soft and hypocritical atmosphere of an Egyptian palace with its many seductions, he had the inner strength to preserve his unblemished nature. Qutb here castigates the medieval interpreters who "under the influence of *isra'iliyyat* transmitted fables that depicted Joseph in the folly of natural impulse, propelled by sexual desire, from which he was only dissuaded by God's many 'signs'";[16] indeed, according to Qutb, it was Joseph who saved himself because his moral strength outweighed his human weakness (IV:1980–1982).

Joseph's main adversary was the *jahili*[17] Egyptian environment. Its representatives were the highborn, spoiled and headstrong Aziz's wife and her women friends, members of that society's aristocracy who spent their days in idleness and materialistic pleasures; representatives also were the prince al-Aziz and the king, both arrogant men too weak to deal with manifest injustice and who merely concealed a scandal even at the expense of imprisoning an innocent man (IV:1952, 1982, 1983). The story, then, has become a paradigm for contemporary Islamic society. Qutb describes it as "a representation of the upper class in the *jahiliyya* thousands of years ago, and yet it is as if looming before our eyes today. Laxity in confronting sexual scandals, the desire to conceal these from society . . . preservation of appearances . . . This is the aristocracy, made up of courteous and polite men, in every *jahiliyya*. How very close it is" (IV:1983). In Qutb's interpretation, Sura 12:52 and 53 (declaration of enduring loyalty and acknowledgment of blame) are attributed to the woman in indication that she remained in love with the blameless prophet because of the true faith his example had taught her (IV:1995). The theme, then, is the ultimate victory of individual righteousness over communal corruption. Qutb sees Joseph as a figure of great relevance for the present age in that all righteous believers are engaged in similar struggles against materialistic and hypocritical society. Ultimately, like Joseph, they will prevail.

It is noteworthy that Zulaykha's story is not a prominent feature in the exhortations of contemporary Muslim literature on women. Certainly the themes of "women's cunning is enormous" and "women are *fitna* [sources of social anarchy]" continue to echo in the contemporary conservative insistence on, for example, the duties of veiling and segregation; but such is usually stated in general moral and legal terms without reference to the female protagonist of the Joseph story with whom these themes appear in Qur'an and medieval Tafsir.[18] That the story will not do for contemporary exhortations undoubtedly comes from its medieval transformation into a tale of romantic love and true mutual devotion, as elaborated in the *qisas al-anbiya'* ("Tales of the Prophets") genre,[19] and a number of medieval romantic and mystic epics the most famous of which may be the Persian *Mathnawi*[20] of Jami of Herat (d. 1492).[21] More important now may be its ongoing popularity in the contemporary pious storytelling tradition.[22] To the medieval popular imagination, Zulaykha's true persona emerged when she repented her betrayal of Joseph and remained loyal to him for many years (cf. Qur'an 12:52–53). When she was old and impoverished (even enslaved), she came face-to-face with Joseph who restored her to her former social position. Then he married her,[23] and God restored to her both beauty and youth. When Joseph lay with her he found her to be a virgin, because her husband "the Notable" had been a eunuch, or he had been impotent because he was prideful. And Joseph and Zulaykha had a happy marriage and were blessed with several children.[24] With contemporary Muslim audiences, the old themes of true love and deliverance continue to sound their echo as the star-crossed lovers live on as symbols of human devotion and its reward. Not unlike the man Majnun in "Majnun and Layla,"[25] the woman Zulaykha in the popular tales of "Joseph and Zulaykha" stands for the power of human love.[26] This, however, can rob her story of the moralistic punch that contemporary Muslim preachers and writers would need to construct of this tale a warning example of what happens to "a cunning woman."[27]

Surely this Qur'anic figure, like many others beside her, exemplifies the richness and subtlety of the Qur'an's lessons, which mere exegesis can but partially explore. In Zulaykha's case, censorship of her weaknesses and celebration of her strengths have been formulated in different genres and areas of Muslim culture, the scholarly-legalistic and the imaginative-artistic, yet her Qur'anic figure remains bigger and more complex than either formulation. This, then, is perhaps also one of this example's lessons to the faithful: That while many readings are possible of the Qur'anic text, that text itself is greater than the sum total of its many readings.

5

The Women in the Life of the Prophet Moses

The Women Surrounding the Prophet Moses (Musa) in the Qur'an

The Qur'an tells the stories of several women connected with Moses:[1] mother, sister, foster mother, and wife. His foster mother was the righteous wife of the tyrannical Pharaoh; it was she who saved his life and raised him from infancy "under God's eye" in the household of God's enemy. Moses' wife was the daughter of an old Madyanite flockherder in whose service he spent some years before God's initiation of his prophethood. The Qur'anic revelations on the events in Moses' life in which these women played a part belong into the middle Meccan and late Meccan periods. Only the verse on Pharaoh's wife whose righteousness is revealed as "an example to the believers" (66:11) is dated into the late Medinan period, and there she is linked with the virgin Mary (66:12).

The Qur'an tells that Pharaoh had elevated himself in the land of Egypt and had broken up its people into fragmented groups. Of these, he oppressed a small minority, the Israelites, killing their sons (or: men) and keeping their daughters (or: women) alive (28:4; 14:6; 40:25; 7:127,141; cf. 2:49). To release the Children of Israel from their bondage and defeat Pharaoh, Haman, and their hosts (28:5–6), God sent an inspiration to the mother of Moses that she should throw her child into a "chest" (or "ark," tabut)[2] and the chest into the river, which would cast it upon the bank, so that he would be taken in by "an enemy of God and an enemy to Moses" (20:38–39). God also inspired Moses' mother to suckle the child; but when afraid for his life, she should cast him into the river without fear or sadness, since God would restore him to her and make him one of His messengers (28:7). Pharaoh's family rescued Moses "in order that he would be their enemy and a cause of sorrow for them, because Pharaoh and Haman and their hosts were men of sin" (28:8). Pharaoh's wife found joy in the infant and prevailed on the Pharaoh not to kill him, saying that he would be useful to them or they might adopt him as a son[3] (28:9). But Moses' (natural) mother was grieving and almost told about him, had not God strengthened her heart so that she remained a firm believer (28:10). Moses' mother told his sister to follow the baby and observe all that was happening while no one knew who she was (28:11). God ordained that the child Moses refused to nurse until his sister recommended their mother as nursemaid for him. In this manner, Moses' mother was reunited with her son (20:40; 28:12–13). Moses' foster mother, the Pharaoh's wife, was a righteous woman, "an example for the believers." She prayed to God to build her a house with Him in paradise, deliver her from the Pharaoh and his doings, and deliver her from the sinful people.[4] (66:11).

When Moses had reached adulthood, God bestowed power of judgment and knowledge on him (28:14). Then he killed an unbeliever (28:15–16); he fled from Egypt and stayed for a number of years with the people of Madyan (28:15–22; 20:40). When he first arrived at the watering place in Madyan, he found there some men who were watering their flocks, and also two women who kept their flocks back. These said that they could not water their animals until the shepherds were done with their work; and they added that their father was a very old man (28:23). Moses watered the women's animals for them, and one of them returned to him, walking bashfully, and invited him to her father's house (28:25). One of the two women then said to her father that he should hire Moses, because he was strong and trustworthy (28:26). The patriarch wedded one of his daughters to Moses on condition that he serve him for eight or ten years, and Moses accepted (28:27–28). When Moses had fulfilled the term and was travelling with his family, he perceived a fire (in the direction of Mount Tur) and told his family to stay behind while he would go to obtain some tiding of the way there, or a burning brand to light their fire and warm them (20:10; 27:7; 28:29). But when he reached the fire, a voice told him that he was in the presence of God (27:8–9). The voice commanded that he take off his shoes because he was in the Lord's presence in the sacred valley of Tuwa (20:12). He heard a voice from the right bank of the valley, from a tree in hallowed ground, which called to him: "Moses, verily I am God, the Lord of the Worlds" (28:30). Thus began the prophethood of Moses.

The Women Surrounding the Prophet Moses in Islamic Interpretation

Moses' father is identified as Amram (Imran),[5] chief of the Israelites. When the Egyptian Pharaoh had a dream that his rule would be ended by a child, he had the Israelite male children in Egypt "and their mothers" killed to ensure that his reign would endure. Seventy thousand Israelite male babies and twelve thousand Israelite mothers are said to have been slaughtered. Amram, however, was appointed the Pharaoh's grand vizier and became "imprisoned" in the palace.[6] Moses' mother conceived this child close to the purple, in Pharaoh's own bedroom. This occurred when Amram, while sitting at the head of Pharaoh's bed as was his custom, saw his wife arrive on the wing of a bird; he lay with her on Pharaoh's rug, and then the bird carried her back to her own house.[7] Ibn Kathir reports that the woman showed no signs of her pregnancy which thus escaped detection.[8] The argument that her husband was "imprisoned" in the castle, however, did not hold back the Egyptian soldiers in search of newborn Israelite males. Legend tells that Moses' mother used to secretly hide the infant in the oven when she had to go out on an errand. One day her daughter lit a roaring fire in the oven where Moses was, and the military search party did not detect him. The baby was miraculously saved and called to his mother to pull him out of the blaze.[9] Then God inspired her[10] to save her son by placing him in an ark and casting the ark on the waters of the Nile where it drifted for forty days, or three, or one night.[11] When the ark was retrieved by Pharaoh's folk and opened,[12] the light of prophethood was seen shining on the baby's face. Then they searched for a nursemaid for him, and through his sister's clever intervention the child's own mother was hired to nurse him, either in the royal palace[13] or in her own home.[14]

From among the women associated with Moses, exegetic literature places the greatest emphasis on Pharaoh's wife. Her name is given as Asya. She was either the daughter of Muzahim ibn Ubayd ibn al-Rayyan ibn al-Walid, Pharaoh in the time of the prophet Joseph, or she was an Israelite of Moses' tribe, perhaps his paternal aunt or first cousin.[15] She was one of the four most beautiful women ever created.[16] Miraculous events surrounded her birth and early life. Her marriage to the infidel Pharaoh was a sacrifice she made for the safety of her people, but this marriage was never consummated since God struck the Pharaoh with impotence.[17] It was Asya who saved the child Moses from the river, brought him up in her palace, and protected him against her husband's murderous wrath on many occasions. Her martyr's death occurred after Pharaoh had killed a number of believers in the palace, among them a ladies' maid, her children, and her husband;[18] when Asya picked up an iron stake to avenge these innocent victims, the Pharaoh had her tortured to death. Iron stakes were driven into her breast, but Gabriel arrived with glad tidings that she would be joining Muhammad in paradise. He gave her nectar from paradise and gently took her soul so that she felt no pain from Pharaoh's torture. Her last words were those of Qur'an 66:11.[19] Ibn Kathir, recording medieval traditions on God's special recompense for this believing woman, speaks of Asya as one of the Prophet's celestial wives, supreme honor that she will share with the Prophet's earthly wives and also the virgin Mary.[20] A number of traditions on the authority of the Prophet establish that Asya and Mary, Muhammad's wife Khadija bint Khuwaylid and Muhammad's daughter Fatima are "the best women of the world" and also the ruling females in heaven.[21] While Asya's and Mary's merit is established on the basis of the Qur'an (66:11–12), Khadija's merit is seen in her support of the Prophet from the day they met to the day she died. Fatima's merit (in Sunni exegesis) lies in her grief over the Prophet's death whom of all his children she alone survived. (In Shi'i tradition, the theme of Fatima, "mistress of sorrows," is much more prominent, and the figures of Fatima and Mary bear many similarities).[22]

This scripturalist connection of historical Islam's holy women with those of earlier sacred history goes beyond reaffirmation of the Qur'anic theme of Islam's position as interpreter of all past revelations. The women have here been joined in an archetype of righteousness.[23] Its core is female commitment to God and obedience to His command. Secondary aspects are virginity and/ or freedom from female physical symptoms such as menstruation and post-partem bleeding. Asya's Hadith-recorded marriage to an impotent Pharaoh here equals Mary's virginity which, in turn, is connected with Fatima's Hadith-recorded freedom from defilement.[24] Likewise, Khadija is given the honorific title *al-tahira*, "the pure."[25] (Even though the classical Hadith records that Khadija was married twice before her marriage to Muhammad,[26] a contemporary pious reader on her life even makes her Muhammad's virgin bride who had previously spurned all suitors from among the "Arab nobles and princes").[27] Virginity and purity are then, thirdly, conjoined with motherhood: Asya's by adoption, Mary's by the power of God's spirit. Khadija was the mother of all of the Prophet's children but one,[28] and Fatima the mother of Muhammad's grandsons Hasan and Husayn who, to many Muslims, were his true heirs.

This paradigm no longer informs contemporary writings on Asya's righteousness. Her story now exemplifies the believer's duty to testify to God's Oneness even at the peril of life. Neither spouse nor relatives can stand in the way of true devotion to God. With Asya, it was the Pharaoh's claim to be a god and his people's fearful prostrations before him that struck her as madness. The torture of innocent believers then prompted her to declare her faith openly; when she would not be dissuaded even by her own mother, she suffered a martyr's death.[29] "Closest to Pharaoh, her spirit was farthest away."[30] Asya now proves to the Muslim woman that (in Islam) the female has the freedom to choose her faith, even if against the will of a tyrannical husband.[31]

Of Moses' wife the Qur'an only tells that she was an old Madyanite sheepherder's[32] daughter. In some *qisas al-anbiya'*, she is identified as Zipporah (Safura),[33] the young woman who "walked bashfully" (Sura 28:25) and suggested to her father that he hire Moses (Sura 28:26).[34] The story has also been embellished with some further details. It is said that the sheepherder's daughters could not water their small flock because the shepherds had placed a large stone on the well, which only Moses could remove.[35] Else, they lacked the strength to jostle the male crowd.[36] Greater emphasis is placed on the "bashful gait" (28:25) of the Madyanite girl who returned to Moses still sitting at the well.[37] "She walked in the manner that free [not slave] women walk,"[38] to invite him to her father's house. On the way to her home, and while she was walking in front of Moses, the wind lifted up her garment and he saw her thigh.[39] It was then that Moses asked the young woman to walk behind him and throw pebbles to show in which direction he should proceed, so that neither her figure nor her voice would be apparent to him, the male stranger.[40]

In contemporary Muslim literature, the daughters of the Madyanite patriarch loom even larger as models for emulation by the righteous Muslim female. Their model behavior, firstly, is seen in their attitude toward work in the public sphere, that is, outside their home; secondly, a paradigm is once again derived from the personal comportment (of one of them). On the former point, the conservative Muslim argument is as follows:

> Islamic morality requires that the woman work in her home and refrain from participation in public life and public affairs; Islam has established that women's work should be done within the parameters of the family, except in cases of established and unavoidable necessity. Now the two young women in Madyan were obliged to water their animals in public because their father was a very old man. This is an example of "the need to work"; but here the two women's righteousness consisted in the fact that "they held their animals back until the male shepherds were done," so that they avoided mingling with the men in their work.[41]

This Qur'anic story, then, here serves as scripturalist proof that Muslim women's work outside of the home is religiously acceptable only as long as it is truly unavoidable and does not entail association with strangers (that is, nonrelated males).[42] Moses' righteousness prompted him to do the job for the women in order to relieve them of what contemporary conservatives assert was a moral burden. Here the understanding is that what Moses did for the two young women in Madyan must now be done by Muslim society at large. Muslim society, be it the immediate neighborhood or society at large, must take cognizance when a woman is compelled by circumstances to leave her "natural arena" to work elsewhere, and it must help her out so that she may safely return to her home. As for the woman, she must strive with all her might to settle the contingency at the earliest moment possible. The two women in Madyan did this by asking their old father to hire Moses since he was "strong and trustworthy." They had not worked outside of the home because of preference but because of need; and they eliminated this need at the earliest possibility. This, then, presents a model to be followed by all believing Muslim women.[43] Contemporary conservative teaching continues to find a second paradigm in this story in the old sheepherder's daughter's "bashful gait" when it emphasizes that this young woman "walked like a true female, not trying to behave like a man. . . . Therein lies another lesson for the contemporary Muslim woman."[44] In the medieval model, the "bashful gait" separated the free-born (respectable) Muslim woman from the (not-so respectable) slave; at present, the "bashful gait" separates the traditional Muslim woman from her modernist sister who "tries to behave like a man."

6

The Chapter of Bilqis, Queen of Sheba

From among the Qur'ans women figures, the queen of Sheba has, perhaps, remained the one most elusive of the Muslim (scholarly) exegetic grasp. In some measure, even in the Qur'an this figure remains a foreign entity, a strong and enigmatic presence resisting paradigmatization. Sovereign ruler of her pagan, sun-worshipping nation, she ably engaged in political negotiations with God's prophet Solomon; then, when she had recognized Solomon's God-given powers of control over nature and its forces, both seen and unseen, she joined his Cause and "submitted with Solomon to God, the Lord of the worlds" (Sura 27:43).

To traditionalist Islamic exegesis, this queen's story was clearly obscure inasmuch as the notion of female political sovereignty lay outside of the accepted paradigm of women's societal status. More importantly, the Qur'anic accounts of Solomon's supernatural powers, augmented in pious legend, endowed this queen's story with more miraculous detail than was useful for sober scripturalist exegesis. Therefore, the Qur'anic image of the queen of Sheba in Islam has on the whole been more productive in fanciful storytelling than scholarly *tafsir*.

In the Qur'an, this woman's story is relayed sequentially within a single Sura that, however, bears as its title neither the name of Solomon nor the queen of Sheba but that of "The Ants" (*al-Naml*), lowly creatures who feared Solomon's advance into their valley until Solomon smiled at their fear and asked God to grant him righteousness (Sura 27:18–19).

The Queen of Sheba (Saba') and
the Prophet Solomon (Sulayman) in the Qur'an

God's apostle Solomon[1] son of David is frequently mentioned in the Qur'an. His prophetic career unfolded mainly in the arena of public life, where he became renowned for his wise and skilfull administration of justice and also his God-given (esoteric) knowledge and powers. The Qur'an denies that Solomon was a magician, since magic was revealed not to Solomon but two Babylonian angels, Harut and Marut, as a trial for humankind (2:102). Nevertheless, the (Qur'anic) prophet Solomon was endowed with knowledge of the speech of animals, such as birds and ants (27:16,19).[2] He ruled the wind(s) (21:81, 38:36–37), commanded legions of satans who did his bidding (21:82, 38:37), and ruled the *jinn* who labored for him (34:12–13). Solomon's armies were recruited from men, jinn, and birds, all drawn up in ranks.

The story of the prophet Solomon and the queen of Sheba[3] is relayed in Sura 27, a Middle Meccan Sura, in the following terms: It was the hoopoe (*hudhud*) who first informed Solomon of what he had seen in Sheba. He said:

(23) I found a woman ruling over them who has been given of everything, and she has an enormous throne. (24) I found her and her people bowing to the sun instead of God,[4] and Satan made their deeds appear to them in a favorable light and kept them from the [right] path, so they are not rightly guided. (25) So that they do not bow to God who brings out [into the open] what is hidden in the heavens and on earth and knows what you hide and what you disclose. (26) God, there is no god but He, the Lord of the tremendous Throne. (27) He [Solomon] said: We shall see whether you have told the truth or are one of the liars. (28) Take this letter of mine and throw [or, deliver] it to them. Then turn away from them and see what they reply. (29) She [the queen] said: Oh notables, a noble letter has been thrown [or, delivered] to me. (30) It is from Solomon and says: In the name of God the Compassionate the Merciful. (31) Do not be arrogant against me but come to me in submission [or, as Muslims]. (32) She said: Oh notables, advise me in my affair. I will never decide a matter until you are present [with me]. (33) They said: We possess power and great fighting strength. It is for you to command. So consider what you will command. (34) She said: When kings enter a city, they ruin it and make the noblest of its people its most lowly. Thus they do it. (35) I will send them a present and will see what the emissaries bring back. (36) When he [the envoy] came to Solomon, he [Solomon] said: are you indeed supplying me with wealth? What God has given me is better than what He has given you. Yet you delight in your gift. (37) Go back to them, surely we will come to them with armies against which they cannot prevail, and we will drive them out of it [the city], submissive and humiliated. (38) He [Solomon] said: Oh notables, who of you will bring me her throne before they come to me in submission [or, as Muslims]? (39) An *'ifrit* ["demon"] of the jinn said: I will bring it to you before you get up from your place. I have the strength for it and am trustworthy. (40) He who had knowledge of the Book said: I will bring it to you in the twinkling of an eye. Then when he [Solomon] saw it [the throne] standing in his presence, he said: This is of the kindness of my Lord so that He test me whether I be

grateful or ungrateful. Who is grateful is grateful for himself [does so for his own benefit], and who is ungrateful, God is rich [free from need] and noble. (41) He said: Disguise her throne for her, so we see whether she will [or, can] be rightly guided or be of those who are not rightly guided. (42) And when she came, it was said: Is your throne like this? She said: It is as though it were the one. And before her, we were given the knowledge, and we were Muslims [or, we submitted].[5] (43) And what she used to worship instead of God impeded her, she was from a people who were disbelieving. (44) It was said to her: Enter into the palace! And when she saw it, she thought it was a deep water and she uncovered her legs. He [Solomon] said: This is a palace paved with slabs of glass. She said: My Lord, I have committed an outrage against myself. Now I submit [in Islam] together with Solomon to God, the Lord of the worlds.

The Queen of Sheba and the Prophet Solomon in Islamic Interpretation

Qur'anic consort to the prophet Solomon,[6] Islamic exegesis has identified the queen of Sheba as Bilqis. She is commonly placed into, or in relation to, the Yemenite Ma'rib-based Himyarite royal house.[7] According to some sources, her father, Dhu Sharkh ibn Hudad, was vizier to the tyrannical Himyarite king Sharakh ibn Sharahil. Her mother was Umayra, daughter of the king of the jinn. Dhu Sharkh was a most handsome man and an avid hunter. One day in the forest he heard the jinn singing their poetry and caught a glimpse of Umayra. He fell in love with her, asked her father for her hand, and became her husband.[8] Bilqis was born and raised among the jinn and grew to such beauty that she came to be known as the Venus of the Yemen. After her return to humankind, the tyrannical Himyarite king whose habit it was to ravish a new maiden every week heard of her beauty and wished to marry her. Bilqis accepted but persuaded the king to come by himself to her splendid jinn-built palace where she made him drunk and cut off his head. Then, with the help of gold (to bribe them) and wine (to besot their senses), she enticed the king's viziers to rebel against the king and swear fealty to her instead. Thereafter, she showed the viziers the king's head as though she had just killed him at their behest.[9]

Of Solomon's hoopoe, exegesis reports that he accompanied a relative, a Yemenite hoopoe, to his home and there witnessed the queen's military might, which consisted of an army of ten thousand leaders, each in command of ten thousand soldiers. Of Solomon's letter to the queen it is said that it was dictated to Aseph ben Berakhiah (Asaf ibn Barakhya);[10] that it was then sealed with musk, and that the hoopoe took it to the queen's palace. Entering through an open window into her private chamber and finding her asleep, the hoopoe threw the letter on her chest and then, "politely", "in good manners," flew back toward the window sill whence he watched all that was happening in order to report it to his master.[11] After consultation with her ministers, Bilqis ordered that gifts for Solomon be made ready. The queen's presents for Solomon (which were to test whether he was "a pious prophet" or "a worldly prophet") consisted of one hundred bricks each of gold and silver; one hundred young slave boys dressed as girls and one hundred young slave girls in boys' clothing; also one hundred horses, an unpierced pearl and an onyx vial, each linked to a riddle Solomon was able to solve. Solomon, in turn, had his courtyard paved in precious metals to show that he was in no need of the queen's presents.[12] Then queen Bilqis set out to visit Solomon. According to some interpreters, Solomon had her throne magically moved[13] to his court in order to prove his prophethood and its powers,[14] while others say that he wished for the throne and knew that he would have to appropriate it before the queen's and her followers' conversion to Islam, at which time their lives and property would become inviolable.[15] The fact that the queen recognized the throne as her own inspite of its transformation is reckoned as proof of her intelligence and powers of understanding. (Here, as also in her style of rulership over the Yemen and her political decision not to wage war against Solomon, queen Bilqis is presented as possessing "male powers of discrimination").[16] She was less astute when confronted with the palace floor made of thin glass under which, some say, there was real water with fishes and other creatures. Deeming the floor to be water, she uncovered her legs, and thus Solomon could verify whether she had hairy legs;[17] else, he could see that she did not have donkey's feet as his satans had insinuated.[18] In any case, the splendor of the palace is said to have so impressed Bilqis that she accepted Solomon as God's noble prophet and submitted to God in Islam.[19] Pious legend further reports that Solomon married Bilqis after her conversion and that she bore him a son.[20] According to some, she returned to the Yemen as its queen and Solomon visited her there for three days every month.[21] According to others, Solomon married her off to Dhu Bat', or Dhu Tubba', king of Hamadan.[22]

Concerning the story of the queen of Sheba, medieval exegesis is on the whole content with providing some legendary materials without searching for the story's "applicability," that is, its sociomoral "lesson" for Islamic society. This lack of interest to paradigmatize Bilqis[23] may have to do with the fact that her Qur'anic story deals with events prior to her acceptance of Islam; indeed, her Qur'anic story begins with evidence of her (pagan) political wisdom and ends with her submission to God. What distinguishes the medieval interpretations is merely the degree of credibility attributed to fanciful detail thought to derive from *isra'iliyyat* traditions. Here, Qur'an exegesis proper (*tafsir*) is on occasion more critical of such "fanciful tales" than is historical legend (*qisas al-anbiya'*),[24] even though the materials are presented in both genres. It is also important, however, to recall that, according to the Qur'an, Bilqis was the competent sovereign ruler of her country, a notion that neither classical nor modern conservative and fundamentalist religious interpreters have accepted as part of the Islamic paradigm. A faint echo of this political theme is found in medieval exegetic literature. Ibn Kathir, for example, quotes a tradition according to which the Prophet said that "a people who entrust their command to a woman will not thrive," and that the Prophet said this "when Bilqis was mentioned in his presence." The tradition in question, however, is here judged "weak" because "the authenticated Hadith establishes that the Apostle of God uttered these words after he had heard that Khosroe's daughter had acceded to the Persian throne."[25] Even though this tradition is recorded in the latter form in the authenticated Hadith collections, for example, Bukhari's *Sahih*,[26] it has here recently been criticized as "weak" on other grounds as well; indeed, in her book *The Veil and the Male Elite*,[27] Fatima Mernissi has deconstructed this tradition by quoting reports on false testimony given by the tradition's first transmitter, the Prophet's freedman Abu Bakra, which prove this trans-mitter's moral deficiency and, hence, the tradition's whole chain of authenti-cation (*sanad*) as "faulty." While this hadith remains an important scripturalist argument in the conservative Islamic stand against women's rights to share in, let alone assume, political power, to my knowledge most medieval and all mod-ern references to it fail to connect this Prophetic verdict with the queen of Sheba.

In contemporary pious legend, the queen of Sheba continues to appear as a fanciful historical figure.[28] More important at present, however, may be her story's reading as parable of the might, incorruptibility, and convincing power of righteousness. Sayyid Qutb, for instance, once again stripping his interpre-tation of all medieval Hadith lore, uncovers this story's meaning in Solomon's true prophetic devotion to his faith and mission (*da'wa*, "Call"). Solomon's true wealth lay in his God-given knowledge and prophethood. Thus he saw no need to accept the queen's presents; in any case, a prophet cannot be bought with material goods.[29] To Qutb, these facts, together with the miracles of the "transported throne" and the "slabs of glass" in the palace, are the reasons that by divine design led the "smart and independent" queen of Sheba to submit to God.[30] At this point, this fundamentalist writer comes forth with an "applica-tion" of Bilqis' story to Muslim society but in a manner that excludes all gen-der issues. The queen's Islam, according to Qutb, made her Solomon's equal, since in Islam the vanquished and the victor are equal brothers, as are the "called" and the "caller," the "followers" and the "leader." The pagan Meccans who rejected Muhammad's mission because they were too arrogant to accept his leadership should have heeded "this woman of history," the queen of Sheba, whose lesson teaches that Islam is submission not to a leader, not even a prophet, but to God—the God in whose sight all true believers are the same.[31]

7

The Chapter of Mary

The figure of Mary, mother of Jesus, looms very large in Qur'anic scripture, scripturalist exegesis, and popular Muslim piety. In the Qur'an, Mary is the only female identified by name, and her name appears far more frequently in the Qur'anic text than in the entire New Testament. Her name is also the title of a Qur'anic Sura (Sura 19). From birth she was surrounded by miracles of divine favor. As a young woman, she received the angelic annunciation of a child from God's spirit, a word from God cast into Mary, whose name was the Christ Jesus son of Mary, chosen to be one of God's righteous prophets. The angels also gave Mary glad tidings that God had chosen and purified her, had chosen her above the women of the worlds. And the Qur'anic revelation celebrates Mary as "an example for the believers" because of her chastity, obedience, and faith.

In the Qur'an, the story of Mary is intertwined with that of her guardian, the prophet Zacharia (Zakariyya). The Qur'anic accounts of Zacharia's prayer for a child in old age and the glad tidings of the birth of John (Yahya) (19:2–15; 21:89–90; 3:38–41) in all instances directly precede Qur'anic passages on Mary's sinless conception of the prophet Jesus (19:16–35; 21:91; 3:42–51); in Sura 3, Zacharia's story (3:38–41) is inserted between verses on Mary's birth and childhood (3:33–37) and the angels' annunciation of the birth of Jesus (3:42–51). The angels' words on the birth of John to Zacharia (3:39) are almost identical with those on the birth of Jesus to Mary (3:45). Both Zacharia (3:40) and Mary (3:47) question the message—"my Lord, how shall I have a son"—and both are told that God "does" (3:40), "creates" (3:47) what He wills. Furthermore, the wording of God's praise and blessing of John (19:12–15) is almost identical to Jesus' words about himself, spoken in the cradle (19:30–33). In this manner, a strong affinity is established between the figures of Zacharia and Mary on the one hand and those of John and Jesus on the other (except that the Qur'an overall awards much greater prominence to Mary and Jesus). Zacharia's wife here remains a figure apart. It is only in Qur'anic exegesis and pious tradition that she is linked with Mary by ties of kinship, gender, and shared life experiences.

The Wife of the Prophet Zacharia and Mother of the Prophet John in the Qur'an

The Qur'an renders the story of the motherhood of Zacharia's wife in Suras 19, 21, and 3.[1] The woman's name is not mentioned, but the revelation speaks of her righteousness and God's favor in restoring her from barrenness and granting her motherhood.

The aged Zacharia[2] prayed to God in secret in the *mihrab*[3] for a son who would be his successor and equal in righteousness (19:2–6; 21:89; 3:38). The prayer was answered, and God (19:7; His angels, 3:39) gave him tidings of a son named John (Yahya), a name not before given (19:7); he would witness to the truth of a word from God and be a lord, an ascetic, and a prophet (3:39). Zacharia doubted because his wife was barren and he himself had grown very old; God restored his wife for him, God's will was done, and the task was very easy for God (19:8–9; 21:90; 3:40). Zacharia asked for a sign, which God granted him; it was that he would not speak for three nights (19:10; three days, 3:41) and would communicate through motions or signs only (19:10–11; 3:41). Zacharia thus (silently) suggested to his people to celebrate God's praises in the morning and in the evening (19:11); he himself was commanded to celebrate God's praises in the evening and in the morning (3:41). The child John was given *hukm* ("jurisdiction;" in Islamic exegesis usually understood as "the wisdom of prophethood") even while still a young boy. He was compassionate, pure, and devout, kind to his parents, neither arrogant nor rebellious (19:12–14). God ordained "peace on him the day he was born, the day he dies, and the day he will be raised alive" (19:15). Zacharia, his wife and their son were a righteous family. They competed in good deeds, prayed to God in longing and fear, and were humble (21:90).

The Wife of the Prophet Zacharia and Mother of the Prophet John in Islamic Interpretation

Islamic tradition has identified Zacharia's wife as Elisabeth (Ishba', daughter of Faqudh).[4] Zacharia,[5] before his prophethood a frugal and devout carpenter, is said to belong into the Solomonic line; indeed, he and Amram (Imran), father of Mary, are called the children of Solomon. Elisabeth is the sister of Mary's mother Anna (Hanna)[6] and also appears in some traditions as the sister of Mary.[7] Information on this figure is scanty. She is seen as resembling Sara in that both were blessed with a child, a future prophet, in old age after life-long barrenness. Other traditions tell of her meeting with Mary when both were pregnant. The women embraced, and Elisabeth told Mary that her own unborn child was prostrating himself in obeisance before the child in Mary's womb. This, the commentators explain, was in fulfillment of the Qur'anic words that John would "testify to the truth of a word from God"(3:39),[8] and that the prostration meant obedience and glorification, as had the angels' prostration before Adam. It signified that the prophet Jesus stood above the prophet John "because God made him resurrect the dead and heal the blind and the leper."[9] In contemporary works on Qur'anic women figures including those of the *qisas al-anbiyā'* genre,[10] Elizabeth is not mentioned; to my knowledge, she also plays no role as "example" in the contemporary pious literature for and about women.

Mary (Maryam) the Mother of the Prophet Jesus (Isa) in the Qur'an

Mary[11] is the only female identified in the Qur'an by name. Her name appears in a large number of Qur'anic verses[12] and is also the title of a Sura (Sura 19). Most other personal names used as titles of Qur'anic chapters are those of prophets—for example, Sura 10: Yunus; Sura 11: Hud; Sura 12: Yusuf; Sura 14: Ibrahim; Sura 47: Muhammad; Sura 71: Nuh.[13] Before birth, Mary's mother consecrated her to God's service. After the baby was born, she invoked God's protection for her and her progeny from Satan. According to authenticated tradition, both Mary and her son Jesus thereby escaped "the pricking of the devil" at birth, which tradition is said to have played a role in the formation of the later Islamic doctrine of prophetic *'isma* (innate quality of "impeccabil-ity," "immunity from sin and error" of prophets).[14] Mary served in the *mihrab*[15], where she received miraculous sustenance. While a virgin, God's angels spoke to Mary to give her glad tidings of a word (*kalima*) from God; God cast of His spirit (*ruh*) into Mary; He sent His spirit to Mary to give her a pure son. Was Mary, then, a Qur'anic prophet? Classical Islamic theology debated this issue, especially after it had been championed by the Zahirite school, a relatively marginal and in any case short-lived medieval *madhhab* ("school of scriptural interpretation and religious law"), whose focus on the literal (*zahiri*) meaning of the sacred text found proof for Mary's prophethood in the fact that God's angels had informed her of things to come. Neither consensus-based main-stream doctrine nor public piety, however, came to recognize Mary's prophet-hood. Exegetes have consistently extolled her high Qur'anic rank; but their images of Mary have also reflected the fact that she differs from other Qur'anic women figures in nature and life experiences and also, at least in part, from the Islamic ideal of womanhood as elaborated in Islamic law.

The Qur'anic story of Mary is related in three Meccan[16] and four Medinan[17] Suras. The earliest and longest account is found in Sura 19, the *Sura of Mary*, which relates the annunciation, Jesus' birth, and Jesus' first words, spoken before birth(?) and in the cradle. According to this Sura,

(16) Mary withdrew from her family to an eastern place.[18] (17) She took a screen [or, curtain, *hijab*] [to screen herself] from them. And We sent Our Spirit to her, and it took the shape of a well-proportioned human. (18) She said: I take refuge with the Compassionate from you. [Go away] if you fear God. (19) He said: I am only your Lord's messenger, to give you[19] a pure boy. (20) She said: How could I have a boy when no human has touched me and I am not a whore? (21) He said: Thus. Your Lord says: It is easy for Me, and so that We make him a sign for the people and a mercy from Us. It is a settled matter. (22) So she was pregnant with him, and she retired with him to a remote place.[20] (23) And the pains of childbirth drove her to the trunk of a palm-tree. She said: If only I had died before this and were completely forgotten. (24) And he called her from below her[21]: Do not grieve, your Lord has placed beneath you a little brook. (25) And shake the trunk of the palm-tree toward you, so it will drop juicy fresh dates upon you. (26) And eat and drink and be joyful. And when you see a human being, then say: I have vowed a fast to the Merciful, and I will not speak with a human being today.[22] (27) Then she brought him to her people, carrying him. They said: Oh Mary, you have done something unheard-of. (28) Oh sister of Aaron,[23] your father was not a bad man nor was your mother a whore. (29) Then she pointed toward him. They said: How can we speak to someone who (as) a small boy is [still] in the cradle? (30) He said: I am God's slave. He has given me the Book and has made me a prophet. (31) He has made me blessed wherever I be and has charged me with prayer and almsgiving as long as I live,[24] (32) and filial piety toward my mother.[25] And He has not made me tyrannical and villainous. (33) And peace be upon me the day I was born and the day I die and the day I am resurrected alive.[26] (34) Such is Jesus, the son of Mary—to say the truth which they doubt. (35) It is not for God to acquire [or, take to Himself] any child.[27] Praised be He! When He decides a matter He only says to it: Be! and it is.

In the short verses of Suras 23 and 21, Mary and her son Jesus are revealed to be "a sign" (*aya*) from God: (23:50) "And We made the son of Mary and his mother a sign, and We granted both of them shelter on a hill with *qarar* ["fertile ground," or, "a secure abode," "a hollow"],[28] and spring water"; (21:91) "And she who guarded her chastity [literally, her shame]. Then We breathed into her of Our spirit, and We made her and her son a sign for the worlds."

A second annunciation scene is related in Sura 3,[29] where it is preceded by the story of Mary's consecration to God's service, Zacharia's guardianship of Mary, and the miraculous sustenance she received while serving in the temple as a young girl.

(33) "God chose Adam and Noah and the family of Abraham and the family of Amram above the worlds. (34) Progeny one from the other. And God hears and knows. (35) [Then] when the wife of Amram said: My Lord, I have pledged [or, I herewith pledge] to you what is in my womb as consecrated.[30] So accept [it] from me. You are who hears and knows. (36) And when she had given birth to her, she said: My Lord, I have given birth to her, a female. And God was most aware of what she had borne. The male is not like the female. And I have named her Mary, and I place her and her offspring under

your protection against stone-worthy Satan. (37) And her Lord accepted her graciously and made her grow up in a goodly manner. And He put her charge with Zacharia. Whenever Zacharia entered upon her in the *mihrab*,[31] he found sustenance with her. He said: Oh Mary, from where do you have this? She said: This is from God. God provides for whom He wills, without accounting.[32] (42) And [then] when the angels said: Oh Mary, God has chosen you and purified you and chosen you above the women of the worlds. (43) Oh Mary, be devoutly obedient toward your Lord, prostrate yourself, and bow down with those who bow down.[33] (44) This belongs to the stories of what is hidden. We reveal it to you. You were not with them when they cast their reed-stalks as lots [to establish] who of them would provide for Mary. And you were not with them when they quarreled. (45) And [then] when the angels said: Oh Mary, God gives you glad tidings of a word from Him whose name is Christ Jesus son of Mary, highly regarded in this world and in the hereafter, and one of those brought close [to God]. (46) He will speak to the people in the cradle and as a grown man, and be of the righteous. (47) She said: My Lord, how shall I have a son when no human has touched me? He said: Thus. God creates what He wills. When He has decreed a matter He only says to it: Be! and it is. (59) Jesus is before God like Adam. He created him from dust, then said to him: Be! And he is.

Sura 66 establishes Mary's status as "example for the believers" because of her chastity, faith, and obedience. (11) "And God has given an example to those who believe . . . (12) (in) Mary the daughter of Amram who remained chaste [literally, protected her shame] and We blew into it of Our spirit. And she testified to the truth of her Lord's words and His books and was of the devoutly obedient."[34]

Suras 4 and 5 emphasize Mary's chastity but also her and Jesus' full humanity; here the language includes the refutation that Jesus and Mary formed part of a "trinity":

(4:156) [Among the sins the Jews committed were . . .] their unbelief and their uttering of an enormous slander against Mary.

(4:171) Oh people of the Book! Do not go too far in your religion, and do not assert against God, except the truth. Christ Jesus son of Mary is only God's messenger and His word which He conveyed to Mary, and a spirit from Him. Therefore believe in God and His messengers and do not say: Three. Cease. It is better for you. God is only one God. Glory be to Him. [He is exalted above] that He should have a son. To Him belongs what is in the heavens and on earth. And God is the best caretaker.

(4:172) Christ does not disdain to be the slave of God, nor [do] the angels brought close [to God]. He who disdains His worship[35] and is arrogant, He will gather them all together to Himself [for judgment].

(5:19) Unbelieving are those who say that God is Christ the son of Mary. Say: Then who would prevail against God if He wished to destroy Christ the son of Mary and his mother and all who are on earth? God has the dominion of the heavens and the earth and what is in-between. He creates what He wills. And God is capable of everything.

(5:75) Unbelieving are those who say: God is Christ the son of Mary.

And Christ said: Oh children of Israel, worship God, my Lord and your Lord. He who ascribes partners to God, God has forbidden him paradise. His abode is the fire, and the sinners have no helpers.

(5:78) Christ the son of Mary is only a messenger. Before him have the messengers passed. And his mother is a woman of truth. The two of them used to eat food. See how We clarify the signs for them, then see how they are turned away?

(5:119) And [then] when God said: Oh Jesus son of Mary, did you say to the people: beyond God, take me and my mother as gods? He said: Praise be to you. It is not for me to say what is not my right. If I said [or, had said] it, you knew it. You know what is in my mind, while I do not know what is in your mind. You are the knower of hidden things. (120) I only said to them what you commanded me, to worship God my Lord and your Lord, and I was a witness over them as long as I was among them. And then when you took me unto you, it was you who watched over them. You are witness over everything.

Mary the Mother of the Prophet Jesus in Islamic Interpretation

The medieval Hadith[36] relates different "occasions of revelation" of the story of Mary.[37] The verses of Sura 19 are said to have been revealed before the first Muslim migration to Abyssinia, where they impressed upon the Negus Islam's status as a monotheistic faith and, consequently, his obligation to protect the Muslim migrants in his realm against their pagan Meccan compatriots.[38] Conversely, the verses of Sura 3 are said to have been revealed during meetings that the by then victorious Prophet held in Medina with a large delegation of sixty horsemen from the Yemenite Christian community of Najran. "These began to argue about God and the Messiah, and God revealed the beginning of Sura 3 (*Al Imran*) about that and clarified that Jesus was created, as was his mother before him."[39] These traditions may give an inkling not only of the chronology of the sequential Qur'anic segments of Mary's story but also of early Muslim perceptions of the unfolding story's import. Post-Qur'anic Islamic exegesis, however, came to perceive the main purpose of all of the revelations on Mary[40] as divine clarification of the true natures of Jesus and Mary in order that their creaturedom be but another sign of God's Oneness and Omnipotence. In contemporary exegesis, the reading of Mary's story in terms of *tawhid*, unicity of God, is even more clearly stated.[41]

Hadith and Tafsir have dealt with the figure of Mary in several different ways. Firstly, the miraculous events surrounding her birth and childhood, the annunciation and the birth of Jesus were developed and expanded upon in the hagiographic mode. Secondly, the scholars of Islam found in the Qur'anic text a number of theological problems for debate and dogmatic formulation. Among these has been the meaning of "spirit" (*ruh*) and "word" (*kalima*) that the virgin received from God. The debate has also involved the question of whether Mary was one of God's prophets, and how her Qur'an-proclaimed qualities of purity and obedience should be defined. The Hadith has probed Mary's relationship with Eve and, in consideration of her Qur'an-established rank "above the women of the worlds" has asked if she was, indeed, superior to earlier figures, such as Pharaoh's wife, or later ones, such as Khadija, Fatima, and A'isha. Thirdly, as with all other exemplars in Qur'an and/or Sunna, the religious authorities have attempted to define the social applicability of Mary's qualities, that is, the facets of her model status suited for emulation by the Muslim woman. Modern interpretations show some change from the classical on all three themes. The old hagiographic dimension (based in part on Bible-related Hadith materials) is now largely eliminated. Scholastic probings into the dogmatic significance of key issues in Mary's story are of low priority compared to exegetic emphasis that the story's core is the affirmation of God's Oneness and unlimited power. And while the problematic of Mary's model status for emulation by Muslim females is now addressed with greater purpose and vigor, modern theological efforts in this latter area have not been "pervasive" in that the figure of Mary remains *sui generis* and thus presents problems for Islamic paradigmatization.

The Story in Hagiographic Extension

Mary's Consecration, Birth, and Childhood in the Temple

Traditions report that Mary's mother Anna (Hanna),[42] wife of Amram (Imran), was longing for a child. The sight of a bird brooding over its young moved her to tears, and she entreated her husband to pray for a child. Both prayed, and Amram dreamed that he should lie with his wife. He did and she conceived.[43] Else, Anna began to menstruate (i.e., she was once again awarded the physical state of women who can conceive); having been purified from her menstruation, she conceived from her husband.[44] Assuming that she was carrying a boy, Anna consecrated her unborn child to God's service in the temple, and God accepted the offering even though the child was female.[45] Anna named her daughter Mary.[46] Because of Anna's prayer that God protect Mary and her offspring from Satan, neither Mary nor her son Jesus were "touched," or "pricked," or "kicked," or "squeezed," or "pierced in the side" at birth by Satan, which is what happens to all other human beings and explains why babies cry when they are born.[47] After the infant was weaned, Anna took Mary to the temple. Then Amram died,[48] and lots were cast for the privilege of the child's care. Of the reed stalks cast into the well of Seloam (or, other bodies of water), only that of Zacharia consistently floated on the surface (or, against the current), and therefore it was he to whom was awarded the privilege of her care.[49] Mary grew up in the temple a beautiful young girl. She worshipped day and night, her feet swollen and oozing with pus, until her unequalled piety and righteousness became known among the Israelites.[50] She lived in the *mihrab* to which only Zacharia had the key. He would lock her into the room, but whenever he visited her, he found wondrous provisions: winter fruit during summertime, and summer fruit during wintertime. Mary gave some of these to Zacharia, and it was then that he lay with his wife and she conceived John (Yahya); else, Zacharia prayed to God, provider of "fruit out of season," to give him "a son out of season."[51] When Mary had attained the age of puberty, she told Zacharia that "she had seen a horrible thing," (i.e., she had begun to menstruate), and from then on Zacharia removed her from the place of worship to his wife's (her maternal aunt's) care until she returned to a state of purity.[52] Among the people who served with Mary in the temple, mention is made of Joseph son of Jacob,[53] a carpenter, who is identified as Mary's cousin on her mother's side.[54]

Annunciation, Pregnancy, and the Birth of Jesus

In Tafsir literature, the annunciation of the angels (Sura 3) is generally interpreted in light of Mary's visitation by God's spirit in the form of a man (Sura 19), and both instances are said to refer to the angel Gabriel (Jibril).[55] When the angel(s) approached, Mary was alone. Some traditionists say that this was at a well in the wilderness ("desert") to which Mary and Joseph had walked to fill their water jugs.[56] According to others, Mary had withdrawn to an isolated place for the duration of her menstrual period, as was her habit, and that she had just cleansed herself when the angel(s) appeared. Else, she is said to have sought solitude in order to pray.[57] God's spirit, that is, the angel Gabriel, approached her in the form of a handsome, beardless young man who had a pure face and curly hair.[58] Other traditions maintain that God's spirit (Gabriel) took the form of Mary's companion Joseph.[59] Mary's surprise at the annunciation is explained by the fact that she had no husband.[60]

Identification of the spirit with the angel Gabriel, however, presented the interpreters with a textual problem in that the Qur'anic "spirit" speaks to Mary in the first person, announcing "I am only your Lord's messenger, that I give you a pure boy" (19:19).[61] Exegesis solved the problem by making the angel Gabriel the medium, or means, or instrument, of God's "blowing of His spirit" into Mary (as established in 21:19 and 66:12). "Gabriel could not create life in her, because he himself was a created body."[62] The theme of Gabriel's blowing, however, was thereafter elaborated with the loving detail of popular legend. Exegesis ponders at length whether Gabriel blew into the *jayb* ("breast-pocket," or "fold," or "neckline") of Mary's chemise, or whether he blew at its hem, or into its sleeve. Some say that the fold of her chemise was ripped in the front, so that the breath reached her breast. Else, the breath entered through her mouth.[63] In any case, the breath reached her womb and she conceived her child.[64] Traditions go on to tell that Joseph was the first to notice Mary's pregnancy, and that he was much astonished and troubled. Eventually, he confronted her by asking whether a crop could grow without seeds, and a child without a father? Mary answered yes, since God had created the first crop from nothing, just as He had created Adam without father or mother. Her answer convinced Joseph that Mary's child was also the result of God's creative power beyond the customary course of nature.[65]

Mary's pregnancy is said to have coincided with that of her maternal aunt Elisabeth, Zacharia's wife. When the two women met and embraced, John prostrated himself in Elisabeth's womb before the unborn Jesus.[66] When Mary was alone, her unborn child would speak with her, and when she was among people, she could hear him praise God in her womb.[67] Most traditions relate that Mary carried Jesus for nine months, "as women carry." Some assume a shorter pregnancy, such as eight, seven, or six months, nine or three hours, one hour, or no time at all, with the delivery occurring immediately after conception.[68] That Mary was generally thought to have been pregnant for some time is affirmed in the stories involving Joseph and Elisabeth. Furthermore, exegesis perceives Mary's withdrawal "to a remote place" (19:22) as selfprotection against "the heretics among the Israelites," the gossipers and slanderers who would accuse her of an immoral relationship with Joseph, or even Zacharia.[69]

It was then that the birthpangs drove Mary to the trunk of a palm tree and she wished that she had died before any of this happened, and to be completely forgotten.[70] God's favor and blessing then came to her in the form of fresh dates and clear drinking water. Some say that the date palm in that place was a dried-up tree that miraculously began to sprout; others say that it was a living tree that bore no fruit, because these events took place in winter when fruit are not in season. The gifts, when miraculously provided, gave Mary the nourishment "most appropriate for women in labor," and also confirmed the noble status the date palm holds in God's creation. A number of traditions, however, see God's gifts to Mary as greater than physical nourishment in that God's creation of fresh dates in the winter "without pollen" was, primarily, miraculous proof of Mary's sinlessness.[71] Mary stayed with her child in the place of his birth for forty days, that is, until she had regained physical purity.[72]

According to medieval scholarly Qur'an interpretation, Mary then returned home to her people. The more popular and hagiographic *qisas al-anbiya'* genre of pious legendary tales here records some additional events. Some traditionists "who transmitted from the *ahl al-kitab*" relate that a search party went out for Mary.[73] When they came upon Mary and her newborn child, they found them both surrounded by lights.[74] According to Wahb ibn Munabbih,[75] the idols East and West collapsed on that day and the satans were confused until Iblis told them about Jesus . . . and they found Jesus lying in his mother's lap, while angels stood all about him. A brilliant star rose in the sky. The priests of the Persian king took this as the sign of an important birth. The Persian king then sent his emissaries to Jesus with gold, myrrh, and frankincense. The Syrian king, however, planned to kill Jesus. When Mary was informed of his intentions, she fled with Jesus to Egypt, where they stayed until Jesus was twelve years old.[76] Medieval scholarly Tafsir rejects this story by denying that anyone went out in search of Mary. Modern exegesis, much more critical of hagiographic detail in general and Bible-related lore (*isra'iliyyat*) in particular, has labeled tales of this nature "fables and legends" which obscure the main Qur'anic issue, that is, God's reminder to the faithful that He is One and His power is absolute.[77]

When Mary returned to her family, she left her defense to her child. The interpreters here speak of the anger of Mary's people at the suggestion that a mere infant would speak to them to exonerate his mother.[78] The effectiveness of Jesus' defense is seen in the fact that his (Qur'an-recorded) words concerned himself as God's prophet and thereby established Mary's virtue within the parameter of prophetic veracity.[79]

Some Doctrinal Issues in the Qur'anic Revelations on Mary

Spirit (ruh)

Suras 19:17; 21:91; and 66:12 state that Mary was impregnated by "Our spirit."[80] Jesus is identified as "God's prophet, His word that He cast into Mary and a spirit from Him" (4:171). Jesus was supported with the holy spirit (*ruh al-qudus*) (2:87, 253; 5:113).[81] The casting of God's spirit into Mary recalls the gift of God's spirit to Adam shaped from clay (15:29; 32:9; 38:72),[82] while Jesus' support by means of the holy spirit recalls the strengthening of those in whose hearts faith is firmly inscribed "with a spirit from Himself" (58:22). In addition, the Qur'an speaks of "the trusted spirit" (*al-ruh al-amin*) as the agent of God's revelation (26:193; cf. 16:102). The spirit is further mentioned together with, but separate from, the angels (97:4; 70:4; 78:38), and also as something conveyed by the angels to God's chosen servants (16:2). In its role as conveyor of revelation, the spirit is identified as Gabriel (Jibril) (2: 97).[83]

In Mary's story, the spirit is life-creating force of, or from, God. To this day, however, Islamic exegesis has differentiated between "Our [God's] spirit" sent to Mary in the form of a man (19:17) and "Our [God's] spirit [of] which We breathed into Mary" (21:91; 66:12). While the former has been "personalized" by way of identification with Gabriel,[84] the latter is understood as the life substance with which God (directly) awakened Adam to life from clay, just as it (directly) awakened Jesus to life in Mary's womb.[85] Classical exegesis established that Gabriel was the means, or instrument, of God's creative power. But contemporary thinkers perpetuate the notion that, "somehow," "God's spirit in the form of a well-shaped human" *qua* Gabriel in human form was a different "entity" than the spirit which God breathed (directly) into Mary.[86] The issue, however, has not attracted much further attention. On the whole, the conservative shaykhs familiar with the medieval rationalist tradition are merely imitative of medieval authorities. Others find little use in the scholastic tradition since their attention lies with social, economic and political issues, the new agenda of defining Islam in the modern world.

Kalima, God's Word Bestowed upon Mary

In Sura 3:42, the angels announce to Mary that God gives her glad tidings of a word from Him whose name is Christ Jesus, son of Mary. Sura 4:171 speaks of Jesus as God's apostle and His word bestowed upon Mary. Classical Qur'an exegesis has recorded different interpretations of the meaning of Jesus as "a word from God" (3:42) or "God's word" (4:171).[87] Once again, the richest formulation is found in the work of the medieval rationalist theologian Razi[88] and is reiterated, with little change, by the nineteenth century modernist theologian Muhammad Abduh. To these authorities, use of the term "word" is mainly metaphorical. The term can be interpreted as:

1. God's creative power and His act of creation of Jesus.
2. "word" indicates the gospel, essence of Jesus' prophetic mission.

3. Else, Jesus himself is figuratively referred to as "God's word" in order to define his mission, which is to clarify God's message to the world and cleanse the record of past revelations from [Jewish] distortion.
4. The "word" means God's message to Mary *about* the birth of Jesus.[89]

The fundamentalist Sayyid Qutb sums up the lack of interest of many modern and contemporary religious thinkers in the whole scholastic rationalist tradition when he places the notion of Jesus as God's word among the Qur'an's "implicit" or "obscure" (*mutashabih*) teachings, "a matter above human understanding and, therefore, none of man's concern."[90]

Prophethood
Was Mary a prophet? Some Muslim theologians, especially of the Zahirite ("literalist") school, have argued that Mary mother of Jesus, Sara mother of Isaac, and the mother of Moses are to be reckoned among God's prophets because, according to the Qur'an, angels spoke to them (or God otherwise inspired them). In a controversial tract, the Zahirite Ibn Hazm of Cordova (d. 1064) argued in favor of women's prophethood but distinguished *nubuwwa* (prophethood) from *risala* (messengerhood), the latter restricted to men.[91] According to Ibn Hazm, the knowledge the mothers of Isaac, Jesus, and Moses received from God (through word or inspiration) was as true as the knowledge received by male prophets (through revelation). Ibn Hazm further likens the "inspiration" of Moses' mother (to throw her son into the river) to Abraham's "inspiration" (to sacrifice his son). Both would have been crazy as well as sinful in acting on the inspiration unless they trusted its divine source.[92] According to Ibn Hazm, Mary's prophethood is further clarified in that the Qur'an also calls her "a woman of truth" (5:75) just as it speaks of the prophet Joseph as "a man of truth" (12:46). Finally, the authenticated prophetic tradition that Asya (the Pharaoh's wife) and Mary are "the two perfect women" prompts Ibn Hazm not only to include Asya among the prophets of Islam but also to rank Mary and Asya above the other female prophets in the manner that Muhammad and Abraham are ranked above the male.[93]

Consensus-based Sunni theology rejected this doctrine and labeled it "heretical innovation" (*bid'a*) on the authority of Suras 12:109 and 16:43 ("We sent not before you other than men whom We inspired"). Critical to the argumentation, however, was also the consideration of "purity" as aspect of *'isma* ("innate quality of immunity from sin and error of prophets"). In orthodox definition, purity includes (constant) physical purity, a state unattainable to women because of menstruation. This legalistic notion has informed scripturalist interpretation of the issue of Mary's prophethood and also the definition of Mary's Qur'an-proclaimed purity.

Purity, Sinlessness, Virginity
In Islamic usage, the terms "purity"[94] (*tahara*) and "purification" (*tathir*) with relation to women usually signify the physical state marked by absence of menstruation, and the ritual (major ablution, *ghusl*) preceding it. In the Qur'an,

the angels announce to Mary that God has "purified" her (*tahhara*) (3:42). The Qur'anic text does not indicate whether this signified a physical state. The Hadith, however, has generally insisted that in the physical sense Mary was a woman like all others. She is said to have begun menstruation during the time of service in the place of worship, from which she was then removed until purification. Most interpreters add that Mary was ten or thirteen or fifteen years old at the time of the annunciation, and that she had completed two menstrual cycles at that time.[95] The forty days of isolation Mary is said to have observed after her delivery "until she was healed of childbirth" further indicate that Jesus' birth was considered ordinary in its physical symptoms.[96]

Conversely, some interpreters have recorded traditions and/or their own scholarly opinions that Mary's purity included freedom from menstruation just as it did "freedom from the touch of men."[97] The modernist Muhammad Abduh speculates that it was this quality that enabled Mary to serve in the temple.[98] In modern as well as classical sources, however, these readings have remained marginal to consensus-based doctrine that defined Mary's purity in ethical terms. While physically a woman like all others, Mary is said to have been excised of all lowly character traits, also disbelief and rebelliousness/disobedience against God, that is, sin.[99] In this context, exegesis has awarded prominence to the Prophet's words, enshrined in several authenticated traditions, that of all humans only Mary and her son escaped Satan's touch at birth. These prophetic traditions are generally linked with Anna's prayer that God protect her daughter and the daughter's offspring against Satan (3:35).[100]

It is, perhaps, because of Mary's holiness (rather than physical purity) that some interpreters have even considered Mary a man, "because of the perfection apportioned to her," (since) "among women are some who are perfect and knowledgeable and who attain the standard of men—they are in a real sense men."[101] The question remains, however, whether such reckoning of (holy) women among men is, or has been, thought to carry true ritual and other legal implications, that is, whether such women are acknowledged full status in the community of believers. Of interest in this context are the scholarly interpretations of 3:43, God's command to Mary to "bow down [in prayer] with those [males] who bow down." According to Smith and Haddad, the modern Qur'anic commentator Muhammad Jamal al-Din al-Qasimi was one of the few Muslim authorities who established the connection between female holiness and women's right to lead the prayer.[102] Traditional exegesis, though acknowledging Mary's sinlessness, interpreted 3:43 as God's call to Mary to pray *with* the congregation, that is, the male members of the community, but nothing more.[103]

According to classical as well as modern Islamic consensus, Mary was virgin (*batul*)[104] when she conceived her child from God's spirit. (The question of whether Mary's virginity prevailed after Jesus' birth is largely disregarded).[105] Clearly controversial (within the Islamic context), then, is the rejection of the notion of virgin birth as advanced by some modernist Qur'an interpreters from among the radical avant garde of modernism on the Indian subcontinent. The nineteenth-century Indian exegete Sayyid Ahmad Khan (d. 1898) interprets the Qur'anic texts on Mary's chastity ("guarding her shame") as the chastity of a married woman who only has sexual intercourse with her husband, while the twentieth-century Pakistani exegete Ghulam Ahmed Parwez argues that lack of Qur'anic detail on Mary's marriage and the identity of Jesus's father is doctrinally insignificant in that such details are also missing in the Qur'anic histories of other Qur'anic prophets; he adds that the words of the angels' annunciation to Mary (3:47) are identical to those given to Zacharia concerning John (3:40), while John was clearly created in the ordinary way, from a father and a mother. Jesus, then, is here perceived as the legitimate son of Joseph and Mary, and the Qur'an-recorded slander of the Jews concerning Jesus's birth is understood as the unfounded Jewish accusation that Jesus was an illegitimate child.[106] Islamic consensus, however, has upheld the tenet of the virgin birth.[107]

Obedience

The Qur'an proclaims Mary as among the devoutly obedient (*qanitin*) of God's servants (66:12). In this context, Mary's questioning of the angel on how she could have a child "while no human has touched me" (19:20), and her outcry at the onset of childbirth, "if only I had died before this and were completely forgotten" (19:23), have attracted exegetic attention in that both could potentially be perceived as rebellious. Exegesis has uniformly upheld the tenet of Mary's obedience. Her words to the angel are seen as the mark of chastity, not doubt in God's omnipotence.[108] Concerning Mary's (more problematic) wish for annihilation, the interpreters emphasize that the very pious are given to such expressions of their unworthiness in situations of distress.[109] Mary neither rejected God's verdict nor did she lose faith in her innocence. Her words of anguish had to do with anxiety about her reputation in that the shame of returning to society with a son would destroy her fame as ascetic servant in the house of worship. Else, she unselfishly worried that her people would fall into sin by doubting the veracity of her story.[110] Some interpreters, however, add that for ordinary human beings and under ordinary circumstances, such behavior would be reprehensible, since "it is a sin to wish for death because of sickness or poverty."[111]

Chosen . . . Chosen Above the Women of the Worlds

In 3:42, the angels inform Mary that God has chosen her, purified her, and chosen her above the women of the worlds. Exegesis interprets the "first choosing" as God's acceptance of Mary for His service, her maintenace in the temple with sustenance from paradise that freed her from all labor, and her miraculous ability to hear the angels' words. The "second choosing" is said to have consisted in God's gift of Jesus without a father, the child's words in Mary's defense from the cradle, Mary's and Jesus's status as a sign (*aya*) for the world, and God's guidance of Mary.[112] This leaves the question of Mary's status "above the women of the worlds," and here the exegetic debate is remarkable both for its intensity and also the lack of consensus. At stake is Mary's ranking among Qur'anic women figures but also, and more importantly, in relation to the elite women of Islam, especially the Prophet's wives Khadija and A'isha and the

Prophet's daughter Fatima. The problem is addressed by questioning whether Mary's preeminence is absolute (over all other women and for all times) or relative (over the women of *her* time). The larger number of traditions recorded in Tafsir and *qisas al-anbiya'* literature establish, on the authority of the Prophet, that Mary and Fatima, Khadija and Asya (the Pharaoh's wife) are the best women of the world and also the ruling females in heaven; traditions on A'isha's inclusion in this group are fewer in number. While Asya's and Mary's merit is established on the basis of the Qur'an (66:11–12), Khadija's merit is seen in her great service to the Prophet's mission, and that of A'isha in her status as Muhammad's most beloved wife and a prominent authority on his legacy after his death.[113] Popular piety has, in some fashion, settled the question of Mary and Asya, Khadija and A'isha by making all four Muhammad's wifely consorts in paradise. Indeed, it is said that Khadija's heavenly mansion will be between the houses of Mary and Asya.[114]

This leaves the question of Mary's ranking in relation to Muhammad's daughter Fatima. In Muslim piety, and here especially Shi'i piety, the connection of Mary to Fatima is such that the two figures at times appear collapsed into one. Mary was one of four miraculous midwives who assisted Khadija in Fatima's birth,[115] and Mary also appeared to Fatima to console her during her last illness.[116] Both were visited by angels, received miraculous sustenance during childhood and also during the isolation preceding the birth of their children, and both are believed to have shared the same miraculous qualities of freedom from menstruation and bleeding at childbirth.[117] What most deeply binds Mary and Fatima together is the joint image of mistress of sorrows. In Sunni tradition, Fatima's suffering is mainly linked with the Prophet's death, whom of all of his children she alone survived. In Shi'i piety, she is also, and primarily, the grieving mother whose short and hard life was made bitter by the foreknowledge of the future martyrdom of her son Husayn, an event of divine redemption and cosmic significance.[118] Although, according to the Qur'an, Jesus was persecuted and rejected by his people but not slain, Shi'i hagiography has recognized strong affinities between Jesus and Husayn[119] as, also, between their holy mothers. Mary and Fatima, holy figures of solace and hope, are at times revered simultaneously.[120] While some traditions reported on the authority of the Prophet award Mary and Fatima equal rank as the two reigning females in the celestial realm hereafter, most Shi'i authorities rank Fatima above Mary; indeed, Fatima is sometimes referred to as *Maryam al-Kubra*, "Mary the Greater."[121]

Creaturedom

Muslim exegetes have consistently seen the affirmation of God's Oneness as central issue and purpose of all of the revelations on Mary. Mary, God's handmaiden, and Jesus, God's slave and prophet, are not "gods" (5:78; cf. 5:19). The refutation of the notion of "three" (trinity) (4:171) is interpreted as divine correction of blasphemous Christian association of Mary "the female consort" and Jesus "the son" with God in a "family setting."[122] It is likened to the Qur'anic refutation of equally blasphemous pagan Arabian allegations that the angels are God's "daughters" whom God begat with the jinn (in interpretation of 37:149–159; cf. 43:19–20), or that pagan deities were God's "daughters" (53:19–23).

Mary and Eve

In clarifying that the nature of Jesus is fully human, the Qur'an likens Jesus to Adam in that both are God's creations, brought forth by the might of divine speech and decree. The Hadith has expanded this equation into a creatural tetragram where Mary parallels Adam and Jesus, Eve. "Just as Eve was created from Adam without a woman, so was Jesus created from Mary without a man."[123] The Qur'an-based Islamic doctrine that Adam's and Eve's disobedience was but a "slip" (or, "error"), repented and forgiven (essentially in the divine gift of prophethood) precludes linkage of Eve and Mary in any other way within the Islamic context.[124]

Mary as Model for Emulation by the Righteous

The Qur'an acclaims Mary "an example for the righteous" (66:12). Exegesis has, of course, affirmed her obedience to God, devoutness in His service, and truthful testimony to His revelations as exemplary qualities that the Muslim woman is called upon to emulate. However, given that the Hadith teaches that "marriage is one-half of the believer's faith," important aspects of Mary's nature and history remain beyond what the Muslim woman can, or should, strive to equal. Exegesis, then, has used some parts of the Qur'anic narrative to draw moral lessons and omitted others. The Qur'anic dictum that, prior to the annunciation, Mary had withdrawn to a place of isolation (19:16–17) has been interpreted as Mary's desire for gender-based segregation at the onset of puberty, and here she is also said to have donned the face-veil (means as well as symbol of Muslim female morality in that it hides the beauty of its wearer).[125] Mary's words to the angel who appeared to her in the form of a young man while she was alone have served as exemplar of female selfprotective virtue at its best.[126] Mary's Qur'an-proclaimed qualities of chastity and obedience have also occasioned exegetic emphasis on the duty of women to come to their husband's bed as virgins, to maintain marital fidelity, and to realize obedience to God through obedience to their husbands in whose charge they are placed by God.[127]

But Mary's importance to Muslims, especially Muslim women, is far different and far greater than what these scholarly formulations might suggest. Recitation of "her Sura" (Sura 19) is a favorite especially with women circles throughout the Muslim world, believed to confer special blessings on reciter and listeners alike. Many women in Syria are said to pray through Mary (and Fatima) in moments of anguish,[128] as women elsewhere pray through (other) female saints. And sightings of Mary, such as were witnessed by throngs of Copts and Muslims in Old Cairo in May 1968 when many reported miraculous healings,[129] further attest to the high status and lasting importance of Mary in Muslim piety.

Conclusion

The preceding has discovered a multiplicity of meanings for the Qur'anic women of the sacred past, both in scripture and also interpretation. From the beginning, the women figures signify themselves and also something else. Actors in Qur'anic history, they function as images, or metaphorical extensions, of that historical reality which God revealed to His Prophet. Thus their stories are specifically Qur'anic, in the casting of the individual tale and also its larger message. Muslim interpretation extended the images' symbolic range to accommodate a variety of later readings that often changed their first, Qur'anic, didactic import. Though differing among themselves, the later formulations share in the fact that they were, and are, culturally determined. In different moldings, the images of the Qur'an's women have thus acted as signs of, and for, cultural self-understanding.

Both the concept of Qur'anic history as "real," that is, "factual," history, and also the place of the female actors within that history represent religious "symbols" in the Geertzian sense. Within this shared worldview, Muslims past and present have developed a number of "paradigms,"[130] that is, specific models that structure perception and also serve as agenda for the future. From Eve to Mary, the interpretations presented above show some measure of internal consistency as to paradigms and paradigmatic shifts on questions of doctrine and ethics. With the modern period, the latter dimension rose to prominence, especially as relating to sociopolitical change in the Islamic world. Like their Qur'anic blueprint, the women of sacred history are still models of guidance and warning, but in a number of new ways. As those of the past, their modern images are occasioned by the need of each generation of Muslims to make sense of the world in light of God's revelation.

II

The Prophet's Wives

8

The Mothers of the Believers in the Qur'an

The Qur'an specifically addresses the Prophet's wives on numerous occasions; many other revelations are linked with members of their group in the Hadith literature. Their honorific epithet "Mothers of the Believers" was revealed in a late Medinan verse (33:6). Muhammad's consorts thus play a prominent part in the Qur'an-as-process. Their reception of specific divine guidance, occasioned by their proximity to the Prophet, endows them with special dignity. But the latter is matched by more stringent obligations. While the Qur'an says of the Prophet's wives that they "are not like any [other] women" (33:32), their peerlessness also entails the sharper rebukes for human frailties as well as the more stringent codes of private and public probity with which the scripture singles out the Prophet's consorts. It is by linking dignity with obligation, elite status with heightened moral responsibility, that an aspect of God's *sunna* (His "law" for the world) is here defined. Numerous divine reprimands addressed to Muhammad's wives in the Qur'an establish their special responsibility to overcome their human frailties[1] and ensure their individual worthiness. In this manner the Prophet's wives emerge within the Qur'anic context as models of the principle of ethical individualism. As divine censure, when heeded, comes to signify divine grace, the women's obedience to censure becomes the basis of their model status. In this world and the next, peerlessness is their reward. Furthermore, just as God's last prophet Muhammad begins a new chapter of sacred history so do his consorts signify a new beginning of the female example in Islam. As historical figures whose lives yield examples for the righteous, their Islamic importance eclipses that of even the most unblemished women of the Qur'an-recorded past, and it was their precedent that served as a foundation of later *shari'a* legal structures.

Even though the role of Muhammad's wives as exemplars *qua* targets of God's revelation is clearly established in the Qur'anic text, the text's wording is general in that it does not identify any of the women by name.[2] It is here that the Hadith as scripturalist exegesis has consistently satisfied pious interest by providing information on the specific individuals involved in the "occasions for revelation" (*asbab al-nuzul*) vouchsafed for the benefit of the members of the Prophet's household. The following summary of the Qur'anic verses directed at the Prophet's wives uses segments of the Hadith and of Hadith-based classical (Sunni) Qur'anic exegesis in order to furnish some narrative background and suggest the chronological sequencing of the revelations. As will become apparent, however, the traditionists' interpretations of the "occasion for" and the "meaning of" a Qur'anic revelation tend to have a dynamic all their own. Neither is, nor is meant to be, a form of historicist inquiry. While pious stories and legends pervade the "occasions" literature, the definitions of a revelation's "meaning" derive from the interpreter's world as he knows it *and also* provide him with the scripturalist *ratio* to apply to his world as it should be. The inclusion of Hadith and *tafsir* as background material, then, here primarily means to serve as (by nature piecemeal) introduction to Muslim perceptions of the meaning of Qur'anic revelations on the Prophet's consorts. To identify the various classical paradigms that constituted that perception, a fuller discussion of the Hadith materials on the Prophet's wives is presented in Chapter 9.[3]

Muhammad's Wives

33:50 (categories of females lawful for the Prophet for marriage)
[a late Medinan verse][4]
While the Hadith is not unanimous on the number of women whom the Prophet married, the majority of traditions put their number at fourteen, of which nine were alive when the Prophet died.[5] Some Muslim thinkers now link the large size of the Prophet's harem to the fact that all of the Prophet's marriages had been concluded by the time that the early Medinan revelation of Sura 4:3 "limited the number of wives (for Muslims) to four."[6] This, however, appears to be a modern argument, or at least an argument favored by modern religious thinkers.[7] By contrast, classical Hadith and Qur'an interpretation maintained that the Prophet's right to unrestricted polygamy was a prerogative that God's *sunna* had extended to all prophets: a "natural right" of His spokesmen on earth.[8] Furthermore, the classical sources found the scriptural legitimation for the Prophet's larger household in Sura 33:50, a late Medinan revelation that determined the "categories of females" lawful for the Prophet for marriage. The verse in question enumerates the following "categories": wives with whom the Prophet contracted marriage involving a dower; female prisoners of war (slaves) who fell to him as part of his share of the spoils; both paternal and also maternal cousins who had migrated with him to Medina; "and a believing woman, if she gives herself to the Prophet, if the Prophet wishes to marry her.[9] *Especially for you, exclusive of [or, beyond] the believers. We*

know what We have imposed upon *them* concerning their wives and slaves. So that there be no restriction [or, "restraint," "anguish," *haraj*] on you. And God is forgiving, compassionate."[10]

Hadith reports agree overall that the Prophet was married to the following women:[11] Khadija bint Khuwaylid (Asad/Quraysh), who died before the hijra;[12] Sawda bint Zam'a (Amir/Quraysh); A'isha bint Abi Bakr (Taym/Quraysh); Hafsa bint Umar (Adi/Quraysh); Zaynab bint Khuzayma (Hilal), who died about eight months after the wedding; Hind (Umm Salama) bint Abi Umayya (Makhzum/Quraysh); Zaynab bint Jahsh (Asad/Khuzayma); Juwayriyya bint al-Harith (or, al-Harth) of the Banu Mustaliq of the Khuza'a tribe, an Arabian war captive; Rayhana bint Zayd ibn Amr, a Jewish woman of the Banu Nadir, also a war captive, who may have been either wife or concubine; Safiyya bint Huyayy ibn Akhtab, a Jewish woman of the Banu Nadir, also a war captive; Ramla (Umm Habiba) bint Abi Sufyan (Abd Shams/Quraysh); and Maymuna bint al-Harith (or, al-Harth) of the Banu Hilal. Furthermore, the Prophet is said to have married several women whom he divorced (or some of whom divorced him?) before the marriage was consummated; mentioned are Fatima bint al-Dahhak ibn Sufyan of the Kilab tribe, Asma' bint al-Nu'man of the Kinda tribe, Amra bint Yazid of the Kilab tribe, Qutayla bint Qays of the Kinda tribe, and Mulayka bint Ka'b of the Banu Layth. But there is little consensus on who belongs in this "category" of women or whether there may have also been some others.[13] To some additional women marriage was proposed but the marriage contract was not concluded.[14] Finally, there were some women who "gave themselves to the Prophet," that is, women who offered themselves directly to Muhammad without participation of a *wali* (guardian) to negotiate a marriage contract, and also without expectation of a dower.[15] In addition, there was a concubine Marya the Copt, mother of Muhammad's son Ibrahim.[16]

For the time being, we will leave the question of numbers and types of marriages, also the tribal backgrounds, family affiliations, and individual character traits of these women aside in order to present in chronological order the Qur'anic revelations believed to concern them. It must be noted, however, that the Prophet's wives figure unequally in Qur'anic exegesis, which is to say that only a small number of their group are consistently presented as key figures in the Hadith accounts of contexts of specific revelations ("occasions for revelation," *asbab al-nuzul*). Their stories are given in what follows, while a more comprehensive Hadith-based account is provided in the second segment of this chapter.

The earliest clusters of Qur'anic verses linked with a particular consort of the Prophet consist of: 33:37–38; 33:4,40; and 33:53,55.

A Marriage Made in Heaven

33:37–38 (lawfulness of marriage with former wife of adopted son);
33:4,40 (adopted sons are not sons)
These revelations, dated by Muslim scholarship into the fifth year after the hijra, are commonly linked with the figure of Zaynab bint Jahsh. Zaynab, a granddaughter of Abd al-Muttalib, was Muhammad's first cousin on her

mother's side. She had migrated early with her family to Medina where the Prophet had arranged a marriage between her and Zayd ibn Haritha, a former (Arabian) slave of Khadija whom the Prophet had freed and adopted for a son.

Ibn Sa'd reports that Zaynab rejected Zayd because of her own high social status and his lowly one, but that the Prophet insisted on the marriage[17] which, however, is said to have not been harmonious. A year or more later,[18] the Prophet happened to call on Zayd at his home but only found Zaynab there, while Zayd was out on an errand. Ibn Sa'd reports that Zaynab had dressed in a hurry when she heard that the Prophet was coming, and that the sight of her pleased him. He did not accept her invitation to enter, nor did he look at her, but Zaynab "heard him mutter words that sounded like 'praise be to God, the changer of hearts.'"[19] Tabari[20] embroiders the story; he quotes traditions that indicate when the Prophet approached Zayd's and Zaynab's house on this visit, Zaynab was wearing but a single slip; at the house entrance was a curtain made of pelts, and when the wind lifted this curtain, it revealed the sight of Zaynab, "uncovered" in her chamber. It was then, says Tabari, that the Prophet began to feel a liking for Zaynab. Thereafter, Zaynab "was made unattractive to the other" (i.e., by God) so that Zayd eventually approached the Prophet to inform him of his desire to divorce his wife.[21] Of the medieval exegetes here considered, it is only the traditionalist interpreter Ibn Kathir who states his opposition to such (by then well-established) "seductiveness" and "desire" traditions. Much like the twentieth century Muslim interpreters considered below, Ibn Kathir regarded these materials on "how," or "why," the Prophet began to like Zaynab as "unsound"; while he mentions that a number of authorities, *including* Ahmad ibn Hanbal, had transmitted such tales, he states that "we would like to omit some pages because they are unsound, and we will not mention them."[22]

"Hiding in (his) heart what God would make apparent, and fearing the people," the Prophet then instructed Zayd to retain his wife (cf. 33:37), but reportedly Zayd could no longer control Zaynab, and therefore he divorced her.[23] According to Tabari[24] and others, what the Prophet was "hiding in his heart" was both his attraction to Zaynab and also the fact that God had given him clear foreknowledge that she would be his wife. His "fear of the people," in turn, derived from the fact that both pre-Islamic custom and also Islam forbade marriage to the former wife of a son because (until this point in time) adopted sons were in all respects regarded as the full equals of legitimate natural sons. According to Zamakhshari,[25] the Prophet's desire for Zaynab did not, however, affect his '*isma* (prophetic state of sinlessness), since the matter was lawful (*halal*): "the matter was permitted, no evil accrued to Zayd or anyone, as Zayd did not want her while the Prophet did. Indeed, only good came of this affair[26]. . . . What was sinful was merely to hide the desire, because, in the righteous, internal conscience and external behavior must be one." For Ibn Kathir,[27] the theme of the Prophet's concealed desire falls into the category of "unsound information" mentioned above; Ibn Kathir's interpretation of what the Prophet was "hiding in his heart," therefore, could concern only his God-given foreknowledge of the marriage. The interpreters agree, however, that the divine reprimand directed at the Prophet in 33:37 for his "fear of the people" was the sternest of its kind in all of the Qur'an, and they quote a tradition on the authority of A'isha that "if the Prophet had [ever] concealed a revelation, he would have concealed this one."[28]

After Zayd's divorce and Zaynab's 'idda (the waiting period of three menstrual cycles) had passed, the Prophet married Zaynab by virtue of the revelation that specifically commanded him to do so as an obligation (fard) (33:38). The Qur'anic rationale for this command is stated in the preceding verse: "that there should be no burden on the believers concerning the wives of their adopted sons, when they [the latter] have terminated a business [or, purpose, desire] with them. And God's command is [inevitably] fulfilled" (33:37). The community, however, is said to have continued in their questioning and criticism, because in their understanding the adoptive relationship between the Prophet and Zayd still rendered Muhammad's marriage to Zaynab incestuous. Some remnants of the communal discussions on the probity of this marriage may perhaps be found in a number of sentimental traditions on Zayd's reaction to it; else, the traditions may be sheer pious embroidery on an interesting story. In any case, the Prophet is said to have sent Zayd to Zaynab's house as his emissary to ask for her hand in marriage. When Zayd arrived, he found her leavening her dough, and the sight of her was so agonizing to him that he could not look at her, knowing that the Prophet was now proposing marriage. So he turned his back to Zaynab and then gave her the good news.[29] "This was an enormous trial [for Zayd], and clear proof of the strength of his faith."[30] Zaynab, in turn, is said to have declared that she would not give an answer until she had received her Lord's command. She went "to her place of prayer (masjid), and it was thereafter that the revelation was vouchsafed to the Prophet."[31]

The communal debate is said to have persevered until two revelations established that "adopted sons are unlike real sons," and that "Muhammad is not the father of any of your men" (33:4,40).[32] Ibn Kathir[33] and others call the revelation of 33:40 "the [divine] rejection of the hypocrites' suspicion surrounding [the Prophet's] marriage with the wife of Zayd, his client and adopted son." This statement is important in that it identifies a prominent hostile faction that influenced the civic atmosphere in Medina during the fifth year after the hijra and in relation to which the largely negative public debate on the Prophet's marriage with Zaynab must be understood. The "hypocrites" (munafiqun) of Medina were in name Muslims but in fact of unreliable loyalty to the Prophet. In times of Muslim military setbacks and other difficulties (such as the battle of Uhud in year 3 and the Meccan siege of Medina in year 5 after the hijra), hypocrite influence increased to the detriment of the Islamic cause.[34] This group spread vicious rumors to divide the community and also harrassed women, including the Prophet's wives, especially by night.[35] According to the Moroccan sociologist Fatima Mernissi, it was the core of hypocrite strategy to attack the Prophet through his wives,[36] of which the rumors surrounding Zaynab's marriage are but an example.

The Beginning of Seclusion

33:53 (the "hijab" verse) and 33:55 (exemptions thereto)

Zaynab bint Jahsh's marriage to the Prophet, likewise said to have occurred during the fifth year after the hijra, is identified in the majority of Hadith and *tafsir* accounts as the occasion for God's legislation of the *hijab* ("curtain," "screen")[37] imposed by God to shield the Prophet's women from the eyes of visitors to his dwellings. Most traditions maintain that this revelation was vouchsafed after some of the wedding guests had overstayed their welcome at the nuptial celebration in Zaynab's house. On this occasion, the *hijab* "came down" in a double sense: Firstly, it was, literally, a "curtain" the Prophet loosened while standing on the threshold to Zaynab's chamber, with one foot in the room and the other outside, in order to bar his servant Anas ibn Malik (main authority of the traditions on this event) from entering; secondly, the *hijab* also "came down" by way of God's revelation of 33:53, which the Prophet recited to Anas at that time.[38] Other traditions report that the *hijab* was decreed after the Prophet saw some men loitering in the vicinity of Zaynab's house on the morning after the wedding night,[39] or after the hand of one of the Prophet's wives had touched a man's hand at a common meal, or after A'isha's hand had accidentally touched the hand of Umar ibn al-Khattab while they were eating together.[40] A third strand of traditions mentions Umar ibn al-Khattab in the role of "counselor," who urged the Prophet to conceal and segregate his wives, because "both the righteous and the wicked enter into your houses."[41] In this context, it is important to note that, firstly, Umar ibn al-Khattab appears with some consistency in Hadith and classical *tafsir* as spokesman in favor of the segregation, domesticity, and marital obedience of the Prophet's wives. Secondly, the sources record some spirited opposition on the part of the Prophet's wives to Umar's "interference." The aristocratic Umm Salama of the noble Meccan clan of Makhzum here frequently appears as group spokesperson, with Muhammad's other wives in grateful support of her initiative.[42] Thirdly, for some of the later medieval exegetes such as Baydawi and Ibn Kathir, Umar's vigilance "for the good of the Prophet's wives" rates greater consideration as "occasion for revelation" (of 33:53) than do the accounts of the Prophet's annoyance at the guests who lingered in Zaynab's house on the wedding eve.[43]

The *hijab* verse (33:53) reads:

> Oh believers, do not enter the Prophet's houses except that permission is given you for a meal, without waiting for its time. But when you are invited [or, called], enter, and when you have eaten, disperse, without seeking familiarity for talk. This used to cause the Prophet annoyance, and he is ashamed [or, bashful] of you. But God is not ashamed of what is right. And if you ask them [the women] for a thing, then ask them from behind a *hijab*. That is purer for your hearts and their hearts. And it is not for you to cause annoyance to God's Messenger, nor that you should marry his wives after him. Truly this with God would be enormous.[44]

The *hijab* verse is followed by a revelation that establishes the classes of individuals "in whom there is no sin [or, harm] for them; their fathers, sons, brothers, brothers' sons, sisters' sons, their women, and their slaves"[45] (33:55). This revelation is thought to belong together with the *hijab* verse and to concern the categories of relatives and servants with whom the Prophet's wives were permitted to deal face-to-face rather than from behind a partition.

Muslim interpreters past and present stipulate that the Prophet's wives participated fully in the communal affairs of Medina until the revelation of the *hijab* verse. They ascribe their exclusion from public life at that time to several factors. For one, living conditions in Medina were extremely crowded, especially in the area around the mosque, itself the very center of public activity. It was here that the Prophet's wives' quarters were located; indeed, they stood so close to the mosque that the women's rooms were natural extensions of its space. The Hadith gives a vivid picture of throngs of Muslims seeking audience with the Prophet and presenting him with *sadaqa* (free-will offerings), while he sat in the chamber of one of his wives. The *hijab* revelation, then, is seen mainly as the legislation of a means to provide domestic comfort and privacy for the female elite of Islam. This notion, in turn, connotes an element of "privilege." And, indeed, the medieval Hadith informs that the *hijab* was imposed upon the Prophet's wives as criterion of their elite status.[46] In addition, the *hijab* is also seen as a protective device, especially during periods of civic tension when the hypocrites were instigating disorder and stirring up intercommunal fears. The latter has recently been emphasized by Mernissi in her description of the sociopolitical setting of revelations 33:53 and 33:55 as a time of crisis in Medina. According to Mernissi, it was during the aftermath of Medina's siege by the Meccans (year 5 hijra), when the hypocrites had gained influence and communal tensions were rife, that the Prophet felt compelled to heed Umar ibn al-Khattab's council and seclude his wives.[47]

According to Muslim interpretation, then, both the privileges of privacy and also physical protection were accorded Muhammad's wives by way of seclusion in the home which, in turn, was achieved through the architectural means of "a single curtain," *sitr wahid*.[48] While the literal Qur'anic meaning of the term *hijab* in 33:53 is that of a concrete object ("curtain", "partition", or "screen"), the term's meaning in the Hadith evolved to connote both the concrete and also the abstract, a domestic fixture to ensure seclusion and also the seclusion itself.

Soon after the revelation of the *hijab* verse, selfprotection of "the Prophet's wives, his daughters, and the women of the believers" was enjoined in Qur'an 33:59–60 by way of God's command that Muslim women cover themselves in their "mantles," or "cloaks" (*jalabib*, singular: *jilbab*) (when abroad) "so that they be known [as free women, not slaves] and not molested [in the streets] by the hypocrites, and those in whose hearts is a disease, and those who stir up sedition in the City [al-Madina]."[49] This piece of legislation differed from the *hijab* of 33:53 in two ways: Firstly, it concerned individual female appearance when outside of the home, not seclusion within it; and, secondly, it applied to all Muslim women, not just the Prophet's wives. Once again, classical exegesis has here identified Umar ibn al-Khattab as the main spokesman in favor of this clothing law, which he is also said to have "enforced" on several occasions. A subsequent revelation concerning male and female modesty was vouch-safed in Sura 24:30–31, of which 24:30 is directed at Muslim men and 24:31 at Muslim women in general terms. The verses read as follows:

> 24:30: Tell the male believers that they restrain their eyes and guard their private parts. This is purer for them. God is well aware of what they do.
> 24:31: And tell the female believers that they restrain their eyes and guard their private parts, and not display of their adornment [or, finery, *zina*] except for what is apparent [or, external], and draw their kerchiefs [*khumur*, singular: *khimar*] over their bosoms [*juyub*, singular: *jayb*], and not display their adornment except to their husbands, or their fathers, or their husbands' fathers, or their sons, or their husbands' sons, or their brothers, or their brothers' sons, or their sisters' sons, or their women, or their slaves, or male subordinates who have no natural force (*irba*), or the children who have no knowledge of women's private parts. And that they not stamp their feet to give knowledge of the adornment which they hide. Turn to God in repentance, oh believers, perhaps you will prosper [or, perhaps it may be well with you].

With Islam's expansion into areas formerly part of the Byzantine and Sasanian empires, the scripture-legislated social paradigm that had evolved in the early Medinan community came face to face with alien social structures and traditions deeply rooted in the conquered populations. Among the many cultural traditions assimilated and continued by Islam were the veiling and seclusion of women, at least among the urban upper and upper-middle classes. With these traditions' assumption into "the Islamic way of life," they of need helped to shape the normative interpretations of Qur'anic gender laws as formulated by the medieval (urbanized and acculturated) lawyer-theologians. In the latter's consensus-based prescriptive systems, the Prophet's wives were recognized as models for emulation (sources of *sunna*). Thus, while the scholars provided information on the Prophet's wives in terms of, as well as for, an ideal of Muslim female morality, the Qur'anic directives addressed to the Prophet's consorts were naturally seen as applicable to all Muslim women.

Semantically and legally, that is, regarding both the terms and also the parameters of its application, Islamic interpretation extended the concept of *hijab*. In scripturalist method, this was achieved in several ways. Firstly, the *hijab* was associated with two of the Qur'an's "clothing laws" imposed upon all Muslim females: the "mantle" verse of 33:59 and the "modesty" verse of 24:31. On the one hand, the semantic association of domestic segregation (*hijab*) with garments to be worn in public (*jilbab, khimar*) resulted in the use of the term *hijab* for concealing garments that women wore outside of their houses. This language use is fully documented in the medieval Hadith. However, unlike female garments such as *jilbab, lihaf, milhafa, izar, dir'* (traditional garments for the body), *khimar, niqab, burqu', qina', miqna'a* (traditional garments for the head and neck)[50] and also a large number of other articles of clothing, the medieval meaning of *hijab* remained conceptual and generic. In their debates on which parts of the woman's body, if any, are not "'*awra*" (literally, "genital," "*pudendum*") and may therefore be legally exposed to nonrelatives, the medieval scholars often contrastively paired woman's *'awra* with this generic *hijab*. This permitted the debate to remain conceptual rather than get bogged down in the specifics of articles of clothing whose meaning, in any case, was prone to changes both geographic/regional and also chronological. At present we know very little about the precise stages of the process by which the *hijab* in its multiple meanings was made obligatory for Muslim women at large, except to say that these occurred during the first centuries after the expansion of Islam beyond the borders of Arabia, and then mainly in the Islamicized societies still ruled by preexisting (Sasanian and Byzantine) social traditions. With the rise of the Iraq-based Abbasid state in the mid-eighth century of the Western calendar, the lawyer-theologians of Islam grew into a religious establishment entrusted with the formulation of Islamic law and morality, and it was they who interpreted the Qur'anic rules on women's dress and space in increasingly absolute and categorical fashion, reflecting the real practices and cultural assumptions of their place and age.[51] Classical legal compendia, medieval Hadith collections and Qur'anic exegesis are here mainly formulations of the system "as established" and not of its developmental stages, even though differences of opinion on the legal limits of the *hijab* garments survived, including among the doctrinal teachings of the four orthodox schools of law (*madhahib*).

The Prophet's Medinan-born biographer Ibn Ishaq, an early source (d. 767), makes an interesting remark on the face veil while describing the nasty end of Muhammad's uncle Aby Lahab (an enemy of Islam) who died in Mecca of "pustules"; in fear of the disease, Abu Lahab's sons left his body unburied for three days, then "threw water at the body from a distance [instead of properly washing it] . . . they did not bury Abu Lahab, but he was put against a wall and stones were thrown against him from behind the wall until he was covered. It is said that when A'isha passed the place she used to veil her face."[52]

For the later scholars of Islam, the female face veil would be a hotly debated item; not, however, in the context of individual choice, such as horror of a place, but within the parameters of the *hijab* as legally prescribed female "concealment." For the Shafiites and Hanbalites, the entire female body, including face, hands, and below the ankles, was *'awra* and thus to be covered, while Malikites and Hanafites considered face and hands as excluded from *'awra*.[53] Malikites and Hanafites here based their paradigm on a number of authenticated traditions that the Prophet himself instructed "the believing woman" to bare her face, hands, and "one hand's breadth" of the forearms.[54] The differences between the law schools were perhaps not always this clear cut, however, since authorities belonging to the same *madhhab* registered different opinions over time. A chronological factor appears to have prevailed here in that with the progression of time *'ulama'* opinion within a particular *madhhab* could prescribe the female face veil as part of the obligatory *hijab* in increasingly absolute and categorical terms. Tabari (d. 923), a *Shafi'ite* who later founded his own short-lived law school,[55] maintained that women's "lawful" dress permitted her to leave hands and face uncovered.[56] By contrast, the popular

Qur'anic exegete Baydawi (d. 1286 or 1291), also of *Shafi'ite* affiliation, opined that the Muslim freeborn woman must conceal her whole body, including face and hands, except during prayer and in cases of "necessity" such as medical treatment and the bearing of witness in court.[57] This restrictive position was later heightened and emphasized by, for example, Khafaji (d. 1659), author of a *Hashiya* ("marginal commentary") on Baydawi's Qur'anic commentary who, again on the authority of *al-Shafi'i*, argued in agreement with Baydawi that "the whole body of the Muslim woman, including face and hands, is *'awra* ["pudendal"] and must, therefore, be concealed."[58] While Khafaji continued to allow for women's bare-facedness in cases of prayer, medical emergency, and testimony in court as lawful exceptions from "the established rule," he also presented these cases as more marginally acceptable than did his thirteenth-century source.[59]

Slandering the Prophet's ("Favorite") Wife: The Affair of the Lie

24:11–26 (the Qur'anic injunctions against slander)
In chronological terms, the next block of Qur'anic legislation consistently linked in the Hadith with a member of the Prophet's household is found in 24:11–26, the Qur'anic injunction against slander. The verses in question are dated into the fifth or sixth year after the hijra and are said to have been occasioned by A'isha bint Abi Bakr's involvement in "the affair of the lie [or, slander]" (*al-ifk*).

The medieval Hadith consistently describes A'isha as the Prophet's favor-ite wife. The only virgin among Muhammad's brides, she was betrothed to the Prophet in the tenth year of the prophethood, that is, three years before the hijra, when she was 6 or 7 years old. The marriage was concluded and consummated when she was 9. She still played with her dolls, including a toy horse, after she had moved into her husband's house as a wife.[60] The "affair of the lie" thus occurred when she was 11, 12, or 13 years old. On the trip back to Medina from the military expedition against the enemy tribe of Banu Mustaliq, on which A'isha and Umm Salama had accompanied the Prophet, A'isha left the camp in the darkness of early morning to heed the call of nature. She delayed when she discovered that she had lost her necklace of Yemenite onyx, or agate. She was able to retrieve the necklace, but when she returned to camp, she found the grounds deserted. Her curtained litter[61] had been placed on a camel and been led away; since she was slight and slim, the carriers had not realized that she was not inside the litter. A'isha then waited in the deserted camp, until a young man by the name of Safwan ibn al-Mu'attal al-Sulami (or, al-Salmi) arrived with his camel, on which he took A'isha back to Medina. A scandal broke, and malicious gossip and unproven accusations spread through-out the community. It is related that the main instigator was Abdallah ibn Ubayy (a dangerous Medinan hypocrite of the Khazraj tribe); he had found some allies in Awf ibn Uthatha (nicknamed Mistah, a kinsman of Abu Bakr), also Hamna bint Jahsh (sister of the Prophet's wife Zaynab bint Jahsh), and Hassan ibn Thabit (later known as the eulogist of the Prophet and his family). Communal tensions erupted in mutual public recriminations of the indigenous Medinan tribes of Aus and Khazraj, both now supportive of the Islamic cause but who had shared a long history of mutual feuds and warfare. The Prophet chose two character witnesses for questioning, Usama ibn Zayd and Ali ibn Abi Talib. Usama recommended that A'isha be considered innocent. Ali's role in this consultation, however, was ambiguous. He is reported to have remarked to the Prophet that "women are plentiful, and you can easily change one for another"; then he recommended the questioning of A'isha's slave girl, whom he beat "so that she would tell the truth." The girl, however, had nothing to report. A'isha herself maintained her innocence in the face of her parents' doubts and the Prophet's questioning. A full month later, the revelation of 24:11–26 was vouchsafed, which established A'isha's innocence, severely criticized the believers for their unrighteous behavior, and announced grievous penalties for all who would perpetrate unfounded slander of chaste women.[62] In Mernissi's words, this crisis was just another example of the threat of hypocrite manipulation of communal unity. By defaming A'isha, the hypocrites had "sexualized their attacks" on the Prophet himself.[63]

Additional legislation on slander (*buhtan*) is found in Sura 24:4. The transgression was later classified in Islamic jurisprudence as one of the *hudud* offenses[64] and carries the *hadd* (divinely defined punishment) of flogging. The punishment is based on the legislation of Sura 24:4, "and those who launch a charge against chaste women and then do not produce four witnesses, flog them with eighty stripes, and reject their witness ever after, because they are sinful." In the eyes of the Qur'an, slander is both a crime against society and also an act of sinfulness "enormous in the eyes of God" (24:15). The Qur'anic revelation, then, provides protection for righteous women against unfounded accusations of unchastity, since the Qur'an here defines slander as a crime directed at females, not males. Elsewhere, the Qur'an also establishes that women are forbidden to perpetrate this transgression (60:12). Both sexes in equal measure lose their right to marry righteous spouses when they commit this offense. "Bad [wicked, malicious] women are for bad men, and bad men are for bad women, and good women are for good men, and good men are for good women, these are cleared from what they say, for them is forgiveness and a splendid provision" (24:26). While godliness, then, lies with the innocent victim of slanderous accusations, the accuser, male or female, loses his righteousness in the sight of God and also his membership of good standing in the community.

Disturbances in the Prophet's Household

33:28–29 (God's order that the Prophet's wives be made to choose between "God and His Prophet" and "the world and its adornment")[65]

The traditions do not reflect a consensus on the incident or incidents that led to the Prophet's seclusion from all of his wives for a month and culminated in the revelation instructing him to have his wives choose between "God and His Prophet" and "the world and its adornment" (33:28–29). This revelation has been dated into the fifth, seventh, eighth, or ninth year after the hijra.[66] Traditions specify several factors that may have triggered this crisis, such as the Prophet's wives' desire for more possessions, especially clothes, or the women's bickering over shared food; else, the crisis is said to have occurred because of the Prophet's relations with his concubine Marya the Copt, of whom his wives were jealous. Other traditions link the domestic disturbance with the fact that two of the wives "made common cause against the Prophet" (66:4), which led to the divine warning of divorce of all of them (66:5).[67] It is also possible that the exegetes have here compounded several different episodes of household disagreement into one "crisis." By all accounts, however, the domestic turmoil was of major proportions, even if its historical "reason" or "reasons" may not have been clearly or fully recorded. Ibn Sa'd gives six different "sets" of traditions in exegesis of 33:28–29 which, taken together, indicate that the "crisis" preceding the "verse of choice" occurred because:

1. the Prophet's wives, in the manner of the Ansar women of Medina, had become argumentative and given to insubordination and backtalk (*muraja'a*) against their husband.
2. the Prophet's wives made material demands that the Prophet could not fulfill because of poverty.
3. the Prophet had sexual relations with his concubine Marya in Hafsa's house on A'isha's "day," or on Hafsa's "day"; when confronted, he made an oath that Marya would henceforth be *haram* (forbidden to him for sexual contact) if Hafsa kept this information secret, but she betrayed it to A'isha (this account of the "crisis," then, links 33:28–29 with 66:1–5, cf. below).
4. Hafsa was not satisfied with her share of presents (or, meat) distributed by the Prophet among his wives; she sent the gift back several times to bargain for more, until A'isha blamed the Prophet that he had "lost face" in these dealings, an accusation that is said to have angered him.
5. Hafsa was jealous of A'isha's beauty and the Prophet's love for her (or, she was jealous of A'isha's favored position and Zaynab's beauty).
6. The Prophet's wives bragged about the unequalled value of their dowers.[68]

In any case, the Prophet is said to have segregated himself from all of his wives for the period of a month ("twenty-nine days"), instead of beating them.[69] Once again, the Hadith here furnishes the figure of Umar ibn al-Khattab as the voice of censorship of the Prophet's wives (especially in relation to their material demands); again, Umar's interference is said to have been rejected as "meddling" by at least one of the women (usually identified as Umm Salama, the Meccan aristocrat).[70] Other traditions tell of the outrage of Abu Bakr and Umar at the behavior of their daughters, A'isha and Hafsa, and of their fears that the Prophet's month-long seclusion might signify divorce for his wives, including, of course, their own daughters.[71] When the Prophet then returned to his wives, he repeated the newly revealed "verse of choice" to each of them.

Thereupon, all of the women, beginning with A'isha, decided to choose "God and His Prophet" over "the world and its adornment."[72] The traditions emphasize that A'isha reached her decision swiftly and on her own, without consulting her father (or parents), and that the Prophet was gladdened by her choice.[73]

Peerlessness and Special Obligations

33:30–34 (double punishment/double reward for the Prophet's wives; their peerlessness; injunction against their complaisant speech; command that they stay in their houses, avoid "tabarruj," be pious, obedient, etc.)
The "verse of choice" (33:28–29) is followed in the Qur'anic text by a group of verses which, firstly, were addressed (most likely in their totality) to the Prophet's wives; secondly, these are generally thought to have been revealed right after the "crisis" that led to the Prophet's seclusion from his wives for a month;[74] thirdly, the verses both acknowledge the peerlessness of the Prophet's consorts and also impose specific and far-reaching restrictions on the women's accessibility, visibility, and manner of comportment.

The Qu'ranic verses in question, 33:30–34, begin by establishing for the Prophet's wives "double punishment" (in case of clear immoral behavior) or "double reward" (for obedience to God and His Apostle, and for godly acts) (33:30–31).[75] Muhammad's wives are then told that they are "not like any [other] women" and are enjoined to abstain from submissive (or, complaisant) speech that might be misunderstood (33:32).[76] In the verses immediately following (33:33–34), the expression "oh women of the Prophet" does not appear. The form of address in both 33:33 and 33:34, however, is to a plurality of women; furthermore, 33:33 begins with the particle *wa-*, which syntactically ties it to the preceding verse. The last third of 33:33 contains the expression "[oh] members of the family [or, [oh] People of the House, *ahl al-bayt*]"; in this latter clause, however, the grammatical cast changes to the masculine plural. Because of the context,[77] Qur'anic exegesis has traditionally understood 33:33–34 as having been addressed to the wives of the Prophet.[78]

The question of context is here especially significant because verses 33:33–34 include important pieces of restrictive legislation. Specifically, the Prophet's wives [or, a plurality of women] are commanded to: stay in their houses; avoid *tabarruj* ("strutting about," or "swaggering," or "displaying of charms," or "decking oneself out"); pray; give alms; obey God and His Prophet; and remember God's verses and the wisdom recited in their houses (33:33–34).

Because of the fact that these verses have loomed large in Muslim theological and legal thought, they are here translated in full. (The following quotation includes the preceding verse as a means to recreate the context.)

> 33:32: Oh women of the Prophet, you are not like any of the women. If you fear God, do not surrender in speech [or, be complaisant of speech], so that he in whose heart is a disease should desire, but speak with conventional [or, befitting, good] speech [*qawlan ma'rufan*].
>   33:33: And stay in your houses [*wa-qarna fi buyutikunna*],[79] and do not strut about [or, display your charms] [*wa-la tabarrajna*][80] in the manner of the

former [or, first or foremost] Jahiliyya [*tabarruja l-jahiliyyati l-'ula*],[81] and perform the prayer and give the alms, and obey God and His Prophet. God wishes but to put all filthiness away from you, People of the House [*ahla l-bayt*], and to cleanse you with a cleansing.[82]

33:34: And recollect what is rehearsed to you in your houses of God's verses [or, signs, *ayat*] and of wisdom [*hikma*];[83] God is indeed keen-sighted, cognizant.

In terms of medieval Islamic legal-theological institution building, most important among these three verses was clearly 33:33 when applied to Muslim females in general. Classical exegesis gives the meanings of *tabarruj* (33:33) as (1) strutting, or prancing about; (2) flirting, coquettishness; or (3) embellishment, the showing off of finery, the flaunting of bodily charms, "as was practiced by women in the period before Abraham's prophethood, when women wore shirts made of pearls, open at the sides, or other garments which did not conceal their persons."[84] Some said that *tabarruj* included "the unfastened head-veil which permits glimpses of the neck and necklace, ears and earrings of its wearer."[85] In general terms, *tabarruj* meant a woman's public display of her physical self, including her unrestricted gait and the wearing of revealing garments that aided to display physical features, ornaments, makeup, and the like. Today, the meaning of *tabarruj* includes everything from uncovered hair to the elaborate salon-type coiffure, the hairpiece, and the wig; facial foundation, powder, and blushers; lid color and mascara for the eyes; manicure and enamel for the nails; "revealing" dress of any sort, but also including all Western clothing in generic terms, especially if it is of the *couture* kind or has intentions of being fashionable in the Western sense.[86] While the exact definition of what constitutes *tabarruj* has varied over the ages, its condemnation by the custodians of communal morality has always included the Qur'anic reference that it is un-Islamic, a matter of *jahiliyya* (33:33) and thus a threat to Islamic society. Applied to all women, *tabarruj* thus came to signify the very antithesis of *hijab* in the latter's extended meaning of a concealing garment worn outside the house.

The Qur'anic command to Muhammad's wives to "stay in your houses" (33:33) was likewise applied to Muslim women in general; in tandem with the *hijab* rule in its original meaning—"screen of separation" from strangers in the home (33:53)—it legitimized the medieval institution of women's segregation[87] that became a distinctive feature of life for at least the upper-class urban dwellers among them. According to some oft-quoted traditions, the Prophet himself is said to have likened the merit that men gain by fighting for God's cause (*jihad*) to the merit gained by women who stay quietly in their houses and thus remove themselves from becoming Satan's tools in societal corruption.[88] Domesticity, then, was defined as core of female social righteousness, indeed the crucial criterion of a Muslim woman's true citizenship in the community of her faith. The "scripture-based" legality of women's seclusion in the house, and even within the house (subsumed under the concept of *hijab*) of needs then also signified the legality of the Muslim woman's exclusion from any institutionalized participation in public affairs. Thus, while the pairing of specific key Qur'anic concepts (*hijab, tabarruj*, confinement) as antonyms or metonyms and tropes of each other led to mutually enforced semantic extensions of the concepts' original meaning, women's secluded space, concealing clothing, and unfitness for public activity emerged as three powerful determinants in the medieval Islamic paradigm on women's societal role.

Status and Exclusivity

33:6 and the last sentence of 33:53 (Muhammad's wives are the Mothers of the Believers; Muslims may not marry them "after the Prophet")
According to Qur'anic exegesis, these revelations were vouchsafed at a later date than the "verse of choice" of 33:28–29 and also the "peerlessness and restriction" verses of 33:30–34.[89] Muslim Qur'an interpretation has recognized a connection between the honorific title of "Mothers of the Believers" (33:6) and the injunction against marriage with the Prophet's wives (33:53) because, according to Qur'an 4:23, marriage with the mother is forbidden (*haram*).[90] Even though 33:6 and 33:53 are not consecutive in the established Qur'anic text, they are generally considered to belong together; by identifying the same "occasion for" revelation of both, some interpreters even place them into the same revelational context. Traditions have here linked the Qur'anic injunction against marriage with the Prophet's wives "after him" with Muhammad's Companion Talha ibn Ubaydallah, A'isha's cousin, who is said to have intended to marry A'isha after the Prophet's death.[91] Others place the verses in context with similar plans voiced by other men, including a boorish Arabian tribal chief. These men's designs were either voiced up front in the Prophet's and A'isha's presence, or they were circulated in the city by way of rumors. Mernissi interprets these events as additional indication of how badly the Prophet's prestige had been damaged in Medina by the danger and expenses of the war of the siege.[92] Regarding 33:6 and 33:53, Qur'anic interpreters point out that the injunction against marriage with the Prophet's wives or widows was divinely enjoined in order to glorify the Prophet, alive or dead; the legislation was, furthermore, revealed to bless the Prophet, while alive, with "the serenity, joy, and gratitude which a man feels when he knows that his wife cannot remarry . . . as this is an issue that a man debates with himself and thinks about constantly; indeed, some men are so jealous that they wish for her death so that she cannot remarry. . . ." The legislation, however, applied only to the Prophet's established wives with whom he had consummated the marriage and upon whom the *hijab* and "the choice" had been imposed.[93]

Household Crisis and Restrictions

66:1–5 (the Prophet's release from some past [voluntary?] restrictions in dealing with his wives/expiation of oaths/the wife who betrayed "the secret"/warning to two women who conspired against the Prophet/threat of divorce and enumeration of wifely virtues)
This group of verses has been dated into the period of, or right after, the "crisis" in the Prophet's household that culminated in the Prophet's month-long seclusion from his wives.[94] The revelation relieves the Prophet of some un-

specified, apparently selfimposed restriction: It asks why, from (mere) desire to please his wives, he should hold forbidden what God had made lawful for him (66:1). Mentioned then is the duty to expiate oaths[95] (66:2). A "secret tale" is mentioned, which the Prophet confided to one woman and which she then divulged to another (66:3). Two women are called to repent, seriously reprimanded, and warned against conspiring against the Prophet: "and if you two back each other up against him, then verily God is his protector, and Gabriel, and the righteous [one] of the believers; and the angels after that [or, furthermore] are a supporter" (66:4). Thereafter, the wives are threatened with the possibility of divorce: "Perhaps his Lord—if he dismiss [divorce] you[96]—will give him in exchange wives better than you, Muslims, believers, devout, penitent, obedient in worship, observant of fasting and contemplation, both formerly married and virgins" (66:5).

Hadith and Tafsir give several different interpretations of the "occasion for" revelation of 66:1–5. Most relate to petty jealousies among the Prophet's consorts. One story has it that Muhammad's wife Hafsa bint Umar surprised the Prophet in the company of his concubine Marya the Copt "in Hafsa's house and on Hafsa's 'day'," or "on A'isha's 'day'"; the Prophet swore an oath to Hafsa to abstain henceforth from sexual contact with Marya, if Hafsa would keep the incident secret, but Hafsa shared the secret with A'isha.[97] Another account attributes the women's jealousy to the extended visits which the Prophet paid Zaynab bint Jahsh (or, Umm Salama) on account of tasty honey drinks offered to him when he came to call. Hafsa and A'isha plotted to terminate these visits, and they succeeded when they told the fastidious Prophet that he smelled badly of *maghafir*, the strong-smelling gum of the *'urfut*-tree (on which the honey bees "had supposedly fed").[98] Else, Muhammad drank the honey in Hafsa's house, and the "plotters" were A'isha, Sawda, and Safiyya.[99] A third account in the exegetic literature, while failing to explain verses 66:1 and 66:2, identifies the "secret" of 66:3 as Muhammad's words to Hafsa that A'isha's father Abu Bakr, and thereafter her own father Umar ibn al-Khattab, would be the Prophet's successors in leading the community of the faithful; as it was, however, Hafsa betrayed this secret to A'isha.[100] Once again, Qur'anic exegesis here casts Umar ibn al-Khattab in the role of zealous critic of the Prophet's wives. It is he who is said to have first suggested to the Prophet that God, His angels, and the righteous would be on his side if he divorced his wives, and who also first warned the women that the Prophet might divorce them and in exchange be given better wives.[101]

The Prophet's Marriages

33:50–52 (classes of women lawful for marriage with the Prophet/special privileges for the Prophet within his polygamous household/injunction against additional marriages)

The Qur'anic verse 33:50[102] specifies the "categories" from which the Prophet was empowered to choose his lawful wives; it also indicates that some special privileges are here involved. This verse has been dated into the late Medinan period.[103] It reads:

Oh Prophet, We have made lawful for you your wives to whom you gave their dowries ["remunerations," "hires," *ujur*], and what your right hand possesses [slaves] whom God awarded you as booty, and the daughters of your paternal uncle, and the daughters of your paternal aunts, and the daughters of your maternal uncle, and the daughters of your maternal aunts,[104] who emigrated with you; and a believing woman if she give herself to the Prophet, if the Prophet [should] wish to marry her. Especially for you, exclusive of [or, beyond] the believers. We know what We have imposed upon them [as duty] concerning their wives and what their right hands possess. So that there be no restriction [or, restraint, anguish, *haraj*] on you. And God is forgiving, compassionate.

Muslim interpretation of this verse is divided. Some interpreters understand it to refer to the *number* of wives simultaneously lawful to Muhammad. These exegetes emphasize that it is a prophet's prerogative to marry as many women as he may desire, since unrestricted polygamy is an aspect of God's *sunna* ("law," "custom") for His messengers.[105] Conversely, a second line of argumentation finds the Prophet's special prerogatives here legislated in the clause "a believing woman, if she give herself to the Prophet, if he [should] wish to marry her."[106] What is at stake for this latter group of interpreters is the institution of *hiba*, the act by which a woman "offers herself" to a man without a guardian (*wali*) to negotiate the union, and without expectation of a dower.[107] The traditions indicate that the Prophet's wives, among them especially A'isha, did not approve of *hiba*. Indeed. A'isha is to have said that "there is no good in a woman when she offers herself to a man"; and after the revelation of 33:50 she is said to have commented to the Prophet: "God verily is in a hurry for you to do your desire."[108] These traditions coincide with the general discomfort of later Muslim interpreters with the institution of *hiba*, which so blatantly went against the type of marriage formulated in Islamic jurisprudence. Indeed, a tradition from al-Zuhri declares that *hiba* was not lawful for anyone "*after* the Prophet."[109]

Sura 33:51, most probably revealed on the same occasion as 33:50, grants the Prophet greater freedom in choosing, or dealing with, his wives, permitting him to "defer" or to "take in" whom of the women he willed; the verse ends with the words: "and if you desire one whom you had sent away, it is no sin for you. This is more appropriate that their eyes be gladdened and that they should not be sad, and all be satisfied with what you have given them. God knows what is in your hearts. . . ." One school of exegesis links 33:51 with 33:50 to indicate divine permission for the Prophet to enter into new marriage arrangements and terminate old ones.[110] Another strand of interpretation stipulates[111] that "the Prophet was restricted to his [established] wives"; thus, 33:51 is here understood as applicable to the Prophet's relations with his existing spouses, that is, as release from the rigid pattern of marital equity which Muhammad had practiced in the past. The latter traditions also indicate that the revelation of 33:51 did away with all jealousies among the women, because they accepted their new domestic arrangement unquestioningly, in obedience to God.[112]

The classical interpreters generally place the following verse, 33:52, into the same revelation as the verses just considered.[113] 33:52 (which appears to contradict 33:50 and 51) addresses the Prophet: "After this, women are not lawful for you, nor that you (ex)change them for wives, even though their beauty please you; except for your slaves. And God watches over everything." Commentators have registered various opinions on the meaning of this verse. According to some, 33:52 put an end to further marriages by the Prophet, and they maintain that this injunction was God's reward for Muhammad's wives' "choice" (33:28–29) and also recompense for their taboo status as "Mothers of the Believers," which precluded (re)marriage with another man (33:6 and 33:53).[114] Others interpret the verse as limitation on the "groups," or "classes," or "categories," from which the Prophet was empowered to choose new marriage partners.[115] A third point of view, expressed in a number of traditions on the authority of A'isha, maintains that this verse was "abrogated" by the preceding one (33:51).[116] The stipulation of abrogation here both eliminates the apparent contradiction between 33:52 and 33:51, and also serves to establish the Prophet's complete freedom with regard to his marital arrangements.

Conclusion

The Qur'anic legislation directed at the Prophet's wives, then, is entirely of Medinan provenance and belongs into the last six or seven years of the Prophet's life. Considered in chronological sequence of revelation, the duty of seclusion behind a partition in the presence of strangers (i.e., nonrelatives) was the first to be imposed. It was accompanied, or soon followed, by stringent codes of modest comportment in private and public. The latter codes, in turn, emphasized the women's duty to maintain seclusion in their houses, charity, piety, and obedience to God and His Prophet. Added thereto were strongly worded warnings against domestic disobedience in the form of plots or conspiracies. While the Prophet was granted unequalled rights concerning the number and type of marriages he might wish to conclude, remarriage of his wives "after him" was forbidden.

To seek to recover the dynamics of the Qur'an-as-process by way of attending to the chronological sequence of revelations is, of course, not a Western Islamicist invention. Indeed, the problematic of time frame and sequence of revelations was clearly an important concern of early Muslim Hadith and Tafsir, made all the more urgent by the doctrine of "abrogation" (*naskh*) of an earlier revelation by a later one.[117] Insofar as the Qur'anic legislation on the Prophet's domestic affairs progresses, in chronological terms, toward Muhammad's increasing control over his women, the time frame of the relevant revelations suggests a trend in the direction of increasing restraint, not increasing "liberation," of the Prophet's wives. The Qur'an itself provides the *ratio legis* for this trend in its repeated statements of concern for the collective wellbeing, indeed, the perfection of the Prophet's household. It is this latter, collective, entity that the revelations mean to strengthen and elevate to model status, and be it at the expense of individual ambitions and idiosyncracies of some of its members. The Prophet's polygamous household here becomes a prime example of Qur'anic reasoning in favor of righteous institutions over individual aspirations.[118] At the same time, as indicated above, the Qur'anic legislation also signifies aspects of the principle of ethical individualism in its linkage between individual select status and individual virtue, clearly expressed in the "verse of choice" (33:28–29). Double shares of divine reward (and also divinely decreed terrestrial rank) are compensation for the Prophet's wives' choice to accept obligations more stringent than those the Qur'an imposed upon Muslim women in general. The Qur'an's promise of everlasting elite status for the Prophet's consorts hinges on their fulfillment of greater and graver obligations because, for their group, the conditions of "obedience to God and obedience to His Prophet" are cast in more exacting terms.[119] But such is God's *sunna*: Human virtue bears rewards manyfold, some individual and eternal, others communal and of this world when virtuous institutions are maintained by the individual virtue of their members.

9

The Mothers of the Believers in the Hadith

The first generation of Muslims surely regarded the Prophet's comportment and way of life as a model they endeavored to emulate, because he was God's spokesman in their midst and also their divinely appointed leader to whom they had pledged obedience.[1] The notion of the Prophet's personal peerlessness expanded and intensified after his death when the victorious wars of conquest that led to the foundation of a vast Muslim empire were triumphant proof of the truth of Muhammad's mission. Within the newly expanded realm of Islam, later generations of Muslims, most of them not of Arab stock, came to see the Prophet in terms of a personal infallibility and sinlessness that had not been perceived by his contemporaries in Mecca and Medina.[2] The Hadith is both a record of what Muhammad actually said and did and also a record of what his community in the first two centuries of Islamic history believed that he said and did. Thus, the Hadith has been called "a guide to understanding the historical Muhammad as well as a guide to understanding the evolution of Muslim piety from the seventh to the ninth centuries."[3] Even in the authenticated Hadith, "history" and "example" were intertwined in that the compilers' intent and methodology were not to record historical data per se but to institutionalize Muhammad's exemplary behavior for the benefit of the community.[4]

The transformation of Muhammad's historic personality into ideal persona is, in part, reflected in the proliferation, content, and function of early

An earlier and shorter version of this and the next chapter appeared in *The Muslim World*, vol. 82, nos. 1–2 (1992), pp. 1–36.

Islamic Prophetic hagiography. Gordon Newby has recently shown the influence of Jewish and Christian hagiography and prophetology (*qua isra'iliyyat* traditions) on the Prophet's sacred biography.[5] During the second quarter of the eighth century (beginning of the second century of the Islamic calendar), Islam began to pull back from such influences as part of pervasive spiritual and intellectual processes that, within the parameters of the formation of Islamic law, elaborated the notion that the Prophet's way of life was *sunna* (sacred precedent and impeccable model). The latter principle was made the cornerstone of legal theory by Muhammad ibn Idris al-Shafi'i (d. 819/20) who, on the basis of Qur'an 24:52 (divine command to obey God and His Prophet) declared that the Prophet's actions were tacitly inspired, beyond human questioning, a source of the divine will complementary to the Qur'an, and therefore an infallible "source," or "root," of the law.[6] In tandem with other factors, this development in Islamic legal theory necessitated the excision of Bible-related foreign "inspirational" models of prophethood[7] and also established the need for greater vigilance in Hadith transmission, especially regarding *isra'iliyyat* materials. Thus, it was the adoption of the Prophet as authority of law that in the generations after al-Shafi'i called forth the great medieval effort of full-scale Hadith criticism and the "sifting out" of the authentic Hadith. The latter was compiled in the ninth century (third century of the Islamic calendar) by a number of renowned traditionists, six among whom authored collections that the Muslim community accepted as authentic, or "sound" (*sahih*). Among the six, Bukhari (d. 870) and Muslim (d. 875) are held in special esteem.[8] By their time, Hadith proliferation had reached such dimensions that of the 600,000 traditions which he examined, for instance, Bukhari is said to have retained as authentic only 7257, when the repetitions, which number 4000, are eliminated.[9] The science of Hadith criticism paid great attention to the question of soundness of "chain of transmitters" (*sanad, isnad*) of each tradition, including reliability of each transmitting authority as examined in biographical dictionaries such as the *Kitab al-tabaqat al-kabir* of Ibn Sa'd (d. 845). While critiquing the authorities, the works of biographical history themselves were, however, less exclusive (i.e., less rigid in the criteria applied) than the authenticated collections that were compiled mainly for legal purposes. Nevertheless, even in Bukhari and Muslim and other *Sahih* collections, contradictory traditions abound that give both sides of an argument, with the noteworthy exception of traditions on some women's issues—especially regarding matters of social status and rights—in which only one side of the argument, the restrictive, is documented.

Similar developments are recognizable in the copious Hadith materials on the Prophet's wives. Although their status and importance, of course, never matched the Prophet's, the women's Qur'an-established rank, also their role as the Prophet's helpmates and supporters in his mission to preach and implement God's truth, and, finally, their intimate involvement with the righteous Prophet in all of the minutiae of daily life elevated them even during their lifetime to a level of prestige above the community's other females. This special status grew more lofty with the progression of time when Muslim piety came to view the women of the Prophet's household as models for emulation. Eventually, the Prophet's wives' behavior as recorded in the traditions was likewise recognized as *sunna* that furnished many of the criteria of what was lawful (*halal*) or forbidden (*haram*) for Muslims, especially Muslim women. These criteria were then codified (*qua* examples) in the works of early Islamic jurisprudence (*fiqh*).

The Hadith, however, portrays the Prophet's wives in several distinctive ways; that is, the women appear in a number of conflicting sets of personae. On the one hand, they emerge as perfect exemplars of their sex regarding virtue and righteousness. On the other hand, they are portrayed as embodiments of female emotionalism, irrationality, greed, and rebelliousness. As discussed below, these divergent "images" of the Prophet's wives appear in the Hadith as *functionally* convergent. That is to say, the "images" as recorded/transmitted by the medieval scholars of Islam provided both the paradigm for the limits that needed to be placed on women's roles in religion and society, and also their justification, that is, scripturalist proof of "women's nature." In the scholars' formulation, then, the Qur'anic revelations of restriction directed at (and obeyed by) the Prophet's wives were made applicable to all Muslim women, while the human frailties of Muhammad's wives, which the Qur'an had sought to rectify, were maintained (indeed, highlighted) as symbolic for all that was wrong with the female sex.

What follows is a representative sampling and classification of the Hadith, here mainly culled from the eighth volume of Ibn Sa'd's (d. 845) *Kitab al-tabaqat al-kabir*, entitled *Fi al-nisa'* ("On the Women").[10] The material available in this and other Hadith collections constitutes three different categories, here entitled: (1) the Prophet's wives as "ordinary women"; (2) the Prophet's wives in early Hadith hagiography; and (3) the Prophet's wives as paragons of virtue and models for emulation by all Muslim women. Of these, the second category is largely linked to the legacy of the *qussas* (popular tellers of pious lore). The first and third are complex mixtures of history and "image," in which close reading can discover concerns and experiences of the early community as understood by medieval traditionalist scholarship; in addition, the third also bears the imprint of development of the terms of Islamic law.

Our approach to the Hadith on the Prophet's wives is to report the traditions in all their variety in order to be able to investigate the modes of their deployment both medieval and also modern. The literary analysis approach pursued here aims to discover paradigmatic meanings of the text and their symbolic functions. The Hadith on the Prophet's wives signifies both itself and also something else. As text, it presents "images" of the Prophet's consorts. As subtext, these images are meaningful in relation to the society of their first formulation and also the societies to which they then were (or are) applied by way of instruction, explanation, to legitimate the status quo or establish the validity of a new paradigm. At present, new uses of the authenticated Hadith on the Prophet's wives often involve some reformulation or tacit, selective elimination of established traditions. But innovation has recently also yielded some direct textual criticism of authenticated texts by Muslim scholarship undertaken with the techniques of classical hermeneutics, that is, by way of proof of unreliability of transmitters of a given item.[11]

Bulky segments of the classical Hadith portray the Prophet's wives as "ordinary women" possessed and motivated by petty jealousies. It is noteworthy that these "anecdotal" household hadiths make up such a large segment of classical Muslim literature on the Mothers of the Believers. Why is it that pious tradition has lavished so much attention on the details of the domestic intrigues, squabbles, jealousies, envies, and other human foibles of the Prophet's wives? Traditions depicting the women as "ordinary females" may, firstly, stem from the Hadith's exegetic function by which the Qur'anic materials of rebuke and censure directed at Muhammad's wives were legitimate topics for pious concern. Secondly, the women's family ties, hence their relations with rival political cadres in early Muslim history, in all likelihood made them fitting targets for enhancing, or, conversely, disparaging detail.[12] Thirdly, the Hadith also developed what may be called a "typology of pettiness" that employed the theme of the women's jealousy in formulaic fashion to "explain" a number of occurrences whose original nature was unknown, or unacceptable, to later Muslim traditionists.[13] Some of the jealousy accounts, then, may be "encodings" of events and practices known only to the original source and transmitter. Fourthly, the fact that scholarly consensus continued to support and make great use of these traditions is related to the generally low opinion of women's nature expressed in medieval religious literature as a whole. Indeed, in its function of providing exegetic material and also raw legal data, the medieval Hadith on the Prophet's wives may well have served in several ways toward the medieval institutionalization of a decline in women's societal rank and obtainable legal rights. By emphasizing the ambiguity (or, two-sidedness) of the materials on the female elite of Islam, the Prophet's wives, whose scripturalist personae it presented as partially flawed, the Hadith in fact questioned the equality of male and female in the early community; in all justice and by necessity, then, the laws governing women's lives had to be more restrictive. Even the Prophet's wives' "image" as blameless saintly women did not substantially alter this state of affairs because (by the consensus of the scholars of Islam) it failed to eradicate the other.

It is symptomatic of a new age and debate on women's questions, then, that modern and contemporary Muslim literature on the Prophet's consorts has largely excized the "anecdotal" materials so copious in Ibn Sa'd and other medieval sources. The same applies, at least in part, to the hagiographic dimension. Excepting the works of popular piety (often with a Sufi bent) and others of general conservative-inspirational character, contemporary Muslim literature now *de*-emphasizes the miraculous experiences of the Prophet's wives, just as it also de-emphasizes their all-too-human frailties. It is as fighters for the establishment of Islamic values, and there mainly by way of their impeccable morality and manner of life, that the Mothers of the Believers are now depicted; as such, they embody that model behavior the contemporary Muslim woman can recognize and must strive to follow.[14]

The Prophet's Wives as "Ordinary Women"

Many of the accounts on life in the Prophet's household contain detailed descriptions of the jealousies and domestic political maneuvers of the Mothers of the Believers. These reports present the Prophet's wives as a petty, greedy, backbiting, and power-hungry group. The unseemliness of their behavior is shown up all the more by the many traditions on the Prophet's impartiality toward his wives. Indeed, the Prophet is said to have been scrupulous in treating his wives equitably. He visited each of them once a day when he made his daily rounds of their houses, usually after the afternoon prayer (Ibn Sa'd, *Nisa'*, p. 59); he would lay his hand on each and kiss her (ibid., p. 122). After a wedding night spent with a new wife he is said to have wished his other wives well and asked to receive their good wishes (ibid., p. 75). In addition, each wife had her turn of a fixed period of companionship and sexual contact with the Prophet.[15] This was a prerogative she guarded zealously as her right (ibid., p. 67) and which she could give to a rival if she so chose.[16] If a new bride opted for a longer period of privacy and intimacy with the Prophet after the wedding, then the other wives were entitled to the same (ibid., pp. 64–66). During his visits to his wives, the Prophet would stand, but when he arrived at the house of the woman whose "day" it was, he would sit (ibid., p. 122). When the Prophet went on travels and military expeditions, he determined by lot which two of his wives would accompany him (ibid., pp. 72, 121–122). The Hadith reports, however, that this equitable system was upset when a wife would think of some trick or other in the attempt to detain the Prophet in her house during his daily visit. An oft-quoted story has it that Hafsa bint Umar, who was aware of Muhammad's love for sweets, detained him by offering a honey drink, until the ruse was discovered and thwarted by a counterruse of A'isha, Sawda, and Safiyya (ibid., p. 59). Or it may have been Umm Salama who detained him, and A'isha and Hafsa who plotted to terminate that stratagem (ibid., pp. 122–123).

New arrivals in the Prophet's household are said to have evoked intense jealousies in the already established wives, who feared that a new rival might replace them in the Prophet's affection. Such jealousies could make a new wife appear more beautiful than she was, as fear of competition played havoc with objective observation. For example, such fears are related of A'isha when the Prophet had married Umm Salama (ibid., p. 66), or when she saw the beauty and sweetness of the Arab war captive Juwayriyya (ibid., p. 83).

A sizeable number of traditions state that the women were dissatisfied with the manner in which food and other presents were distributed among them. The faithful reportedly offered their freewill gifts (*sadaqa*) most frequently on the day the Prophet spent in A'isha's house (ibid., p. 117). The other wives are said to have sent his daughter Fatima to request their fair share, but the Prophet requested that Fatima "love A'isha for the sake of his own love for A'isha"; Fatima, in turn, is said to have been so embarrassed that she vowed she would "never talk to him about her again." (This tradition is given on the authority of A'isha, ibid., pp. 123–124). Thereafter, the wives sent Zaynab bint Jahsh who began to revile A'isha; the latter describes how she looked at the Prophet until she was sure of his permission to avenge herself. Defaming Zaynab, she then silenced her, and "the Prophet smiled and said: verily, she is Abu Bakr's daughter" (ibid., pp. 123–124). The women also competed among themselves by way of boasting how one or the other had played a special role in an "occasion for revelation," or held a special rank with the Prophet. Some traditions, for instance, assert that the wives disliked Zaynab bint Jahsh's reminders that her marriage to the Prophet had occurred by specific divine dispensation (Qur'an 33:37–38, also 33:4 and 40) and the *hijab* verse (33:53) had been revealed on the occasion of her wedding (Ibn Sa'd, *Nisa'*, p. 75) A'isha's status claims involved the fact that of all the Prophet's wives she had been the only virgin bride, "an un-grazed slope as compared to all the others that were grazed over," (ibid., p. 55) and that she was the dearest companion of the Prophet who was always aware of her moods, (ibid., pp. 47, 55) calling her "dearer [to him] than butter with dates," (ibid., p. 55) "as superior to all women as breadsoup is to all foods." (ibid., p. 55).

It may be useful to associate traditions of this genre with the fact that the Prophet's wives hailed from different clans and even tribes;[17] by way of family relationships (a factor of considerable import during the formative years of Islam), these women were thus naturally allied with what were, or later turned out to be, opposing political factions in early Islamic history.

To give a few examples: A'isha was the daughter of the first caliph, Abu Bakr of the family of Amir ibn Amr of the Taym clan of the Quraysh tribe. A'isha, who was childless, derived her *kunya* (honorific title) "Mother of Abdallah" from her sister's son Abdallah ibn al-Zubayr, whom she is said to have "adopted" and loved like a son. Abdallah's father al-Zubayr (i.e., A'isha's brother-in-law) was a rival political candidate at the time of the election of the third caliph Uthman ibn Affan (644 A.D.); after the latter's assassination in 656 A.D., he became a declared enemy of Ali, Uthman's successor and fourth caliph of Islam. In the opposition movement against Ali—who was also first cousin to the Prophet and the husband of his daughter Fatima—A'isha played a leading role. Here, she is said to have galvanized the energies of two important allies, the Companions al-Zubayr and Talha (the former her brother-in-law and the latter her cousin who also, reportedly, thought of marrying her after the Prophet's death, until the Qur'anic revelation of 33:53 made this impossible).[18] Hafsa was the daughter of the second caliph, Umar ibn al-Khattab of the Adi clan of the Quraysh tribe; her father is said to have been "the power behind the throne" during the caliphate of his predecessor, Abu Bakr. Umm Salama was of the family of al-Mughira of the wealthy and influential Makhzum clan of the Quraysh in Mecca, a clan that fought against the Prophet for many years in close alliance with the equally wealthy and aristocratic Meccan clan of Umayya. It is reported that Umm Salama at first supported Ali and Fatima (i.e., she declared in favor of the political aspirations of the Prophet's blood relatives), but that she later became a supporter of the Umayyads. (Umm Salama was also the aunt of the Prophet's general Khalid ibn al-Walid, hero of the *ridda* wars and the early wars of Islamic expansion; at the end of his military career, the latter served as governor of Syria which after him became the crown colony of the Umayyads). Umm Habiba was an Umayyad. She was Ramla, daughter of Abu Sufyan and a half-sister of Mu'awiya; the latter fought Ali ibn Abi Talib for control of the Islamic state in 657 A.D. and then, after Ali's assassination in 661, went on to found the Umayyad dynasty while ruler ("caliph") of Islam. While some of the "jealousy" traditions quoted here may be political statements linked to intercommunal power struggles,[19] later pious understanding took these traditions at face value after the political events in question had long passed. And, indeed, these traditions may very well signify both, their apparent meaning (actual jealousy) and their hidden meaning (support for a group or party against one or a number of other groups and parties).[20]

Not all traditions of this genre relate to the Arabian power struggles of early Islamic history. Some suggest a functionality of a different kind. At least one of the Prophet's wives, the Makhzumite aristocrat Umm Salama, is said to have hesitated in accepting the Prophet's proposal of marriage because she knew herself to be very jealous, "while you, oh Prophet of God, accumulate women" (Ibn Sa'd, *Nisa'*, p. 63). He persuaded her to the marriage by replying that God would take care of such feelings. Nevertheless, Umm Salama's jealousy is said to have erupted on numerous occasions, one of which occurred during her travels with the Prophet when he mistook his wives' litters and by mistake approached Safiyya's litter on Umm Salama's "day." The latter flew into a rage both at the Prophet and also her new rival (ibid., 67). What distinguishes this tradition is that Safiyya was a young Jewish captive whom the Prophet had received as part of his share of booty after the conquest of Khaybar, and that Umm Salama's anger at being neglected led her to say that "you are talking with the daughter of the Jews on my day, when you are God's Apostle!"[21] Many other traditions contain similar elements of prejudice of the Prophet's wives toward his Jewish consorts, which may indicate a common subtextual meaning in these traditions. It is reported, for instance, that when the Prophet brought Safiyya home to Medina, she was riding behind him on his mount, fully concealed by a wrap. The camel stumbled and threw off both riders in sight of Muhammad's watching wives who said: "May God banish the Jewess, and do 'that and that' to her" (ibid., pp. 87–88). A'isha is said to have left her house "disguised by a head veil" in order to mingle unrecognized among the throngs of women who welcomed, and inspected, Safiyya; the Prophet reportedly recognized A'isha inspite of her veil, but when he asked her opinion of the new arrival, he received an insolent answer (ibid., p. 90).[22] All of the Prophet's Arab wives are said to have looked askance at the beautiful Jewish woman taken prisoner of war (ibid., p. 90). Backbiting and bragging matches involving a wife of Arab and another of Jewish descent are also recorded. For example, A'isha and Safiyya are said to have reviled each other's father (ibid., p. 56) until the Prophet reportedly suggested to Safiyya that she should have stood her ground by saying that "her father was Aaron, and Moses was her uncle" (ibid., p. 91). Muhammad's (other) wives are also said to have mocked Safiyya when she expressed the wish that God inflict the Prophet's illness upon herself in his stead; the Prophet is said to have censured them (ibid., p. 91). Such unseemly behavior is said to have included unwillingness to help a co-wife in need. Zaynab bint Jahsh, for instance, is said to have refused to lend one of her camels to Safiyya, whose mount had become defective. When the Prophet suggested this loan, she answered: "Should I give anything to this Jewess?" The Prophet is reported to have shown his displeasure by avoiding her for two or three months, until she had given up all hope of reconciliation, but he forgave her in the end (ibid., pp. 90–91). These and many other similar traditions, then, hinge on prejudice shown by the Prophet's Arab wives toward his Jewish consorts, but one may well understand their meaning and purpose in relation to larger and also later sociopolitical developments. Several of the reports indicate that the Prophet censured such behavior on the part of his wives of Quraysh descent. The traditions, then, may have some antitribal and also anti-Arab signification.[23]

The theme of jealousy of the Prophet's wives appears in a set of curious traditions on marriages that the Prophet intended to conclude, or did conclude, with Arabian tribal women but which were dissolved before consummation. In all cases, the women under consideration were "strangers" (*ghara'ib*), that is, not of the Quraysh tribe or other tribes located in the area of Mecca and Medina.[24] A'isha is reported to have lamented the Prophet's desire to marry such strangers: "he has placed his hands on strangers, they are about to turn away his face from us" (Ibn Sa'd, *Nisa'*, p. 104). It is related that the Prophet sent A'isha on a mission to "look over" a woman of the Kalb tribe to whom he had proposed marriage. A'isha declared her to be "nothing worthwhile," but the Prophet answered: "What you saw was, indeed, worthwhile; you saw a beauty spot on her cheek, and every hair of yours trembled (in apprehension)." A'isha then knew that nothing was concealed from the Prophet (ibid., p. 115). The explanation of the failure of this union by reason of A'isha's jealousy, however, is formulaic and does not make much sense.[25] Ibn Sa'd[26] furthermore reports on three instances in which a marriage of the Prophet with a tribal woman was dissolved before consummation by a repudiation formula, *a'udhu billahi minka*, "I seek refuge with God from you," pronounced by the woman. According to some of these traditions, the woman repeated the formula three times while the Prophet covered his head with his sleeve. In all cases, he released the woman and sent her back to her tribe.[27] Fatima Mernissi[28] sees in these traditions remnants of the Arab woman's pre-Islamic customary right to repudiate the man, a counterpart to her right to "bestow herself" (*hiba*). The Islamic Hadith, however, ascribes the dissolution of these marriages to the jealousies of Muhammad's established wives.[29] It is A'isha and Hafsa who are said to have suggested use of the "formula of refuge" so that the new bride would "win the Prophet's favor."[30] Reportedly they used this ruse while preparing the beautiful Asma' bint al-Ma'mun of the Kinda tribe for her wedding night, "while one applied henna dye to her hands and the other combed her hair."[31] Thereafter, "the Prophet walked on foot into (the new bride's) presence, then he dropped down on his knees, then reached for her to kiss her, as he used to do when he unveiled women, and she said: 'I take refuge with God from you;' he turned away from her with the words: 'you have certainly sought refuge,' and

he jumped away from her, then gave orders . . . to return her to her tribe."[32]
Thereafter, when the Prophet was informed who had suggested that she utter
these words, he said: "They are surely Joseph's companions [cf. Qur'an 12:28]
and their cunning is enormous," *while his anger showed in his face* (Ibn Sa'd, *Nisa'*,
pp. 103, 106).

Finally, the jealousy of the Prophet's wives emerges as the dominant theme
in all reports on domestic and communal events involving the Prophet's concubine Marya the Copt, mother of his son Ibrahim. Her figure looms large in
the interpretations of Qur'an 33:28–29 ("the choice") and 66:1–5 ("censure
of the woman who betrayed the secret"), which Qur'anic exegesis has consistently linked with disturbances in the Prophet's household brought on by
intense sexual jealousy of the Prophet's wives toward this concubine. It appears that these reports, however, can likewise be read on several levels.
Marya,[33] whose *kunya* (honorific title) was, of course, "Umm Ibrahim," is said
to have pleased the Prophet because she was "white and beautiful, and her
hair was curly." He lodged her in a piece of property later called "the loft of
Umm Ibrahim" where he visited her frequently. Reportedly he imposed on her
the *hijab* (segregation in the presence of strangers as imposed on the Prophet's
wives by Qur'an 33:53), surely to signal special status, even though she remained his concubine. Marya gave birth to Ibrahim in this loft. Salma, the
Prophet's "client" woman, acted as midwife, and it was her husband Abu Rafi'
who gave the Prophet the glad tidings of the birth of a son. Abu Rafi' was
rewarded with the gift of a household slave. This is said to have occurred in
the eighth year after the hijra (Ibn Sa'd, *Nisa'*, p. 153).

As an afterthought to a long and detailed description of her feelings of
intense sexual jealousy of Marya, a tradition from A'isha states: "then God gave
the child from her, while He had deprived us of a child from him (the Prophet)"
(ibid., p. 153). This phrase may give a clue to some otherwise unintelligible
information on Marya found at the end of her "chapter" in Ibn Sa'd's *Tabaqat*.
The traditions in question (Ibn Sa'd, *Nisa'*, pp. 154–155) appear to echo rumors
that Ibrahim was not the Prophet's son but the progeny of a Copt who had
taken refuge with Marya in her loft. The Hadith refutes this accusation without clearly stating it. Reportedly the Copt did household chores for Marya
and the people gossiped that there was "an infidel man who has access to an
infidel woman." The Prophet sent Ali ibn Abi Talib to investigate the matter.
When Ali, sword in hand, approached the Copt, the man was either sitting on
a date palm and threw his clothes away, or he climbed up on a date palm and
his garment slipped off. In either case, Ali saw him to be without genitals,
"without a penis or testicles." Ali sheathed the sword and returned to the
Prophet but he was worried (the implication being that he had not carried out
an order to kill the man). He inquired whether "it was right to check with you
first if one be commanded to do a thing but finds that things are different,"
and the Prophet said "yes." Another tradition indicates that the angel Gabriel
came to the Prophet when Ibrahim was born and greeted him with the words:
"Peace be upon you, father of Ibrahim; and the Prophet found reassurance in
that." Thereafter, he is said to have given Marya her freedom with the words

"her child has given her her freedom," that is, he liberated her as his *umm walad* (ibid., pp. 154–155).[34]

These reports may simply echo "hypocrite" manipulation of Medinan public opinion to the detriment of the Prophet.[35] It is more likely that they hint at communal fears, shared by the Prophet's wives, that the birth of a male child of the Prophet by a foreign woman of Christian faith would have political consequences in the form of dynasty building[36] or possible future Coptic influence in the Muslim community. The latter is suggested by another (although probably much later) tradition reported by Ibn Sa'd in Marya's "chapter" according to which the Prophet said: "Treat the Copts well. They have a covenant (*dhimma*) and also kinship. Their kinship is that the mother of Ishmael son of Abraham (i.e., Hagar) was one of them, and that the mother of Ibrahim son of the Prophet (i.e., Marya) was one of them" (ibid., p. 154). A historical political crisis as well as later Muslim-Coptic relations, then, may be part of the import of copious Hadith materials on the Prophet's wives' intense jealousy of this Coptic slave.

In the preceding examples the theme of wifely jealousy can be linked to a number of political, social, and legal developments that had occupied the early Muslim community. The image of the jealous wife, as transmitted and maintained by the traditionists, thereafter also served another purpose in that the Hadith in question promulgated (formulaic) character traits of the Mothers of the Believers that were consonant with medieval scholarly opinion of women's irrational/lower nature. The image remained in existence long after any "encoded" earlier information had been forgotten, and even though it was in contradiction to the symbolic themes of moral virtue and saintliness.

The Prophet's Wives in Early Hadith Hagiography

The Hadith collections that include the traditions on Muhammad's wives' human frailties also contain reports of miraculous events that studded the women's lives.[37] These occurrences, to be sure, always involve the Prophet, and it is in their relationships with him that the women are granted miraculous experiences or abilities.

The traditions relate such an event in connection with Muhammad's first wife, Khadija bint al-Khuwaylid, said to have occurred during her participation in a popular annual pagan celebration for the women of Mecca that centered around an idol in the shape of a man. This idol began to speak and predicted that a prophet by the name of "Ahmad" would be sent with God's message, and "whichever woman can become a wife to him should do so." While the (other) pagan women pelted the idol with stones, denounced it, and "barked at it," Khadija paid attention to the idol's words and did not treat it as the women did (Ibn Sa'd, *Nisa'*, p. 9). Khadija was the Qurashi "merchant woman of dignity and wealth" who hired Muhammad to trade on her behalf in Syria. It is reported that she *heard about* the miraculous events that occurred on this journey, and that it was *because* of this information that she asked him to marry her.[38]

Ibn Sa'd reports on dream visions experienced by most of Muhammad's other wives prior to their marriage to the Prophet. Sawda, while still married to her previous husband, dreamt that Muhammad approached her and "placed his foot on her neck,"[39] also that a moon hurled itself upon her from the sky while she lay prostrate (ibid., pp. 38–39). When Umm Habiba and her husband lived as temporary refugees in Abyssinia, she had a dream in which she saw her husband disfigured; on the following morning she learned that he had "left Islam" and (some say, again) embraced Christianity. When she rebuked him, he took to drink and died soon afterwards. Then she heard a dream voice addressing her as "Mother of the Believers," and on the following morning the Negus (ruler of Abyssinia) informed her that the Prophet had written a letter asking for her hand in marriage (ibid., p. 68). Similar dreams are reported of Safiyya, the woman of Jewish descent from Khaybar. She is said to have told her Jewish relatives: "I saw as if I were (*sic*) with him who thinks that God sent him, while an angel covered us with his wings," but then they dealt harshly with her (ibid., p. 87). She also dreamt of "a moon that drew close from Yathrib[40] until it fell into my lap," to which her Jewish husband replied "you want to be married to that king who is coming from Medina" and hit her in the face; the mark was still visible when the Prophet married her after the conquest of Khaybar (ibid., p. 86).

With A'isha, it was not she but the Prophet who is said to have been favored with a sign. Reportedly, Muhammad asked Abu Bakr for A'isha's hand in marriage only after the Angel Gabriel had shown him a picture of A'isha (Ibn Sa'd, *Nisa'*, p. 44);[41] according to another account, Gabriel showed him the infant A'isha in her cradle as his future bride and befitting substitute for Khadija, a divine favor to lessen his grief over Khadija's death (ibid., p. 54). Among the wives, it was only A'isha in whose company Muhammad is said to have received revelations (ibid., pp. 43–44). Some traditions report that A'isha could even see the Angel on these occasions and exchanged salutations with him (ibid., pp. 44, 46), while others say that she could not see him but that she and the Angel greeted each other through the Prophet (ibid., pp. 46–47, 55).[42] Zaynab bint Jahsh, in turn, was miraculously blessed by God when the food the Prophet's servant Anas ibn Malik had prepared for her wedding feast multiplied until it sufficed to feed seventy-one guests, possibly even seventy-two (ibid., pp. 74, 125).

The Hadith establishes that all of Muhammad's terrestrial wives will be his consorts in paradise (e.g., ibid., pp. 44–45, 58, 76). Indeed, the Angel commanded the Prophet to take Hafsa bint Umar back after he had divorced her, saying that she was a righteous woman and would be his wife in heaven (ibid., p. 58). In A'isha's case, the Angel even showed the dying Prophet her image in paradise to make his death easier with the promise of their reunion in the hereafter (ibid., p. 45). It was the desire to be resurrected at judgment day as a member of the Prophet's household that led Sawda to implore the Prophet not to divorce her; she wanted no part of men or husbands in this world, she said, but yearned to be his consort in heaven, and therefore offered to assign "her day" with him to A'isha in her stead (ibid., pp. 36–37). The first of the wives to join the Prophet in heaven was Zaynab bint Jahsh. Muhammad had predicted this when he said that the wife who had "the longest arm" would arrive there soon after him. The women later comprehended that by "long-armed-ness" he had meant "charity" because the first to die after him was the charitable Zaynab bint Jahsh (ibid., p. 76).

Traditions of this genre, then, are of inspirational character. In the sample narratives just quoted, the Prophet's wives are depicted as divinely favored individuals lifted high above the realm and ranks of ordinary womankind. God's grace surrounds them because they are His Prophet's chosen consorts.[43] A close reading of the sort attempted above, however, could perhaps find in this hagiographic material a typological resemblance with the Prophet's wives as "ordinary women." The material suggests that one of its functions may have been to elevate the Prophet's wives individually but also unequally (in a sort of competition for miracles). This, in turn, would suggest that such traditions, prestige building as they undoubtedly were, may originally have had a political dimension. What remained when the latter had fallen into oblivion was the linkage between the Prophet's wives' wondrous experiences and their exemplary morality.

The Prophet's Wives as Paragons of Virtue, and Precedent-Setting Models for All Women

A large segment of the Hadith depicts the Mothers of the Believers as models of piety and righteousness whose every act exemplifies their commitment to establish God's order on earth by personal example. Their battlefields are not the plains of war on which Muslim men fight against infidel armies but involve the struggle to implement and safeguard Islamic norms and values. Indeed, the traditions on the women's personal comportment, dress, performance of ritual and worship, and the like must largely be read as (para-)legal texts in that their intended meaning is normative, not descriptive. Each recorded detail represents a facet of *sunna*-in-the-making, while their sum reflects the proliferation of categories of acceptable, forbidden, or value-neutral behavior first debated and then promulgated in early Islamic law. This process, then, involved a dynamic spiral of mutual reinforcement of its two constituent components, that is, the principle of these women's righteousness on the one hand, and their function as categorical norm-setters on the other. This is especially clear in the traditions which deal with modesty, veiling, and seclusion. Here, the Prophet's wives are depicted both as models and enforcers of the then newly imposed Qur'anic norms. It is reported, for instance, that A'isha ripped off the thin, transparent *khimar* ("kerchief") her niece Hafsa wore in her presence; "she chastised her, reminded her of the modesty-verse of the 'Sura of the Light' (24:31), and clad her in a thick cloth" (Ibn Sa'd, *Nisa'*, pp. 49–50). A'isha is said to have worn the "veil" in public at all times, even as a little girl before she had reached puberty (but after the Prophet had asked for her hand in marriage) (ibid., pp. 40, 54).[44] Indeed, the Hadith—in concert with the Qur'anic text—establishes that the invisibility of the Prophet's wives went beyond restrictions placed upon Muslim women in general.[45] Thus it reports that when the Prophet returned to Medina from the Khaybar expedition, he shared his camel with his war captive Safiyya whom he had wrapped in his *rida'* ("cloak") from the top of her head to the bottoms of her feet; no one, so the story continues, dared to look at her when the camel stumbled and threw off its riders, until the Prophet had replaced the wrap (ibid., pp. 86–89).[46] During prayer, A'isha was heavily clad in a *dir'* ("chemise"), *jilbab* ("mantle," "cloak"), and *khimar* ("kerchief"), and she performed the circumambulation (*tawaf*) of the Ka'ba in a *niqab* ("head veil") (Ibn Sa'd, *Nisa'*, p. 49). During prayers, Maymuna is likewise said to have worn a *khimar* ("kerchief"), but no *izar* ("wrap") (ibid., p. 98).[47]

The Prophet's wives were scrupulous in hiding behind the *hijab* (enjoined upon them by the revelation of Sura 33:53) in the presence of individuals who did not belong to the "exempt groups" defined in Sura 33:55. A'isha, for instance, is said to have secluded herself (behind the screen) from Hasan and Husayn, the Prophet's grandchildren (Ibn Sa'd, *Nisa'*, p. 50).[48] She also hid behind the partition in the presence of a blind man, Ishaq al-A'ma, saying that although he could not see her, she nevertheless could see him (ibid., p. 47).[49] During travels, the Prophet's wives were secluded in camel litters so unrevealing and undistinguishable that even the Prophet mistook one woman's litter for that of another (ibid., p. 67). In A'isha's case, her litter was once moved on even though she was not inside it, as related in the "affair of the lie" (*al-ifk*) mentioned above.

Concerning the Qur'anic command to the Prophet's wives to "stay in your houses" (33:33), the Hadith reports that two women of the Prophet's household, Sawda bint Zam'a and Zaynab bint Jahsh, opted for complete confinement and immobility after the Farewell Pilgrimage at which the Prophet is said to have commanded his wives to stick to "the backs of the mats" (*zuhur al-husur*) (ibid., p. 150). Muhammad ibn Umar and others report that the Prophet said on this occasion: "She among you who fears God and does not commit a manifest abomination [*fahisha mubayyina*][50] and sticks to the back of her mat [*zahr hasiriha*] is my wife in the hereafter" (ibid., p. 150). Thereupon, Sawda stayed home, "sitting in [her] house as God commanded (her) to do." She and Zaynab never again went on either the greater or the lesser pilgrimage [*hajj* or *'umra*] (ibid., p. 150), saying that "no mount would move [them] about after the death of the Messenger of God" (ibid., pp. 37–38, 150).[51]

The most notable exception to such righteous immobility on the part of the Mothers of the Believers is, of course, A'isha's well-established active involvement in public affairs after the Prophet's death, which culminated in the Battle of the Camel.[52] A'isha's behavior was clearly outside of the norms reportedly observed by the Prophet's other widows. Here it is noteworthy, however, that the Hadith overall refrains from having others censure A'isha for her role in the "affair of the lie" or the Battle of the Camel. Instead it was she herself who is said to have regretted her part in these events most bitterly; reportedly, she passed her final days in selfrecrimination, sighing that she wished she had been "a grass, a leaf, a tree, a stone, a clump of mud . . . not a thing remembered" (Ibn Sa'd, *Nisa'*, pp. 51–52).[53]

The Hadith also credits the Mothers of the Believers with extending the principle of their segregation from life into death when it reports that Zaynab bint Jahsh was placed into her grave by blood relatives, and that the Prophet's widows prevented Umar, then the caliph of Islam, from descending into her tomb, "as only he may descend to whom it was lawful to look at her while she was alive" (ibid., p. 79).

The righteousness of Muhammad's wives, however, went beyond their role as precedent-setting exemplars of juridic norms put forth in the legalistic reports just quoted. The Hadith, indeed, finds the ideal spirit of a polygamous household embodied in the daily dealings of Muhammad's wives (later, his widows) who coexisted with one another in mutual love and compassion, unified by an intense esprit de corps. The women called each other "sister" (Ibn Sa'd, *Nisa'*, p. 78) and praised each other's uprightness, devotion, and charity (ibid., p. 73). When Zaynab bint Jahsh fell ill, it was Muhammad's other widows who nursed her, and when she had died, it was they who washed, embalmed, and shrouded her body (ibid., pp. 78–79). The Prophet's wives are also credited with that true piety which, in ascetic selfsacrifice, foregoes even lawful pleasures. Of A'isha, for instance, it is said that she fasted continuously (ibid., p. 51), provided freewill alms (*sadaqa*) at the expense of her own already meager food supply (ibid., p. 46), and lived in voluntary poverty that meant only threadbare clothes, which she had to mend with her own hands (ibid., p. 50). According to a tradition, this frugality was in obedience to the Prophet's words: "A'isha, if you want to be joined with me, take of this world [as little as] a rider's provisions, beware of associating with the rich, and do not deem a garment worn out until you have patched it" (ibid., 53).[54] Of Maymuna it is reported that she picked up a pomegranate seed from the ground with the words "God does not approve of waste" (ibid., p. 99). It is especially Zaynab bint Jahsh, "the refuge of the poor,"[55] of whom the Hadith reports that she gave away all her wealth (ibid., p. 81), including her yearly pension of 12,000 dirhams which the caliph Umar sent her for personal expenses (ibid., pp. 77–78). Indeed, Zaynab regarded this wealth as *fitna* ("temptation," "source of corruption") and screened herself from the money with a garment before she instructed her servant to distribute it in handfuls to relatives, orphans, and the poor (ibid., pp. 77–78). A'isha is said to have given away in charity the five camel loads of gold (180,000 dirhams) obtained from the Umayyad caliph for the sale of her house by the Medinan mosque (ibid., p. 117).[56]

Finally, the Hadith emphasizes that the Prophet's wives' righteousness included profound knowledge of matters of the faith and also complete truthfulness in transmitting traditions. For instance, Ibn Zubayr, when transmitting a tradition from A'isha, reportedly said: "By God, she never tells lies about the Prophet of God!" (ibid., p. 47). Indeed, A'isha is said to have been so knowledgeable about the *fara'id* of Islam[57] that very old men who had been Companions of the Prophet came to seek her counsel and instruction (ibid., p. 45). This truthfulness theme is, perhaps, especially meaningful where the women's exemplary behavior is reported on their own authority, that is, in traditions ascribed to one of their group.

Conclusion

To conclude the present section, it may be useful to return to a theme presented above. The elite status of the Prophet's wives, established in Qur'anic revelation and historically realized during their lifetime, was turned into a legal paradigm when Muslim scholarly consensus, and not just pious veneration, established the Prophet's consorts as models for emulation (sources of *sunna*). The latter process unfolded after the women's lifetime, when their historical presence had become but a memory. Its main stages belong into the formation of Islamic law and jurisprudence whose framework was the newly expanded (now multiethnic and multicultural) Islamic realm of the eighth and early ninth centuries where indigenous patriarchal structures predating the Islamic conquests had been retained and strengthened with the emergence of a Muslim urban middle class. Thus, the traditions presented above that extol the Prophet's wives' virtues again signify themselves (the memory of some outstanding women) and also something else (a cultural model of or for Muslim female morality formulated by the medieval urbanized and acculturated scholars of Islam). Main components of their paradigm in this context are: segregation and quiet domesticity; modest comportment, indeed, invisibility through veiling; ascetic frugality; devout obedience to God and His Prophet. Insofar as the latter was these women's husband, special emphasis is also placed on wifely obedience as an important dimension of female righteousness.

10

Modern Muslim Interpretations

A New Paradigm

Muslims and also Western scholars of Islam would agree that the most influential Muslim biography of the Prophet written in modern times is Muhammad Husayn Haykal's *Hayat Muhammad* ("The Life of Muhammad"), which appeared in 1935.[1] To judge by quotations in contemporary Muslim literature, Abbas Mahmud al-Aqqad's works on the Prophet[2] have also been influential. On the topic of the Prophet's wives, a widely read study is the hefty tome *Tarajim sayyidat bayt al-nubuwwa* ("Biographies of the Ladies of the House of Prophethood")[3] by A'isha Abd al-Rahman, who publishes under the pen name Bint al-Shati'. It is noteworthy that these influential works were authored by Egyptian Muslim lay intellectuals familiar with Western history, politics, culture, and literature. Haykal began as a liberal Egyptian nationalist who, through political and journalistic activities, strove to reform Egyptian political and even social structures in the Western mould; like al-Aqqad, he eventually came to adopt an Islamic framework in his work.[4] Haykal (d. 1956), who held an economics degree from the Sorbonne, was a lawyer, university lecturer, and politician, cofounder and sometime president of the Egyptian Liberal Constitutionalist Party, also minister (including of education) on several occasions. al-Aqqad (d. 1964) was a prominent man of letters. Both were cognizant of Western (Orientalist) literature on Islam. In Haykal's case, this influenced his commitment to find "the new scientific way," "the modern method" in writing an historical-critical study on the Prophet Muhammad that would render to the young now under the spell of Western culture an image of their Prophet both culturally authentic and also scientifically sound.[5] Haykal's new approach, combining careful selection of medieval traditions and response to the Orientalist challenge, was initially criticized by the Egyptian "ultra-right" but has continued to find popularity among many Muslims in the Arab world and beyond.[6] Haykal's treatment of Muhammad's wives differs from all others by reason of this new focus. Intent on writing a critical study that would refute the Orientalists' view of the Prophet, including the Prophet's marriages, Haykal was not concerned with recognizing in history or deriving from history a paradigm of gender roles.[7] al-Aqqad's knowledge of the medieval Hadith and the works of Western Orientalism was much more circumscribed. His purpose in writing on the Prophet was to show Muhammad's genius in terms of transcultural human perfection. Innovative as this approach was, however, it also bears emphasizing that al-Aqqad's images of the Prophet's wives are in concordance with the conservative paradigm of their exemplary domesticity. By contrast to the politically engaged Haykal and al-Aqqad, Bint al-Shati' is an academician. Her early career was in Arabic language and literature, after which she became productive in the fields of Qur'an and Hadith studies. Her Qur'an commentary of some early Meccan Suras, entitled *al-Tafsir al-bayani lil-Qur'an al-karim*,[8] is a literary exegesis in which the interpretation is designed to be inner-Qur'anic. This work has been regarded as the "application" of the methodology developed by the Egyptian philologist and theologian Amin al-Khuli (d. 1967), the author's husband.[9] Unlike her Qur'anic work, which is methodologically modernist, Bint al-Shati's Hadith-based account on the women in the Prophet's household is a conservative book. Even though Muhammad's wives are presented with a modern focus, their exemplary qualities are found in their supportive strengths in the domestic arena. Furthermore, unlike Haykal and al-Aqqad, Bint al-Shati's work is based squarely on the medieval sources, even though its often romantic style is that of the storyteller.

All of the works considered here are presented as historical accounts but also address the errors and falsifications committed by Western Orientalists in their portrayal of the Prophet and his household. This combination of themes has remained popular in the religious literature of this genre, as have the main lines of our authors' argumentation. The works considered here continue to be in concordance with much of contemporary Muslim discourse on the Prophet and his wives. At least in Haykal's case, this is a matter of direct and enduring influence of his work on, by now, three generations of believers.[10]

This modern Muslim literature on the Prophet's life and domestic affairs includes long passages on gender issues in general. Dignity, honor, and rights both spiritual and material provided for the woman in Islam are contrasted with woman's chattel status in the Arabian Jahiliyya[11] and other past and present societies, especially of the West. Concerning the latter, the criticism focuses, firstly, on premodern legal inequities and, secondly, on the ongoing exploitation of the Western woman in the workplace and as sexual object, including in the entertainment and advertising industries.[12] While women's exploitation in Western societies undermines Western credibility (i.e., the claim of being "advanced"), women's rights in Islam verify the collective dignity of all Muslims, indeed of the whole Islamic system that the West (missionaries and Orientalists) had set out to defame. History itself proves the Prophet's superior nature in that Muhammad not only founded a legal society in which women were at long last recognized, respected, and honored, but that he also treated women, including his own wives, better than did any other man at any time in human history before or after his lifetime.[13]

What is new in these writings involves: Firstly, either careful choice—to the point of de-emphasis—of the medieval Hadith as a whole (Haykal, al-Aqqad), or a new reading of the old texts (Bint al-Shati'); in either case, excision of traditions on miraculous occurrences in the protagonists' lives.[14] Secondly, attempts to probe the relationship of "Muhammad the man" to "Muhammad the Prophet" in doctrinal and also psychological terms. Thirdly, some changes in the typology of Muhammad's wives, which involve elimination of the medieval dichotomy of their conflicting images by way of social and psychological analysis. By emphasizing that the Prophet's wives were helpmates and participants in the Prophet's mission, their "jealousy," that is, competitive love for him is now frequently attributed to piety, commitment to the cause, and also their lively natures, in humanly attractive and positive terms. Fourthly, attacks on Western falsifications of sacred scripture and history. In some instances, search for the modern and authentic approach (rejection of medieval lore and rejection of alien falsifications) leads to mistaking medieval Islamic traditions for Orientalist fabrications.

The Theme of the Prophet's Polygamous Household

That the topic of polygamy engenders a defensive reaction in modern conservative Muslims is partially due to Western criticism of that institution. While the conservative defense of polygamy is mainly directed at the West, its real target are those modern Muslims who, in accomodation to Western norms, fail to support polygamy as an intricate part of the moral Islamic social order. In the Arab world, this controversy goes back to the nineteenth century when modernist reformism first decried the post-Muhammadan application of this institution as a social problem in modern Muslim societies. The Egyptian theologian Muhammad Abduh (d. 1905) wrote in empassioned language about male tyranny and lasciviousness, female exploitation and oppression, the corruption of the new generation, all features of the nineteenth century reality of polygamy gone wrong. Indeed, it was this theme that inspired Abduh's most daringly innovative Qur'an interpretations and *fatwas* (legal opinions) in which he called for the abolition of polygamy in Islam. Polygamy, he argued, had been a sound and useful practice among the righteous early believers (*al-salaf al-salih*) but had developed into a corrupt practice of unbridled lust, devoid of justice and equity, and thus was no longer conducive to the community's welfare.[15] Conservative and fundamentalist thinkers to this day reject Abduh's conclusions, although not always his methodology. The vast socioeconomic changes of the past century, expressed in ideological pressures of feminist and other liberal movements and even some government-sponsored legislation (proposed, or in the Tunisian case, enacted) have intensified the controversy.[16] It is in reaction to this new world that conservatives rally in strong defense of polygamy. The biographies of the Prophet and his wives here speak out in support of the institution by way of three main arguments. Firstly, polygamy is the more honorable and compassionate system because it protects the older, sick, or barren wife from divorce while ensuring progeny for the man who may take a second young and healthy spouse.[17] Secondly, polygamy is the most equitable solution to demographic problems in times of war, when soldiers are killed and there are not enough men to ensure marriage and motherhood opportunities for all females.[18] Thirdly, polygamy as response to situations of necessity is far superior to the type of monogamy practiced in the West where 'positive laws' leave loopholes (e.g., by tacitly permitting extramarital sexual liaisons) that create grave social inequities and also always lead to social hypocricy.[19]

The main points established on polygamy in general (legality, equity, honor, practicability, necessity) are then pursued specifically in relation to the Prophet's example. Here, a dominant theme is refutation of Orientalist accusations of lustful womanizing on the part of the Prophet.[20] Such refutation of foreign attacks is already found in the medieval Hadith, which identified the detractors as Jews; the latter were refuted by way of traditions on the hundreds of wives of Solomon and David, which exemplified the principle of prophetic prerogative to a large harem.[21] In modern literature, which here again disregards the Hadith, the argumentation is based not on the Prophet's office but his perfected humanity.[22] That the Prophet married his many wives for reasons involving some sexual interest is indication of his *fitra* ("sound original nature").[23] The fact that the Prophet had the power to fulfill the Call (*da'wa*, the mission of Islam) and also his wives' demands is proof of superiority, not deficiency. Indeed, Muhammad here exemplifies the very essence of Islam, because Islam is "life affirming," not "life renouncing."[24] Never, however, was the Prophet lustful. Never was mere pleasure seeking involved in his choice of any of his wives, before or after his Call, in youth or old age.[25] Muhammad had as little use for mere sensual pleasures as he had for material luxuries. He was a man of seriousness and equanimity who could have lived like a king but chose to live like a pauper; he enjoyed what little he had but did not permit material possessions and amenities to control him, even though all Muslims at that time could, and did, attain such pleasures. Muhammad chose frugality even though this went against the wishes of his wives, who craved the means to beautify themselves for him.[26] Clearest proof of the Prophet's freedom from base instincts (especially lust), however, are the historical facts of his celibacy until his twenty-fifth year and his monogamous marriage with a woman fifteen years his senior to whom he was completely devoted until she died and he was more than fifty years old.[27] It was in this monogamous marriage with his earliest follower and supporter, Khadija,[28] that the Prophet is said to have found a substitute mother.[29] With Khadija, "Muhammad drank deep from the spring of tenderness, made up for the deprevations of orphanhood, and gained provisions for the exhausting struggle, the momentous tasks of the future."[30] The many other marriages the Prophet concluded after Khadija's death, that is, during the last eleven years of his life, were either means to cement political alliances with friends and foes alike or were concluded in order to provide a safe haven of refuge or rank and honor for noble women whom the Islamic struggle had left unprotected and destitute.[31] This was true even for the Prophet's marriage with A'isha, which he concluded in order to strengthen his relationship with her father, Abu Bakr. It was only later that she emerged as his most beloved wife, but even then she could not take Khadija's place in his heart.[32] The marriages with Hafsa bint Umar, Umm Habiba bint Abi Sufyan, Juwayriyya of the Banu Mustaliq and others were likewise primarily political unions, but the compassion motif was never absent. The biographers sum these marriages up under the maxim that "it was the Prophet's *sunna* to honor those who had been brought low after they had held high rank."[33]

The Theme of a Marriage by Divine Dispensation

Since the nineteenth century, Arab Muslim modernists have addressed the problematic of the Qur'an as Gods eternal word and final revelation to mankind, which was also revealed in history to a historical Prophet and his specific society. Challenged by this new focus, conservatives have insisted on the Qur'an's noncontextual eternity in more outspoken form than did their premodern predecessors. Their wish to abstract the Qur'an "from the temporal order, or rather have it within that order in unconditioned terms"[34] grows from a keen anxiety for the Book's abiding total relevance. This has complicated the conservatives' stance toward historical context, the "occasions for revelation" (*asbab al-nuzul*), which, to their mind, in the wrong hands stand in danger of being mistaken for "reasons for revelation."[35] This inner-Islamic tension was ascerbated by awareness of Orientalist attacks along the same lines. The great interest given by our sources to the divinely revealed dispensation for the Prophet's marriage with Zaynab bint Jahsh is related to both of these factors. The literature sees the events here involved as acts of selfless service rendered by both Zaynab and also the Prophet. Zaynab, highborn though she was, obeyed the Prophet when he betrothed her to his former slave and adopted son, Zayd ibn Haritha, in order to exemplify the new democratic spirit of Islam; and when the Prophet later married her himself, he did so by reason of the *jihad* he had been called to wage against pagan institutions (here, "adoptive relationships"), even though the community reacted with disapproval.[36] The modern biographers point out that the Prophet had known Zaynab, his cousin, from early childhood on and knew very well whether she was beautiful or not, "which rules out as utterly fictitious and groundless all the stories . . . attributed to Zaynab's attractiveness."[37] To Haykal,

> There is . . . no ground for these fictitious stories woven by Orientalists and missionaries and repeated by Muir, Irving, Sprenger, Weil, Dermenghem, Lammens and other biographers of Muhammad. Their so-called scholarship is a scandalous piece of missionarizing. It is a masquerade of science. Their traditional antagonism to Islam, going back to the Crusades, has simply taken possession of their conscience, dictating and determining all that they write

on the subject. It is this fundamental prejudice which vitiates their writing. Their "history" is a crime against history itself, for they choose to see, to note, and to report only the most scurrilous and fictitious reports to satisfy this end.[38]

Among our biographers it is only Bint al-Shati' who insists on the validity of such background tales[39] promulgated in the medieval Hadith. Her defense of the stories, however, here concerns more than the question of Hadith relevance. By maintaining the traditions' validity, Bint al-Shati' is also reacting to Haykal's exclusion of the sexual motif in Muhammad's marriages, a stance Haykal adopted in reaction to Orientalist refutation of sexuality in a true prophet.[40] While supportive of Haykal's attacks on Orientalist and missionary slander of Islamic scripturalist truths, Bint al-Shati' feels that she has to set the record straight. "How noble is his [Haykal's] answer," she writes, "were not the story told by our own righteous forefathers . . . long before the world heard of crusades, missionary activities, and orientalism."[41] She then emphasizes that the story exemplifies the Prophet's wondrous humanity, itself a principle of Islamic doctrine, in its most sublime and model-providing form; for though Muhammad did feel a (sudden) liking for this woman, "he turned his face away, praised God, 'the changer of hearts,' and advised her to stay with her husband. Related as it is by authorities above suspicion, the story thus elevates our lord Muhammad to the highest level of virtue and self-control, and it counts as a glorious feat for Muhammad and also for Islam."[42]

The Theme of Revealed Proof of Innocence of the Slandered Wife

A similar reading is given to the Qur'anic and Hadith materials on "the affair of the lie" (*al-ifk*), which involved communal slandering of the youthful A'isha. On the one hand, modern biographers see in this incident a proof of the Prophet's personal nobility, kindness, and generosity toward a wife whom all others would have treated harshly under the circumstances.[43] Such ideal conjugal trust and tolerance, lived by the Prophet and ideally demanded of his followers, is the real key to universal marital harmony, far superior to other models now pursued "in the era described as 'the woman's age,' so-called because woman's concerns are exaggerated and the woman, supposedly, is to be treated without discrimination."[44] On the other hand, the "affair of the lie" also serves to defend two Islamic institutions: punishment of slander by flogging, and the canons of women's modesty and segregation. Both are protective devices, the former of women's honor, the latter of communal order.[45]

The Jealousy Theme Revisited

Modern Muslim biographers do not exclude the jealousy theme from their descriptions of the Prophet's domestic relations. Their use of the theme, however, differs from the medieval Hadith in both mood and purpose in subtle but telling ways. Firstly, the modern material in many instances now equates jealousy with the power of love and other attractive traits that distinguish full-blooded and lively women. The theme, then, is reinterpreted in psychological terms to indicate strength rather than weakness, loyalty and devotion rather than a flawed nature. A'isha's jealousy, writes Bint al-Shati', "was but an aspect of her deep love for her unique man and was proof of devotion to the Prophet, [constituted by] desire not to be opposed in taking exclusive possession of him. We do her injustice, as we do our noble Prophet, if we negate this jealousy of hers and describe her relationship with her co-wives as one of splendid agreement. Why should not the likes of her be jealous for the likes of him?"[46] Episodes recorded in the medieval Hadith are read in a new way. For example, the grim story of the Kindite princess Asma' bint Nu'man—said to have "taken refuge with God" from the Prophet during her wedding night because some of his jealous wives had suggested it—is now interpreted as a wifely prank, basically playful and harmless, to which the Prophet reacted *with a smile*; tolerance of his wives' whims, a certain pride in their resourcefulness, and incredulity that this ruse had, indeed, worked, are all suggested in the modern rendition of this episode.[47] Secondly, remnants of the old jealousy theme (where retained) now serve to elucidate the Prophet's perfected humanity. Muhammad was both Prophet and also perfect man, whose human nature was sounder, purer, and more virtuous than that of all other men. This is demonstrated by way of his contentment with his many jealous wives; "since he was of sound human nature, he allowed his wives to fill his private world with warmth, emotion, and excitement, to turn away from it all stagnation, listlessness, and dryness."[48] Except for the few instances when they went out of bounds and he had to deal with them sternly, the Prophet did not mind spending his free hours observing "his wives' small battles . . . which were kindled by their love and jealousy for him, and perhaps, like any man, he felt satisfaction that the likes of them were jealous about him."[49] Since the Prophet was the perfect husband, all of his wives found honor and happiness with him such as no other, monogamous marriage could have entailed, "because not all men are equal, and a woman may gladly opt for half of one man's life than have the whole life of another."[50] The Prophet's nature is also exemplified by the manner in which he punished his wives if such became necessary. He neither divorced nor beat them, but preferred to punish the rebellious among them by withdrawing from social and sexual contact.[51] Thirdly, large-scale replacement of the medieval jealousy theme with the (humanly attractive) modern one of the lively and loving spouse signifies the end of the classical construct of female weakness, including female powerlessness. The transformation of the old manipulative jealousy into a positive aspect of the female psyche fits in with the widespread and increasingly influential modern Muslim typology of the Prophet's wives as soldiers who fought for the establishment and also the protection of Islamic values.

A Modern Version of the Theme of Ideal Womanhood

In this literature, the Prophet's wives once again emerge as ideal women, but the qualities now emphasized as the ideal's constitutive traits differ from its

medieval predecessor. Firstly, emphasis now lies with the women's active role
as helpmates on the homefront whose domesticity has a new spirit and function.
Secondly, prominently featured is the women's participation in the Prophet's
struggle for the Cause. The domesticity theme involves the glorification of the
female in her God-given roles of wife and mother. The fact that of Muhammad's
wives only Khadija bore him children may be one of the reasons why it is she
who now emerges in the debate as the most prominent figure.[52] Khadija is
celebrated as both wife and mother, the Prophet's tender "rest and refuge."
She is, furthermore, his fellow struggler in his great *jihad*, which she waged as
his *vizier* ("second in command") from the moment of their first meeting until
the day of her death. As loving wife, housewife, and mother, she was Muhammad's "psychological shield against the trauma of enemy violence."[53] Khadija
not only supported the Prophet and his mission with her great spiritual, moral,
and emotional strengths, but also placed her considerable wealth at his dis-
posal for the Islamic cause.[54] After her death, she remained a nurturing spectre that continued to inspire, strengthen, and comfort the Prophet.[55] The interrelationship of domestic support and shared struggle for the Cause is also
pursued in the examples of the Prophet's later wives. "They nourished the
Prophet's heart, gratified his emotions, and renewed his energies . . . so that
he could carry his heavy burden and overcome the obstacles which he encountered on the path of his eternal call."[56] These noble ladies also accompanied the Prophet in his wars and on his raids; but they made their contribu-
tion as nurturers and supporters, not fighters on the fields of battle.[57] Bint
al-Shati' gives the modern equivalent of the medieval ideal personae of the
Prophet's wives when she defines their virtues as follows: constancy in worship;[58] charity;[59] living for the husband's contentment;[60] bringing up the children by herself in order to free the husband for participation in the *jihad*;[61]
self-control, dignity, and pride;[62] courageous defense of Islam against unbelievers, even if these be blood relatives;[63] knowledge of the doctrines and laws
of Islam;[64] and wise counsel in religious matters.[65] The ideal also includes the
women's commitment to "stay in their houses."[66]

With its emphasis on the family centeredness of the Prophet's wives as
Islam's ideal women, the literature reviewed here defines women's role in moral
society as domestic and nurturing. Indeed, the Mothers of the Believers embody the female's function in patriarchal society. Their realm is their husband's
house, their energies are spent in his and his children's service, but public affairs
are the domain of the male. The modern Muslim woman must strive to follow
the ideal exemplified by the Prophet's wives in all of its dimensions. Specifically, she must fight for the Cause by way of providing that nurturing support
which will enable her man to fight. "Women should take the Prophet's many
wives as righteous examples and follow their chastity, frugality, household
management skills, contentment with whatever goods this life has to provide.
In this fashion, the family is happy and can perform its duties toward God
and human society. If Muslims and others contemplated the Prophet's domestic life and imitated it in their own [regarding the relations among spouses,
children, and relatives], as God has enjoined them to do, they would [all] live

a satisfied and satisfying life. . . ."[67] By keeping the family united and strong, the Muslim woman will ensure the survival of moral society and, thus, the values of the Islamic way of life.

The Cultural Significance of the Hijab

Of all scriptural legislation concerning the Prophet's wives, the *hijab* (33:53) and its medieval semantic and legal extensions have during the last century gained prominence as focus of Muslim paradigmatic selfdefinition. Attacked by foreigners and indigenous secularists alike and defended by the many voices of conservatism, the *hijab* has come to signify the sum total of traditional institutions governing women's role in Islamic society. Thus, in the ideological struggles surrounding the definition of Islam's nature and role in the modern world, the *hijab* has acquired the status of "cultural symbol."[68]

When the nineteenth-century French-educated, pro-Western Egyptian journalist, lawyer, and politician Qasim Amin first spoke about bringing Egyptian society from its state of "backwardness" into a state of "civilization" and modernity, he did so by lashing out against the *hijab*, in its expanded sense, as the true reason for the ignorance, superstition, obesity, anemia, and premature aging of the Muslim woman of his time.[69] As Amin pitted the objectionable, because "backward" *hijab* against the desirable modernist ideal of women's right to an elementary education, supplemented by their ongoing contacts with life outside of the home to provide experience of the "real world" and combat superstition,[70] he understood the *hijab* as an amalgam of institutionalized restrictions on women that consisted of sexual segregation, domestic seclusion, and the face veil. He insisted as much on the woman's right to mobility outside the home as he did on the adaptation of *shar'i* Islamic garb, which would leave a woman's face and hands uncovered.[71] Women's domestic seclusion and the face veil, then, were primary points in Amin's attack on what was wrong with the Egyptian social system of his time. Thereafter, both of these items came to be the focus of the conservative Islamic defense, in Egypt and elsewhere. This reaction is recorded, for instance, in a monograph on *The Hijab* by the Indian Muslim Abu al-A'la al-Mawdudi, whose writings have since inspired conservatives and fundamentalists all over the Islamic world.[72] Mawdudi's Islamic formula to avoid the tragic societal consequences of the secularization of culture as it had occurred in the West[73] lay in the preventive measures of the established, that is, traditional Islamic social system,[74] of which women's segregation was the main feature. According to Mawdudi, the Qur'anic injunctions of Sura 33:33 and 53, even though addressed to the Prophet's wives, were and are binding on all Muslim females.[75] For Mawdudi, the laws of what constitutes Islamic dress (*satr*, "coveredness") fall *within* the social system of the *hijab*; that is, they are but one of its many features.[76] Like his medieval predecessors, Mawdudi here infers from the Qur'anic *jilbab*, or "mantle," verse (33:59) that the woman's Islamic dress must include the face veil and also gloves. The question of female concealing garments, including the face veil "except in cases of necessity," stirs this author to a passionate defense of their Islamic nature.

"Though the veil has not been specified in the Qur'an, it is Qur'anic in spirit"; indeed, the Muslim women living in the time of the Holy Prophet were attired in these very garments, which symbolized their commitment to a righteous way of life. According to Mawdudi, the clear and rational laws of Islam stipulate that the modern believing Muslim woman must do likewise, even if this means ridicule by the West and also its hypocritical pseudo-Muslim spokesmen. The latter speak of "progress" and "civilization" while they engage in unprincipled behavior and are beset by bankrupcy of reason and the lack of moral courage.[77]

Amin's call that the bare-faced Muslim woman be given access to the outside world in order to acquire knowledge of "what is real," and Mawdudi's call to uphold and defend the moral and authentic Islamic tradition of woman's segregation, including the complete veiling of her body and her face, both bear a close relationship to the history of European imperialism in the Islamic world. As most recently shown by Leila Ahmed,[78] women's seclusion and veiling in Muslim societies acquired multiple "symbolic" meanings when the Western colonialist establishments, although themselves patriarchal, began to attack these traditions as primary reason for the Muslims' "backwardness" and the obstacle to their progress toward "true civilization," that is, their remaking in the Western mould. Western missionaries and feminists further strengthened this imperialist formula, which resulted in a fusion of Muslim women's issues with Islamic culture as a whole. The formula acquired an inner-Islamic class dimension when indigenous but Westernized, upper-class intellectuals such as Qasim Amin criticized traditional, that is, lower-class Muslim society by focusing on women's issues while using the foreigners' language on the inferiority of Muslim traditions and the superiority of the West. The indigenous Islamic response of resistance was as complex as the original challenge. As here exemplified in Mawdudi's passages, it embodied the call to pitch Islamic cultural authenticity (formulated in terms of Islamic morality) against foreign colonialism, neocolonialism, and their pseudo-Muslim Westernized mouthpieces. True to the challenge, however, the focus of the debate remained on women's issues, especially female domestic seclusion and the veil, as symbol of the validity and dignity of Muslim tradition as a whole.[79] While the linkage of women and culture continues as a dominating theme in Muslim religious theory, socioeconomic changes have now also left their mark on the precise "meaning" of the *hijab* in its practical, although not its symbolic, terms.

Today's Muslim societies have largely developed beyond the past paradigm of gender segregation, no matter how fervently Islamic conservatives and fundamentalists would wish it otherwise. On the one hand, upper and upper middle class women, formerly the only truly "house bound"/"segregated" ones, now have access to education and thereby to professional careers that spell the end to their institutionalized domestic seclusion. If given a choice, the women of these classes tend to favor modes of dress different from the traditional. Simultaneously, middle class women have gained access to education as well, and many of them are now taking on paid jobs outside of their homes, motivated sometimes by choice, but perhaps also more frequently by economic necessity. For the lower middle class women, the situation may not be new, since the women of this class have traditionally had to work both inside and also outside of their homes. Consequently, the Islamic call for women's *hijab* has changed its tenor. On the one hand, the religious message is now addressed to the Muslim woman herself rather than to her man (formerly "her guardian" in all things); this is so because the Muslim woman now listens to the radio, watches television and, most of all, is now able to *read*. On the other hand, the Islamic call is now also directed at a new constituency, the women of the urban middle and lower middle class, in a quasi-"democratized" fashion. Inasmuch as its target audience are Muslim women often compelled to work, the Islamic call for the *hijab* has also shifted in semantic content. By socioeconomic necessity, the obligation to observe the *hijab* now often applies more to female "garments" (worn outside of the house) than it does to the ancient paradigmatic feature of women's domestic "seclusion."

True to the fact that any religious paradigm is persistent by nature, the issue of women's *hijab qua* spatial seclusion *qua* domesticity continues to linger in the discourse of Muslim conservatism. In the sermons and writings of the popular Egyptian preacher Muhammad Mutawalli al-Sha'rawi, for instance, "the house" is celebrated as woman's God-given space. As is predetermined through her God-given physical and mental attributes, the woman's place is in her home. Here she may pursue the noblest of all professions on this earth, which is to raise the next generation. When a woman stays at home, she contributes through her domestic labor far more to the family budget than when she earns a salary outside but has to pay for the support staff who replace her.[80] Other conservative voices point to the disastrous cost of woman's outside work in terms of the damage done to the Islamic family order. A woman who contributes part of the household expenses undermines both her man's divinely appointed obligation to be the family's provider (Sura 4:34) and also his *qiwama*, "guardianship," over her (Sura 4:34); indeed, a working woman's husband is selling his *qiwama* for a trifle, since she takes away his manhood in exchange for a mere portion of her salary. By permitting his wife to work, the man loses his dignity, his substance, and his willpower.[81]

A woman's best *hijab*, then, to those such minded, is still her home.[82] But "necessity" here represents the extenuating circumstance. Even the spokesmen of conservatism now agree that in emergency situations the Muslim woman may work abroad, provided that she behave with all modesty and also return to domestic life as soon as the emergency has been taken care of.[83] Since it is economic necessity that drives increasing numbers of middle class women, the conservatives' new target group, to work without the prospect of early retirement, however, this formula is becoming more and more untenable. By consequence, in the contemporary normative Islamic language of Egypt and elsewhere, the *hijab* now denotes more a "way of dressing" than a "way of life," a (portable) "veil" rather than a fixed "domestic screen/seclusion."

It is indicative of this semantic shift that in conservative primers for the Muslim woman, the material on "the veil" holds center stage.[84] Echoes of past imperialist attacks on this garment and also awareness of its discarding by members of the upper class, but mainly the purpose to salvage at least some aspects of the hallowed *hijab* complex of old now lead conservative writers and preachers to exhort the Muslim woman to "wear the *hijab*" for the sake of God, her own dignity in youth and old age, as protection of her own morality and also that of all males whom she encounters in her daily life outside of her home. In partial continuation of traditional pre-modern usage, then, *hijab* is here used as a generic term for women's clothing. On the basis of Sura 24:31, Egyptian conservatism, for instance, reckons that this *hijab* must cover the woman's head, throat, and upper part of the chest; on the basis of the Qur'anic reference to hidden anklets in Sura 24:31, it must also be a long and loose-fitting gown that reaches to the heels; as established by Prophetic tradition, only hands and face should remain visible. Other hadiths are quoted to prove that the material of the *hijab* should be heavy, not light; that the garment should not be molded to the body and revealing of its contours; that it should not be perfumed or smell of incense; that it should not resemble men's clothing; and that it should not be "showy."[85] As in past tradition, however, its precise cut is not prescribed. Indeed, concerning the shape and "doing-up" of the head cover, the conservative preacher Sha'rawi leaves that to the individual wearer, because "you women know more about this than we men do."[86]

In terms of "garment," the *hijab* has in some Arab Muslim contexts acquired a spectre of meanings that span the semantic field from a specific article of clothing to the general concept of modest female attire reflecting religious commitment. In Egypt, for instance, the *hijab* as specific garment presently denotes the basic head covering ("veil") worn by fundamentalist/Islamist women as part of Islamic dress (*zayy islami*, or *zayy shar'i*); this *hijab*-headcovering conceals hair and neck of the wearer and resembles the "wimple" of Catholic nuns of the reformed orders but that for Muslims the throat is also covered. The Egyptian fashion industry, however, has begun to market new designs of *hijab* headcoverings as well, some of which consist of whimsical ornaments, berets, or pill-box hats to be worn with and over the "veil," so that the whole effect resembles the 1001 Nights more than it does the chaster "wimple." In categorical or generic terms *qua* "modest attire," the *hijab* simultaneously stands for a variety of dress. It can typically mean a bulky, high-necked, long-sleeved, ankle-length robe in a muted color worn with the "wimple." Simultaneously, a long-sleeved blouse and long, tightly belted skirt ensemble with head veil, even if colorful and/or of tailored elegance, also qualifies as *hijab*. In her guide to the symbolic functions of dress in contemporary Egypt, Andrea B. Rugh here differentiates between "fundamentalist" and "pious" styles of dress, indicating that both styles can accomodate grades of (externalized) pious commitment whose final stage includes full face veiling and also the wearing of gloves.[87] While the *hijab* qua "fundamentalist" dress is now mainly a middle class phenomenon that serves to distinguish between educated and uneducated classes, the lower-class women in Egypt still wear folk dress styles that accomplish the same modesty aims but are more related to community norms than to pretensions of piety;[88] consequently, their wearers are also not referred to by the term of *muhajjabat*.

In traditional Sunni countries like Saudi Arabia, itself a main part of the Arab world that was never colonized, the religious debate on women's issues (including the *hijab* in its multiple meanings) remains within the parameters of the established Sunni *shari'a* as formulated by conservative juridic authorities of the Hanbali *madhhab*. While contemporary Shi'ite Iran is worlds apart from the contemporary Wahhabi-based paradigm of Saudi Arabia, the *hijab* issue regarding women's clothing laws in Iran has also seen enforcement by the state. Most other Muslim countries are not quite that *shari'a* ruled. In many, the *hijab* has to some degree become an "option" that entails a spiritual, ideological, and social dimension. When European colonialism first attacked the *hijab* as an obstacle to Muslim "progress" (in the Western mould), the Arab/Middle East conservative establishment, on this issue later joined by fundamentalism both past and present, responded by redefining traditional women-related institutions as the core of Islamic "authenticity," while modernism's response, in some measure acculturationist, sought and continues to seek for legitimate change on these issues within the parameters of the Islamic scripturalist paradigm. All the while, however, the core meaning of *hijab* in this debate has undergone a semantic shift from women's general societal segregation and invisibility to "a garment" (a "portable" veil) which educated and working women for the great part of the middle and lower middle class now wear as badge of both morality and also cultural authenticity, while performing new tasks in the public sphere.

Some Remarks on Islamic Modernism

By virtue of its provenance and role in shaping the Islamic order, the Hadith, as indicated above, is both record of the way of life of the early community and also record of post-Muhammadan processes of Islamization. Given the inevitable gap between the actual and the idealized as well as between the genuine and later ascriptions, (even) the authenticated Hadith contains contradictory information on the social order it describes and prescribes. This has made of the Hadith an instrument of potential flexibility in the hands of lawyer-theologians, now also lay thinkers who have used the Hadith in its normative function as source of Islamic values. Since its compilation in the ninth century, Hadith usage by the faithful has included choice of some traditions over (contradictory) others, and also discovery of new meaning in old texts. As documented above, both approaches were employed in the modern biographical literature here analyzed as basis for an essentially conservative paradigm of gender segregation but that also recognized important societal roles and cultural functions for women. The modernized image of the Prophet's wives of, especially, Bint al-Shati' symbolizes that Muslim women are not just men's followers and wards but are the very support structure of man, family, and society; they are, themselves, prime guardians of cultural and spiritual values, Islam's most precious heritage. They will fulfill this task as long as they, in the image of the Prophet's wives, give their whole energy to the family in seclusion from public life.

Modernists have long opposed the notion that women's segregation is a necessary aspect of moral Muslim society. Starting with Muhammad Abduh's call for the restoration of dignity to the Muslim woman by way of educational and some legal reforms, the modernist blueprint of women's Islamic rights eventually also included the right to work, vote, and stand for election—that is, full participation in public life.[89] Modernism's most crucial difference with conservatism lies in its theoretical stance toward past sociopolitical legislation in both Qur'an and also Hadith. In the Arab world, modernism's theoretical basis was first formulated by Abduh when he separated the forever-valid-as-stipulated laws of *'ibadat* (religious observances) from the more time-specific *mu'amalat* (social transactions) in Qur'an and *shari'a*, which latter included the Hadith as one of its sources.[90] To Abduh and the modernists who followed him, then, *'ibadat* do not admit of interpretative change while *mu'amalat* allow for, indeed require, interpretation and adaptation by each generation of Muslims in light of the practical needs of their age. Because modern Islamic societies differ from the seventh-century *umma*, time-specific laws are thus no longer literally applicable but need a fresh legal interpretation (*ijtihad*). What matters is to safeguard "the public good" (*al-maslaha al-'amma*) in terms of Muslim communal morality and spirituality. The methodology here involved has been termed the discovery of the "spirit" ("values," "objectives," *rationes legis*) behind the literal meaning of the text.[91] Some modernists maintain that the Qur'an established women's equality with men in all essential respects, a fact misunderstood by medieval Muslim lawyers. Here the modernist approach (in development of Abduh's earlier ideas) also entails "hierarchization" of categories of revelation when the Qur'an-proclaimed equality of male and female in the eyes of God is proclaimed a principle of higher value than the disparate legal items revealed to guide and govern that first Muslim society.[92] The latter, of course, include the restrictions God placed on the Prophet's wives for the sake of the first community's wellbeing. For modernists, these (in their literal sense) were directed at Muhammad's consorts only, and for historic reasons. The *hijab* (33:53), for instance, was revealed as a measure of protection of the Prophet's household and did not apply to other females in the community. Modernists also quote authenticated Hadith materials that portray the Prophet's wives and other women of the first *umma* in full participation of communal life.[93] This serves to shore up an Hadith-based Islamic model on women's sociopolitical rights far different from the conservative one. But on the whole, and quite unlike conservatism, modernism is less engaged in Hadith study because of the stipulation that the "literal" relevance of such historical data has been superceded by the need to search for their transtemporal meaning of principles and values.

Stretching the Paradigm: A Feminist Reading of Scripture on the Prophet's Wives

A recent feminist book on the Prophet's household goes one step further in its approach to Qur'an and Hadith than does Islamic modernism. In *Le harem politique,* English translation *The Veil and the Male Elite: A Feminist Interpretation of Women's Rights in Islam,*[94] the Moroccan sociologist Fatima Mernissi attacks the age-old conservative focus on women's segregation as mere institutionalization of authoritarianism, achieved by way of manipulation of sacred texts, "a structural characteristic of the practice of power in Muslim societies."[95] Mernissi's own, feminist model of the Prophet's wives' rights and roles both domestic and also communal rests on a new, although "literal," interpretation of Qur'an and Hadith, of which the former pays great attention to timeframe and sociopolitical circumstances of Qur'anic revelations and the latter to selection and interpretation of traditions, including discreditation of some textual items as inauthentic by the criteria of classical Hadith criticism (even though authenticated long ago by communal consensus). In Mernissi's reading of Qur'an and Hadith, Muhammad's wives were dynamic, influential, and enterprising members of the community, and fully involved in Muslim public affairs.[96] The women were Muhammad's intellectual partners. Accompanying him on his raids and military campaigns, "[they were] not just background figures, but shared with him his strategic concerns. He listened to their advice, which was sometimes the deciding factor in thorny negotiations."[97] In the city, they were leaders of women's protest movements, first for equal status as believers and thereafter regarding economic and sociopolitical rights, mainly in the areas of inheritance, participation in warfare and booty, and personal (marital) relations.[98] According to Mernissi, Muhammad's vision of Islamic society was egalitarian, and he lived this ideal in his own household. However, the male members of the community were not ready to accept such dramatic changes and therefore organized an opposition movement under the leadership of the stern Umar ibn al-Khattab.[99] Finally, during extended periods of military and political weakness (between the third and eighth year after the hijra), the Prophet had to sacrifice his egalitarian vision for the sake of communal cohesiveness and the survival of the Islamic cause. To Mernissi, the seclusion of Muhammad's wives from public life (the *hijab,* Qur'an 33:53) is a symbol of Islam's retreat from the early principle of gender equality,[100] as is the "mantel" (*jilbab*) verse of 33:59 which relinquished the principle of social responsibility, the individual sovereign will that internalizes control rather than place it within external barriers.[101] Concerning A'isha's involvement in political affairs (the Battle of the Camel) after the Prophet's death, an occurrence much criticized in Hadith and religious literature as a whole, Mernissi engages in classical Hadith criticism to prove the inauthenticity of the (presumably Prophetic) tradition "a people who entrust their command [or, affair, *amr*] to a woman will not thrive"[102] because of historical problems relating to the date of its first transmission and also selfserving motives and a number of moral deficiencies recorded about its first transmitter, the Prophet's freedman Abu Bakra.[103]

Modernists in general disregard Hadith items rather than question their authenticity by scrutinizing the transmitters' reliability. Mernissi's approach, then, a very old one here revived, so far remains a minority voice. It is especially in the Qur'anic portions of her model of the Prophet's household, however, that this feminist author leaves most modernists behind. At Mernissi's hands, the Qur'anic verses are related so closely to the historical events surrounding their revelation that a "causal" relationship between the two would logically follow; the *asbab al-nuzul*, "occasions of revelation," have (tacitly) become "occasions for revelation" and the verses themselves but a record of early *umma* history, while the question of their enduring relevance is (also tacitly) omitted. Nevertheless, the message is clear. In pitting the Prophet's early vision of gender egalitarianism against demands later imposed upon him by Medinan *realpolitik*, this author stipulates that the Qur'anic dicta on Muhammad's wives and also women in general are of unequal "value." Even within the Qur'an, then, hierarchization of aspects of the message is here employed to yield that early, pristine, enduring ideal of an Islamic society in which men and women are truly equal.[104]

Conclusion

The preceding analysis has established, firstly, that the medieval biographical Hadith on the Prophet's wives played many roles in the formation of what became the official (here, Sunni) ideogram on the Mothers of the Believers. The gathering of historical data was only one of the many processes here involved. Even within the parameters of history writing, the Hadith, by nature of its authoritative and normative character, operated and was meant to operate on several levels at once. Historical political, social, and cultural realities and aspirations, also inner-Islamic and even extra-Islamic relations from the beginning provided a "subtext" to the biographical materials that, while clear to their original audiences, in many cases became unintelligible to later generations. Secondly, the fact that the traditions retained their importance oftentimes had to do with the fact that the "surface text" supported later medieval sociomoral paradigms as elaborated by the lawyer-theologians. Thirdly, the fact that wherever the medieval models are no longer seen as relevant or completely relevant for contemporary Muslim societies, elimination but also reinterpretation of the tradition materials has ensued. Changed in essence but not always in form, this contingent of the Hadith thus continues to play an important role as framework of religious selfunderstanding, as "normative mirror-image" of contemporary Muslim societal realities and plans for the future. Fourthly, reflecting "the intellectual dynamism and diversity that characterize contemporary Muslim life,"[105] some Muslim thinkers have now begun to look beyond efforts of "reforming" inherited structures by way of integration of modern and traditional Islamic elements. Radically, their efforts now concern a complete "re-interpretation" of Islam, which includes new approaches to the Qur'anic text itself.

Notes

Introduction

1. Marilyn Robinson Waldman, "New Approaches to 'Biblical' Materials in the Qur'an," *The Muslim World*, vol. 75 (1985), p. 8.

2. Waldman, "Approaches," p. 13.

3. Richard C. Martin, "Structural Analysis and the Qur'an: Newer Approaches to the Study of Islamic Texts," *Journal of the American Academy of Religion*, no. 47 (1979), p. 668.

4. Clifford Geertz, *The Interpretation of Cultures* (New York: Basic Books, 1973), pp. 91ff.

5. Clifford Geertz, *Islam Observed* (New Haven: Yale University Press, 1968), p. 98.

6. Geertz, *Interpretation*, p. 123; cf. p. 112.

7. Jane I. Smith, *An Historical and Semantic Study of the Term 'Islam' As Seen in a Sequence of Qur'an Commentaries* (Missoula: Scholars Press, 1975), pp. 183–190.

8. Yvonne Y. Haddad, "Sayyid Qutb: Ideologue of Islamic Revival," in *Voices of Resurgent Islam*, ed. John L. Esposito (New York: Oxford University Press, 1983), pp. 67–98; and Smith, *Historical and Semantic Study*, pp. 203–207.

9. Cf. Leila Ahmed, *Women and Gender in Islam*, (New Haven: Yale University Press, 1992), pp. 82ff.

10. On the Mu'tazila and al-Ash'ari, cf., e.g., Tarif Khalidi, *Classical Arab Islam* (Princeton: The Darwin Press, 1985), pp. 82–87; and John L. Esposito, *Islam: The Straight Path* (New York: Oxford University Press, 1988), pp. 71–74.

11. A fuller identification of the intellectual background and orientation of Tabari, Zamakhshari, Razi, Baydawi, and Ibn Kathir are provided in Smith, *Historical and Semantic Study*, pp. 57–134.

12. Reuven Firestone, *Journey in Holy Lands: The Evolution of the Abraham-Ishmael Legends in Islamic Exegesis* (Albany: State University of New York Press, 1990), pp. 168 and 243, nn. 29 and 30; and W. M. Thackston, trans., *The Tales of the Prophets of al-Kisa'i* (Boston: Twayne Publishers, 1978), p. XIX.

Chapter 1

1. Sura 18:27: "and recite what has been revealed to you of the Scripture of your Lord; no one may alter its (or: His) words."

2. E.g., Sura 10:15–16, 25:32, 17:106.

3. Sura 33:40.

4. Sura 2:97. The Qur'an also identifies the Trustworthy Spirit (26:193), the Holy Spirit (16:102) as the agent of revelation.

5. Sura 85:22.

6. E.g., Sura 3:4; also *umm al-kitab*, "the source, or mother, of Scripture," or "Scripture *par excellence*" (43:4).

7. E.g., Sura 2:185, 34:28.

8. Sura 3:81, 6:92, 35:31, 46:12, etc.

9. Sura 3:23, 4:44.

10. *Ahl al-kitab*, "people of the (original) Scripture."

11. E.g., Sura 2:174, 4:46, 5:13–6, 5:20, 9:30–31.

12. The Qur'anic doctrine of the falsification of earlier books (Torah, Psalms, Evangel) is now said to underlie the general Muslim disinterest in the study and use of the Bible and Bible-related materials. Historically, Jewish and Christian scripture and apocrypha were important sources of early Islamic Qur'an exegesis and prophetology; various processes of rejection of such foreign materials began during the eighth century, i.e., a century or more after the rise of Islam (cf. below). From the vantage point of Christian theology, the Qur'an's teaching of the flawed nature (partial falsification) of the Bible has sheltered the Muslim community from the problematic of diversity in revealed texts (cf. Louis Gardet and M.-M.Anawati, *Introduction à la théologie musulmane: Essai de théologie comparée* (Paris: Librairie philosophique J. Vrin, 1970), pp. 26–27. "Recognizing only the Qur'an as true and authentic scripture, Muslims also recognize only one style of revelation, the literally divine Qur'anic style that is absolutely free of any human imprint" (J. Jomier, "Quelques positions actuelles de l'exégèse coranique en Egypte: Révélées par une polémique récente (1947–1951)," in *Mélanges*, vol. 1 (Institut Dominicain d'Etudes Orientales du Caire, 1954), p. 71.

13. E.g., Sura 5:16–18.

14. On the basis of the Qur'anic doctrine, Islamic scholastic theology formulated the dogma of the Qur'an's Miraculous and Inimitable Nature (*i'jaz*). An important aspect of the Qur'an's flawless nature is the tenet that the Prophet Muhammad was merely the intermediary in the Qur'an's transmission, i.e., neither his person nor his environment were involved in the process of its formulation. From the vantage point of Christian theology, then, Islamic theology does not distinguish between "the principal cause" and "the instrumental cause" of revelation and thus has no room for the concept that God—the first and absolute cause of revelation—would use the mental resources of His "instruments" (His spokesmen, the prophets) to cast His revelation into a specific human setting of place and time (cf. Jomier, "Quelques postions actuelles", pp. 70–71). Gardet and Anawati speak of the Prophet's role as "instrumental cause," but in the sense of "instrumental cause in bondage," i.e., recipient and word-by-word transmitter of the revelation (*Théologie musulmane*, pp. 392–393).

15. E.g., Sura 30:2–10. The third form in which God's revelation occurs is in nature, as nature abounds in "signs" (*ayat*) of God, its Creator and Sustainer.

16. E.g., Sura 33:62.

17. E.g., Sura 8:38.

18. E.g., Sura 40:78. Cf. Fazlur Rahman, *Major Themes of the Qur'an* (Minneapolis: Bibliotheca Islamica, 1980), pp. 51ff; also Michael Zwettler, "A Mantic Manifesto: The Sura of 'the Poets' and the Qur'anic Foundations of Prophetic Authority", in *Poetry and Prophesy: The Beginnings of a Literary Tradition*, ed. James L. Kugel (Ithaca: Cornell University Press, 1990), pp. 75–119.

19. While God reveals Himself in His works (50:6–11) and also in human history (47:10), His more complete message has been to the prophets as His chosen spokesmen (21:7, 25). For this reason, Satan has consistently desired to interfere in the process of revelation (22:52). The following segment on God's prophets is based in part on the Qur'anic data in Arthur Jeffery, "The Qur'an as Scripture," II, *The Muslim World*, vol. 40 (1950), pp. 117ff.

20. Verses such as 40:78 and 4:164 have been understood to indicate that not all of the prophets of the past are identified by name in the Qur'anic text. Exegesis clearly stipulates, however, that the prophetic line extended in continuous succession from Adam to Muhammad.

21. Rearrangement of the Qur'anic verses on the basis of historical sequence of revelations has been undertaken by a number of European scholars among whom are R. Blachère, T. Nöldeke, W. Muir, and H. Grimme. Nöldeke's, Muir's, and Grimme's proposed chronological order is conveniently reproduced in schematic form, together with a standard Muslim sequencing of revelations according to the official Egyptian Qur'anic text, in (*Richard*) *Bell's Introduction to the Qur'an*, second edition, ed. W. M. Watt, (Edinburgh: University Press, 1970), pp. 205–213. In what follows, chronological attribution of Qur'anic passages is based on Nöldeke's work, mainly as schematized in Bell/Watt. Wilfred Cantwell Smith and others have decried undue emphasis on the chronology of revelations as representative of Western interest in the Qur'an's form "before it became a scriptural book for Muslims, not after" (W. C. Smith, "The True Meaning of Scripture: An Empirical Historian's Nonreductionist Interpretation of the Qur'an," *International Journal of Middle East Studies*, Vol. 11 [1980], p. 498). However, the problematic of timeframe and sequence of revelations was also clearly an important concern in early Hadith and *tafsir*, made all the more urgent by the legal-theological institution of "abrogation" (*naskh*) of an earlier revelation by a later one. Some modernist Muslim thinkers, furthermore, have formulated new sociopolitical paradigms within the context of chronological sequencing of the Qur'anic revelations. To indicate the chronology of revelations here means to serve two purposes: firstly, to point out the Qur'anic text's internal dynamics as seen by a non-Muslim, and, secondly, to establish the framework for divergent Muslim readings of the Qur'anic text if and when the question of chronology comes into play.

22. Hud of the tribe of Ad and Salih of the tribe of Thamud are from the Arab tradition; Shu'ayb, the prophet of Midyan, is sometimes considered a Bible-related figure (Rahman, *Themes*, p. 82). Structural analyses of Sura 26 have been presented by Richard C. Martin, "Structural Analysis and the Qur'an: Newer Approaches to the Study of Islamic Texts" (*Journal of the American Academy of Religion*, vol. 47, no. 4S [1979], pp. 665–683); and Zwettler, "A Mantic Manifesto," pp. 75–119.

23. Since most of the Qur'anic prophets are also Biblical figures, some older Western scholars endeavored to make them all Biblical characters. Thus, Idris has been identified with Enoch or Ezra; Dhu l-Kifl with Ezekiel or Obadiah or Elijah; Shu'ayb with Jethro; Hud with Eber; Salih with Salah the father of Eber (cf. Jeffery, "The Qur'an as Scripture," p. 126).

24. Jesus belongs into the family of Imran. His mother Mary is identified as the daughter of Imran (Amram) and the sister of Harun (Aaron). Some Western Biblical scholarship has attributed this to "a confusion of Miriam the sister of Moses and Aaron with Maryam the mother of Jesus" (ibid., p. 125). This controversy is as old as the Muslim-Christian dialogue. The Prophet is said to have refuted similar arguments made by the Christians of Najran during his lifetime; "to confuse Mary the mother of Jesus with Mary the sister of Moses and Aaron in the Torah is completely wrong and in

contradiction to the sound Hadith and the Qur'anic text as we have established it in the Tafsir" (Isma'il ibn Umar Abu l-Fida Ibn Kathir, *Qisas al-anbiya'*, ed. Mustafa Abd al-Wahid, vol. II [Cairo: Dar al-kutub al-haditha, 1968], pp. 393–394; for additional references, cf. Chapter 7 on "Mary").

25. Muhammad belongs into the Abrahamic line of succession (3:68). He has the Scripture (*kitab*) and Wisdom (*hikma*) (4:113), which he has been sent to purify (62:2; 2:151; 3:164). Muhammad's coming is in fulfillment of Abraham's prayer that such a prophet would be sent to the Arabs (2:129), and his mission is foretold in previous Scriptures (7:157; 61:6).

26. *Themes*, pp. 82–83.

27. Of course, God can choose as His messengers angels as well as men (22:75), and angels mediate revelation (16:2).

28. Zwettler, "A Mantic Manifesto," pp. 91–98. Similar work has been done on the exegetic literature. In Ibn Ishaq's biography of Muhammad, the *Sira*, Gordon D. Newby recognizes "already existing ideal types . . . (which) operate as a sort of paradigm on which the sacred biography is patterned. They are a-historic, and in the case of relationships between Muhammad and the other prophets recognized by Islam, we can observe that the telling about Muhammad affects the telling about the other prophets as well as the reverse" (*The Making of the Last Prophet* [Columbia: University of South Carolina Press, 1989], p. 17).

29. Martin, "Structural Analysis," pp. 667–668.

30. For the analyst, Muslim exegesis is, therefore, "an extension of the symbol and must itself be interpreted" . . . (it is not) "exterior to the text but belong(s) to . . . its productivity." Martin, ibid., p. 668, quoting Dan Sperber, *Rethinking Symbolism*, Alice L. Morton, transl. (Cambridge: Cambridge University Press, 1977), p. 34; and Paul Ricoeur, "Biblical Hermeneutics," *Semeia*, vol. 4 (1975), p. 35.

31. That (most) Muslim exegesis is not an interpretation of Scripture but its extension (which must itself be interpreted) here applies to the fact that the Qur'anic text and also its exegesis by the faithful conjoin in the notion of salvation history *qua* history. On a dissenting Muslim model by way of literary analysis, cf. the segment on Muhammad Ahmad Khalafallah, below.

32. Franz Rosenthal, *The History of al-Tabari*, ed. Ehsan Yar-Shater, *Vol. I: General Introduction and From the Creation to the Flood*, translated and annotated by Franz Rosenthal (Albany: State University of New York Press, 1989), p. 157.

33. Rosenthal (ibid., p. 157) reminds us, however, that "neither before nor after Tabari were histories so commonly composed in this manner as is often assumed."

34. Naturally the historical materials appear in the *tafsir* works in the order determined by the Qur'anic text and not chronological sequencing.

35. Much of this interpretative detail is related to biblical lore rather than the text of the Bible. Old Testament apocrypha, haggadic and midrashic sources, likewise New Testament apocrypha and Christian biblical legends found in the writings of the Church Fathers have been identified as containing similar material "which represents much of common Semitic legend and folklore" (Ilse Lichtenstädter, Introduction to W. M. Thackston, Jr., transl., *The Tales of the Prophets of al-Kisa'i* [Boston: Twayne Publishers, 1978], p. XIII.) In medieval and modern Qur'anic exegesis, this genre of Hadith is termed *isra'iliyyat*. For the introduction of these materials into Islamic tradition and the reasons for their exclusion from (sectors of) Islamic tradition during the ninth century, cf. Gordon D. Newby, "Tafsir Isra'iliyyat," *Journal of the American Academy of Religion*, vol. 47 no. 4S (1979), pp. 685–697; also cf. below.

36. Similarity between the two extends to the style of presentation in that Tabari

presents sequential history in the Hadith-based mode employed in his exegesis. Rosenthal concludes that Tabari's approach in both history and exegesis fastened the methodology of history writing to that of traditional religious science. He records the considerable scepticism of later Muslim historians toward the legendary material that Tabari had introduced as historical, and concludes that Tabari's traditionist, i.e., antirational, approach to history writing was itself influenced by the rationalist pressures of his age (*History*, vol. I, pp. 158–159).

37. This identification is from Reuven Firestone, *Journey in Holy Lands: The Evolution of the Abraham-Ishmael Legend in Islamic Exegesis* (Albany: State University of New York Press, 1990), p. 184 n. 8. On this and other *qisas* collections, including of the Sufi genre, and the materials' spread and popularity, cf. Lichtenstädter, Introduction to *Prophets of al-Kisa'i*, pp. XIVff. The oral tradition of popular legend telling continued to flourish independently of the written collections, and it still flourishes in the Islamic world; cf., e.g., Jan Knappert, *Islamic Legends* (Leiden: Brill, 1985), 311 pp.

38. Ibn Kathir (d. 1373) may here serve to prove the case in point. Ibn Kathir was a medieval "scholar" of the Shafii school but with Hanbali leanings, having been trained in Damascus by Ibn Taymiyya (d. 1328). His Tafsir is presently a great favorite with Muslim conservatives and fundamentalists alike. Nevertheless, Ibn Kathir wrote a historical *qisas al-anbiya'* work filled with *isra'iliyyat* traditions, and also used *isra'iliyyat* in his Qur'anic commentary ("for supplementary attestation" *istishhad*, not for "full support" *i'tidad*; cf. Jane Dammen McAuliffe, "Qur'anic Hermeneutics: The Views of al-Tabari and Ibn Kathir" in *Approaches to the History of the Interpretation of the Qur'an*, ed. Andrew Rippin [Oxford: Clarendon Press, 1988], p. 57). On the nature and role of *isra'iliyyat* in medieval Islamic historiography and exegesis, cf. below.

39. E.g., Ibn Kathir (*Qisas al-anbiya'*, ed. Mustafa Abd al-Wahid, vol. I [Cairo:Dar al-kutub al-haditha, 1968], p. 115) ascertains in connection with the story of Noah that only unbelievers would deny the literal truth of Qur'anic history. "Some ignorant Persians and Indians have denied the truth of the flood; others acknowledge it but say that 'it happened in the land of Babel and did not reach us' . . . The Zoroastrians, fire-worshippers and followers of Satan, also deny the flood because of sophistry, fearful unbelief, and profound ignorance which gives the lie to the Lord of the earth and the heavens. The people of the (true) religions who transmit from God's prophets in an unbroken historical tradition . . . have agreed by consensus that the flood did occur, that it involved all lands, and that God did not spare any of the unbelievers . . . in answer to the prayer of His loyal and sinless prophet (Noah) and in execution of what had been preordained." A similar refutation of "the Magians'" denial of the nature of the deluge is found in Tabari's *History*, vol. I, transl. F. Rosenthal, pp. 369–370.

40. As shown below, such dogmatic and legal deductions could be traditionist or rationalist, consensus-based or individual, but even very candid individual opinions on the implications of the Qur'an's history materials were expressed outside of the realm of historical criticism. On this trait in, e.g., Tabari's work, cf. *Shorter Encyclopedia of Islam*, ed. H. A. R. Gibb and J. H. Kramers (Leiden: E. J. Brill; Photomechanical Reprint Ithaca, N.Y.: Cornell University Press, 1965) p. 557.

41. The Qur'an itself suggests such a reading, e.g., in 12:7 ("in the history of Joseph and his brothers, there are signs of God's providence to the inquisitive"), and 12:111 ("in the histories of the prophets and their people, there is an instructive example to those who are endowed with understanding").

42. While Razi's exegesis primarily explored the materials' spiritual and paradigmatic import rather than historical content and meaning, the stories' factual truth was not questioned.

43. al-Sayyid Muhammad Rashid Rida, *Tafsir al-Qur'an al-hakim, al-shahir bi-Tafsir al-Manar* vol. I, (Beirut: Dar al-ma'rifa, second printing, n.d.), pp. 281–283. Hereafter identified as *Manar*. The *Manar* commentary on the Qur'an is based on a lecture course Abduh offered at al-Azhar University. From notes on these lectures, Rashid Rida compiled the interlinear Tafsir work that, revised by Abduh, was first published in installments in the journal *al-Manar* of which Rida was then the editor. In the text, Abduh's statements are introduced with the phrase "the master and guide said" (*qala al-ustadh al-imam*), while statements made by Rida are prefaced by the words "I say." Abduh did not live to complete this Tafsir beyond Qur'an 4:125. Rida continued the project up to Qur'an 12:25. Cf. Jane Y. Smith, *An Historical and Semantic Study of the Term 'Islam' as seen in a Sequence of Qur'an Commentaries* (Missoula: Scholar's Press, 1975), pp. 186–187.

44. Ibid., pp. 283–284.

45. Ibid., pp. 279–280.

46. *Manar*, vol. IV, pp. 324, 326.

47. Ibid., p. 326.

48. In another context, Abduh calls with great fervor for the study of history as an important part of Muslim identity and self-awareness, since without such knowledge the Islamic community "is ignorant of its past and confused about its present, knowing neither why, nor how to find a way out." He blames, especially, the professional theologians (*ahl al-'ilm*) for their ignorance: "these recognize that the community is in dire straights, and plead 'fate' in defense of the fact that they do not know why. . . ." (*Manar*, vol. I, p. 210). The "history" referred to here, however, is that of the Muslim community since its foundation, not Qur'anic scripturalist history (with which, in any case, the *ahl al-'ilm* were most familiar).

49. For some examples, cf. J. M. S. Baljon, *Modern Muslim Koran Interpretation* (*1880–1960*) (Leiden: E. J. Brill, 1961), pp. 4ff.

50. *Themes*, p. 53.

51. Khalafallah was then about thirty years old. He was born around 1916 in the Egyptian Delta.

52. J. Jomier, "Exégèse," pp. 39–41.

53. Khalafallah lost his lectureship at Fu'ad University in 1948. He later received his doctorate with a different dissertation on a nonreligious topic and became a high school teacher. His mentor, Shaykh al-Khuli, was forced to withdraw from the University program of Qur'anic exegesis and was restricted to the teaching of literature. Khalafallah rewrote this book several times. Jomier ("Exégèse," p. 49) reports that while the 1947 dissertation was not available to him, he had access to a typewritten version that preceded the book's first printing (Cairo: Maktabat al-nahda al-misriyya, 1950–1951). According to Jomier, the author had made some (conciliatory) changes in the manuscript prior to publication, but in general the text had remained unaltered. The analysis here following is based on the book's second edition (Cairo: Maktabat al-nahda al-misriyya, 1958). When I interviewed Dr. Khalafallah in Cairo in 1985, he was editor of the cultural journal *al-Yaqza al-'arabiyya* ("The Arab Awakening"). He is presently a prominent voice of Islamic modernism in Egypt and beyond.

54. Khalafallah, *Fann*, pp. 119ff, 151ff, and elsewhere.

55. Ibid., pp. 200ff. Jomier, "Exégèse," pp. 58–60.

56. Khalafallah, *Fann*, pp. 206ff.

57. Ibid., pp. 135ff., 160ff.

58. Ibid., p. 155.

59. Ibid., p. 155.

60. Ibid., p. 133.

61. Ibid., p. 239.

62. "It has been established that the Qur'an is human in expression and human in style, and was revealed according to the norms of style and eloquence of the Arabs" (*Fann*, pp. 135–36); and "the Qur'anic story is built on elements drawn from the Arab environment or the Arab mentality . . . for the single purpose that (thereby) the stories be more influential and powerful. . . ." (p. 231).

63. Cf., e.g., Sura 25:5, of crucial importance in the author's argument and also its rejection by the orthodox majority of his time.

64. Khalafallah, *Fann*, pp. 169ff.

65. Ibid., 185ff, 251, 270ff.

66. Ibid., p. 208.

67. With the exception of Mary, mother of the prophet Jesus.

68. Khalafallah, ibid., pp. 280ff.

69. Cf. Jomier, "Exégèse," pp. 71–72.

70. Cf. Jomier, "Exégèse," pp. 63, 71–72.

71. In what follows, the Qur'anic women stories are presented in the sequence established by this exegetic literature. Among the Muslim scholars who figure with some prominence in the transmission of Biblical lore are: Ka'b al-Ahbar ibn Mati', Abu Ishaq (d. around 652), a Yemenite Jew converted to Islam, said to be the oldest authority for Jewish traditions in Islam; Abu Abdallah Wahb ibn Munabbih (d. around 730), a Yemenite authority on Biblical legend, also South Arabian history; Abdallah ibn Salam (d. 664), a Medinan Jew converted to Islam, who transmitted many Biblical narratives; Abu Hurayra al-Dawsi al-Yamani (d. around 678), Companion of the Prophet and prolific narrator of Hadith; also: Abdallah ibn Abbas (d. 687), a student of Ka'b al-Ahbar; and Ibn Abbas's students: Mujahid, Ikrima, Sa'id ibn Jubayr, Qatada, and Dahhak (cf. Thackston, *The Tales of the Prophets of al-Kisa'i*, pp. 337–339, 344–345, nn. 1, 2, 4, 10, 12, 42, 44, 45, 54). On these and additional collectors and the role of their traditions in Tafsir, biography, and historiography, cf. Newby, "Isra'iliyyat," pp. 685–697; and Firestone, *Holy Lands* (244 pp.; especially pp. 3–21).

72. On "image" in scripture, cf. Gail Paterson Corrington, *Her Image of Salvation: Female Saviors and Formative Christianity* (Louisville: Westminster/John Knox Press, 1992), pp. 15–37; with reference to Sallie McFague, *Metaphorical Theology: Models of God in Religious Language* (Philadelphia: Fortress Press, 1981), p. 74.

73. Cf. Clifford Geertz, "Religion as a Cultural System," in *Anthropological Approaches to the Study of Religion*, ed. Michael Banton (London and New York: Tavistock Publications, 1966), pp. 1–46. By drawing "lessons" of warning and guidance from the Qur'anic dicta, exegesis has approached and appropriated the Qur'anic text in synchronic fashion. Indeed, emphasis on "historicity" notwithstanding, this approach has been the primary framework of Islamic exegetic cognition of the Qur'anic text; therefore, the problematic of historical sequencing and chronology of Qur'anic figures was left to disciplines such as history writing and "story telling," the art of the *qussas*.

74. Carrington, *Salvation*, p. 17; with reference to Paul Minear, *Images of the Church in the New Testament* (Philadelphia: Westminster Press, 1966), pp. 23–24.

75. As indicated above, such traditions are often not related to the canonized text of the Bible but to biblical lore, such as Old Testament apocrypha, haggadic and midrashic sources, and to New Testament apocrypha and Christian biblical legends, sometimes as formulated by the Eastern Church Fathers.

76. Newby, "Isra'iliyyat," pp. 685–697. The quotation is from p. 695.

77. *Holy Lands*, pp. 13–15.

78. Ibid., p. 14.

79. 7 vols.; vol. 1, transl. Henrietta Szold (Philadelphia: The Jewish Publication Society of America, 1909).

80. Louisville: Westminster/John Knox Press, 1991.

81. New York: Random House, 1983.

82. Louisville: Westminster/John Knox Press, 1992.

Chapter 2

1. On Adam and Eve, cf. Genesis chs. 2 and 3. The following segment is largely based on the Arabic sources previously analyzed by Jane I. Smith and Yvonne Y. Haddad, "Eve: Islamic Image of Woman," in *Women and Islam*, ed. Azizah al-Hibri (Oxford: Pergamon Press, 1982; vol. 5 no. 2 of Women's Studies International Forum), pp. 135–144. In addition to this article, also cf. Jane I. Smith and Yvonne Y. Haddad, *The Islamic Understanding of Death and Resurrection* (Albany: State University of New York Press, 1981), p. 11. Also Fazlur Rahman, *Themes*, pp. 17ff.

2. According to the Qur'an, God created humankind from a single *nafs* ("soul," "life energy," "nature," "essence") from which, or of like nature to which, God created its mate (39:6; 7:189; 4:1; 30:21).

3. Of all of God's creation, only Adam was shaped "by God's hands." On the Islamic interpretation of this Qur'anic dictum, cf. M. J. Kister, "Legends in *tafsir* and *hadith* Literature: The Creation of Adam and Related Stories'" in *Approaches to the History of the Interpretation of the Qur'an*, ed. Andrew Rippin (Oxford: Clarendon Press, 1988), pp. 103ff.

4. On the Islamic interpretation of this concept, cf. Kister, "Legends in *tafsir* and *hadith* Literature", pp. 95ff.

5. Was Iblis an angel or one of the jinn? In Tabari's *History*, a number of traditions describe him as angel, as jinni, or the leader of "a tribal group of angels called jinn" (*History*, vol. I, transl. Rosenthal, pp. 252ff). The medieval rationalist Muhammad ibn Umar Fakhr al-Din al-Razi, in reviewing this controversy, indicates that "some scholastic theologians, especially the Mu'tazila" have denied that Iblis was an angel, while "many jurists" have taught that he was (*al-Tafsir al-kabir*, vol. 2 [Cairo: al-Matba'a al-bahiyya al-misriyya, n.d.] pp. 213ff.). For an analysis of the theological debate on this issue, cf. Kister, "Legends in *tafsir* and *hadith* Literature", pp. 88ff.

6. Cf. Abu Ja'far Muhammad ibn Jarir al-Tabari, *Jami' al-bayan 'an ta'wil ay al-Qur'an*, vol. I, ed. Mahmud Muhammad Shakir and Ahmad Muhammad Shakir (Cairo: Dar al-ma'arif, n.d.), p. 512. Also Fazlur Rahman, *Themes*, p. 18. Some traditions indicate that Iblis' arrogance predated Adam's creation, but even here his fall as Satan is linked with his disobedience in connection with the prostration before Adam (cf., e.g., Tabari, *History* vol. I, transl. Rosenthal, pp. 252ff). As shown below, Satan's rebellion was an important issue in the theological debate between the "pre-determinists" and the "free-will-party;" to the former, Iblis' disobedience was God-willed and hence not an act of "true rebellion." Others, especially from among the mystics, have seen the refusal to prostrate himself before Adam as sign of Iblis' "absolute—though one-eyed—monotheism" (cf. Thackston, *The Tales of the Prophets of al-Kisa'i*, pp. 341–342, n. 23).

7. Cf. Watt, *Bell's Introduction*, pp. 206–213.

8. This text is commonly interpreted to mean "prophecy," "prophetic inspiration."

9. Cf. Fazlur Rahman, *Themes*, p. 18, from which part of the translation of this verse is also taken.

10. Again, cf. Smith and Haddad, "Eve," pp. 135–144.

11. Abu Ja'far Muhammad ibn Jarir al-Tabari, *Jami' al-bayan 'an tafsir 'ay al-Qur'an*, ed. Mahmud Muhammad Shakir and Ahmad Muhammad Shakir (Cairo: Dar al-ma'arif, [1950's]–1969).This superb edition of Tabari's *tafsir* is incomplete. Since what is currently available of this edition goes only through Qur'an 14:27, for the remainder of Tabari's *tafsir* I have used the edition *Jami' al-bayam fi tafsir al-Qur'an* (Beirut: Dar al-ma'rifa, 1972). Volume and page of this *tafsir* and also the *tafasir* of other exegetes here quoted will be indicated in the text by way of Roman numerals for the volume and Latin numerals for the page.

12. On the main transmitters of Jewish lore in Hadith form, cf. above—Gordon D. Newby has recently reconstructed one of Tabari's sources, the *Kitab al-mubtada'* ("Book of beginnings"), first portion of Ibn Ishaq's (d. 767) *Sira* (Biography of the Prophet), which Ibn Hisham (d. 834) excised in his recension of this *Sira*. Newby's translation of the reconstructed *Kitab al-mubtada'* is entitled *The Making of the Last Prophet* (Columbia: University of South Carolina Press, 1989). For Ibn Ishaq's materials on Adam and Eve, cf. pp. 33–43.

13. By Tabari's time, Islamic scholarship had rejected many Bible-related traditions by way of labeling them *isra'iliyyat*, a "stamp-of-disapproval" that involved a defective chain of authenticication (*sanad*) or the text (*matn*) itself, especially in cases when the latter contradicted Islamic doctrine and values. Even though the heyday of this process of elimination preceded Tabari's lifetime by a century, Tabari (who wrote both his *History* and also his *Tafsir* in the Hadith-based mode) continued to use many Bible-related traditions but also constantly and courageously expressed his own "independent judgment" (*ijtihad*) on the materials under consideration. Cf. Rosenthal's Introduction in *The History of al-Tabari*, vol. I, pp. 55–56, 63–64.

14. On the creation of Adam from "different earths," cf. Kister, "Legends in *tafsir* and *hadith* Literature", pp. 100ff., and Thackston, *The Tales of the Prophets of al-Kisa'i*, p. 338 n. 7. Rosenthal translates *adim al-ard* as "skin of the earth" (Tabari, *History*, vol. I, pp. 259ff).

15. Cf. Genesis 2:23.

16. On *sunbula* as a term for "wheat" in reference to Rabbinic sources, cf. Rosenthal's translation of Tabari, *History*, vol. I, p. 277 n. 683 and p. 299 n. 814. In his review of this volume, Newby links Rosenthal's translation with "the midrashic word play in Rabbinic sources where *ht'* (sin) interplays with *hth* (wheat)" (*Middle East Studies Association Bulletin*, vol. 25, no. 2 [Dec. 1991], p. 213).

17. On this term and its reference to Jewish literature, cf. Rosenthal's translation of Tabari, *History*, vol. I, p. 276 n. 677.

18. According to other traditions, kneading and baking were women's work, as were spinning and weaving (Tabari, *History*, vol. I, transl. Rosenthal, p. 334).

19. Mahmud ibn Umar al-Zamakhshari, *al-Kashshaf 'an haqa'iq ghawamid al-tanzil* (Beirut: Dar al-kitab al-'arabi, 1966).

20. On the Mu'tazila and its main doctrines, cf. the Introduction, above.

21. Already recorded by Tabari; cf. Rosenthal's transl. of *History*, vol. I, p. 333.

22. Fakhr al-Din Muhammad ibn Umar al-Razi, *al-Tafsir al-kabir* (Cairo: al-Matba'a al-bahiyya al-misriyya, n.d.)

23. On Ash'arism, cf. the Introduction, above.

24. By "free-will party," Razi here specifically means the Mu'tazila.

25. Nasir al-Din Abu Sa'id Abd Allah b. Umar al-Baydawi, *Anwar al-tanzil wa-asrar al-ta'wil*, ed. H. O. Fleischer (Osnabrück: Biblio-Verlag, 1968, reproductio phototypica editionis 1846–1848).

26. Isma'il b. Umar Ibn Kathir, Abu l-Fida, *Tafsir al-Qur'an al-azim* (Cairo: Dar 'ihya' al-kutub al-'arabiyya, n.d.).

27. On these and similar traditions in Tabari, cf. *History*, Rosenthal transl., vol. I, pp. 282–290. Also Kister," Legends in *tafsir* and *hadith* Literature", p. 104.

28. Cf. Tabari, *History*, vol. I, transl. Rosenthal, pp. 290ff.

29. According to Abduh, the Qur'an itself prefigured or, at the very least, implied the findings of contemporary Western science.

30. As documented in the *Manar* commentary, compiled by Rashid Rida during a lecture course which Abduh offered at al-Azhar University, and expanded upon by Rida himself; cf. above.

31. I.e., to its "allegorical," "conjectural," "figurative," "metaphorical," "allusive," "analogical" parts, as opposed to the *muhkamat* or "explicit" verses; cf. Kenneth Cragg, *The Mind of the Qur'an* (London: George Allen and Unwin, 1973), pp. 39–41.

32. Ahmad Mustafa al-Maraghi, *Tafsir al-Maraghi* (Cairo: al-Halabi, first printing 1945, fifth printing 1974).

33. Mahmud Abbas al-Aqqad, *al-Mar'a fi l-Qur'an* (Beirut: Dar al-kitab al-lubnani, 1975), p. 63.

34. Ibid., p. 30.

35. Cf. Qur'an 7:189 and 30:21.

36. al-Aggad, *Mar'a*, pp. 32–35.

37. Ibid.,p. 32.

38. Ibid., pp. 35–36.

39. Cf., for example, A'isha Abd al-Rahman, *al-Qur'an wa-qadaya al-insan*, and Ibrahim Zaki al-Sa'i, *Ma-dha'an Hawwa'*, both quoted in Smith and Haddad, "Eve," pp. 141–144.

40. Muhammad Mutawalli al-Sha'rawi, *Qadaya al-mar'a al-muslima* (Cairo: Dar al-Muslim, 1982), pp. 32–33.

41. God's warning to Adam to beware of Satan's enmity toward him and his wife lest Satan get both of them out of the Garden "so that you (masculine singular) come to toil."

42. Cf. Qur'an 7:189 and 30:21.

43. al-Sha'rawi, *Qadaya*, p. 66; cf. Barbara Freyer Stowasser, "Religious Ideology, Women, and the Family: The Islamic Paradigm" in: *The Islamic Impulse*, ed. Barbara Freyer Stowasser (London: Croom Helm, 1987; reprinted Washington, D.C.: Center for Contemporary Arab Studies, Georgetown University, 1989), pp. 281–282.

44. Sayyid Qutb, *Fi zilal al-Qur'an* (Beirut: Dar al-Shuruq, 1982).

Chapter 3

1. The flip side of this theme—which is righteousness, faith, and obedience of female exemplars who had no conjugal relations with a prophet of God—appears at the end of the Sura (66:11–12) in the examples of the Pharaoh's wife, foster mother of the prophet Moses, and Mary, mother of the prophet Jesus.

2. These verses and their interpretations are analyzed below in ch. 8, "The Mothers of the Believers in the Qur'an."

3. On "the affair of the slander," cf. ch. 8, below.

4. Ibn Kathir, *Qisas*, vol. I, p. 269.

5. On Noah, cf. Genesis chs. 5–7.

6. The Qur'an here mentions the idols Wadd, Suwa', Yaghuth, Ya'uq, and Nasr.

According to the commentators, these idols were worshiped in Arabia "after the deluge" (cf. Thackston, *The Tales of the Prophets of al-Kisa'i*, p. 348 n. 74).

7. Ibn Kathir, *Qisas*, vol. I, p. 267, and Thackston, *al-Kisa'i*, pp. 348–349 n. 77.

8. Ibn Kathir, *Qisas*, vol. I, pp. 100–110.

9. Thackston, *al-Kisa'i*, pp. 100–103.

10. Ibn Kathir, *Qisas*, vol. I, p. 110, in reference to Gen. 7:13.

11. Ibn Kathir, *Qisas*, vol. I, pp. 100–101. Ibn Ishaq's and Tabari's accounts of the deluge do not mention Noah's wife among the people saved on the ark (Newby, *Prophet*, p. 46, and Tabari's *History*, vol. I, transl. Rosenthal, pp. 354–371).

12. Jabir al-Shal, *Qisas al-nisa' fi l-Qur'an* (Beirut: Dar al-jil, 1985), pp. 33–42.

13. It is an essential doctrine of Islam that in this sense the Qur'anic prophets were Muslims and taught Islam.

14. Al-Sha'rawi, *Qadaya*, p. 10; cf. Stowasser, *Impulse*, p. 267.

15. On Lot, cf. Gen. chs. 12 and 19.

16. Early Meccan: Sura 51; Middle Meccan: Suras 54, 37, 26, 15, 27; Late Meccan: Suras 11 and 29. Cf. Watt, *Bell's Introduction to the Qur'an*, pp. 206–213.

17. Her scripturalist twin, Noah's wife, is called Waligha or Wa'ila (Ibn Kathir, *Qisas*, vol. I., p. 267.) The two women's names are sometimes reversed (cf. Thornston, *al-Kisa'i*, pp. 348–349 n. 77).

18. Ibn Kathir, *Qisas*, vol. I, pp. 263, 269.

19. Thackston, *al-Kisa'i*, pp. 157–158. As indicated above, this woman's "treachery" against her husband did not include adultery since Qur'anic exegesis teaches that God's revelation in Sura 24, vouchsafed after "the affair of the slander" of Muhammad's wife A'isha, establishes that no wife of a prophet of God has ever been adulterous (Ibn Kathir, *Qisas*, vol. I, p. 269). On "the affair of the slander," cf. ch. 8. below.

20. Ibn Kathir, *Qisas*, vol. I, p. 269. It is said that "she was transformed into a black stone for twenty years, after which she was swallowed up into the bowels of the earth" (Thackston, *al-Kisa'i*, p. 159).

21. Ibn Kathir, *Qisas*, vol. I, p. 270. He reports that al-Shafi'i, Ahmad ibn Hanbal "and others" in cases of sodomy proscribe the punishment of stoning, while Abu Hanifa establishes that the sodomite be thrown from a mountain and then stoned.

22. Al-Shal, *Qisas*, pp. 42–52.

23. Al-Sha'rawi, *Qadaya*, p. 10; cf. Stowasser, *Impulse*, p. 267.

24. Cf. Darr, *Jewels*, pp. 92–93.

25. On Khadija, cf. Part II, below.

26. Darr, *Jewels*, pp. 120, 148ff, 152ff.

27. Cf. Darr, *Jewels*, pp. 120, 148ff, 152ff.

28. Ibn Kathir, *Qisas*, vol. I, pp. 205ff.

29. Cf. Reuven Firestone, *Journey in Holy Lands: The Evolution of the Abraham-Ishmael Legend in Islamic Exegesis* (Albany: State University of New York Press, 1990), pp. 105–151.

30. *Holy Lands* (159 pp.).

31. On Abraham, Sarah, Hagar, and their children, cf. Genesis chs. 12–18, 20–23, 25.

32. This Sura has been dated into the Early Meccan period.

33. Late Meccan.

34. Ibn Kathir, *Qisas*, vol. I, p. 192; Thackston, *al-Kisa'i*, p. 150; also *Akhbar al-zaman*, sometimes attributed to the medieval historian al-Mas'udi (?) (d.956); ed. Abdallah al-Sawi, fourth printing (Beirut: Dar al-Andalus, 1980), p. 103. Reuven Firestone has collected thirteen exegetic explanations of Sara's kinship to Abraham,

which provide for five different identities. He links the Islamic concern with Sara's genealogy to Muslim familiarity with Genesis 20:12, where Abraham claims that Sarah is his half-sister, and also midrashic interpretations of Genesis 11:27 and 11:29, which make Sarah the daughter of Abraham's brother Haran. Since both would constitute incest in Islamic law, a king (Haran) and a place (Haran or Harran) were brought into play to circumvent this legal problem. See his: "Sarah's Identity in Islamic Exegetical Tradition," *The Muslim World*, vol. 80 no. 2 (1990), pp. 65–71; also *Holy Lands*, pp. 25–30.

35. Ibn Kathir, *Qisas*, vol. I, p. 169. This is a "pre-figuration" of the support of Muhammad's prophethood by his wife Khadija (first convert to Islam) and his paternal cousin Ali (the second to follow Muhammad's call); cf. below.

36. It was from Sara that the prophet Joseph inherited his beauty which is said to have been nine-tenth of the beauty in the world (Ibn Kathir, *Qisas*, vol. I, p. 197). On Sara's beauty in the Bible, see Gen. ch. 12; here cf. Firestone, "Identity," p. 69, and *Holy Lands*, pp. 31ff.; also Franz Rosenthal, "The Influence of the Biblical Tradition on Muslim Historiography" in: *Historians of the Middle East*, ed. Bernard Lewis and P. M. Holt (London: Oxford University Press, 1962) p. 44.

37. Cf. Gen. 12. These Islamic traditions are related to the problem of Sara's kinship with Abraham; cf. above. That Abraham would have lied to save himself creates another difficulty in view of his '*isma* ("sinlessness and infallibility of prophets"). Therefore, the traditions that Abraham and Sara, being at that time the only two believers on earth, were "brother and sister in religion" are the most satisfying from a scholastic point of view (cf. Firestone, "Identity," p. 66).

38. In Gen. 12, the Pharaoh is punished with great plagues.

39. Ibn Kathir, *Qisas*, vol. I, pp. 193–194; Mas'udi (?), *Akhbar*, pp. 230–231, where the name of the Pharaoh is given as Tutis. Al-Kisa'i has a similar story on a king's desire for Sara and the instant punishment that ensues when he tries to touch her, but the land here is Jordan and its ruler is identified as King Zadok. To be released from his affliction, the king has to cede the land of Jordan to Abraham (Thackston, *al-Kisa'i*, pp. 150–151).

40. Else, he marveled at Abraham's and Sara's purity and nobility. (Mas'udi [?], *Akhbar*, p. 231).

41. Ibn Kathir, *Qisas*, vol. I, pp. 193–198. In the "Egyptiana" chapter of the *Akhbar al-zaman*, a book of marvels attributed to the historian al-Mas'udi (?), Sara is said to have refused all other presents. When Abraham and his household were about to depart from Egypt, the Pharaoh's daughter prepared large baskets with foodstuffs among which she hid precious jewels. Sara discovered these during their travel and presented them to Abraham who sold some of them to build a public well; others he distributed among the righteous, some he used to extend hospitality, and Sara stored some of them away (pp. 231–232). This story belongs to the Islamic tradition on the origin of *waqf*, pl. *awqaf* ("pious endowment," "perpetual charitable trust"), which institution is said to have begun with Abraham. Cf. John Robert Barnes, *An Introduction to Religious Foundations in the Ottoman Empire* (Leiden: Brill, 1986), pp. 5–6.

42. On the "suit-case" legend in Judaic literature, cf. Ginzberg, *Legends*, vol. 1, pp. 221. Also Darr, *Jewels*, pp. 95–96.

43. Jan Knappert, *Islamic Legends*, pp. 77–78.

44. Ibn Kathir, *Qisas*, vol. I, pp. 219–220; Thackston, *al-Kisa'i*, pp. 155–156.

45. Ashura is the tenth day of the month of Muharram, first month of the Islamic year, on which day the martyrdom of Muhammad's grandson Husayn occurred at Karbala. Medieval scholarship has also placed the following events on the Ashura: "God bestowed repentance on Adam; Noah's ark came to rest on Mount Judi; Abraham,

Moses, and Jesus were born; Abraham was saved from the fire; Jonah's people were released from torment; Job's affliction was ended; Jacob's sight was restored; Joseph was rescued from the well; Solomon was given his kingdom; Zacharias' prayer for a son was answered; and Moses gained victory over the magicians" (Thackston, *al-Kisa'i*, p. 350 n. 90).

46. Thackston, *al-Kisa'i*, p. 160.

47. Ibn Kathir, *Qisas*, vol. I, pp. 221–223.

48. Ibid., pp. 249–251; Thackston, *al-Kisa'i*, p. 163.

49. al-Shal, *Qisas*, p. 141; for this fact in medieval exegesis, cf. Ibn Kathir, *Qisas*, vol. I, 169.

50. On Hagar, cf. Gen. 16 and 21. On traditional and new approaches in Biblical interpretation on Hagar, cf. Darr, *Jewels*, pp. 132–163. On Hagar in medieval Islamic tradition, cf. Firestone, *Holy Lands*, especially pp. 39–47 and pp. 63–75.

51. Ibn Ishaq, *The Life of Muhammad*, pp. 3–4; additional notes by Ibn Hisham (d. 834), ibid., p. 691.

52. Between the hills of Safa and Marwa; cf. below.

53. Ibn Kathir, *Qisas*, vol. I, p. 194. Al-Kisa'i says she was the daughter of Zadok, king of Jordan, who gave his land to Abraham so that his shrunken hand, which he had stretched out toward Sara, would be cured; cf. above (Thackston, *al-Kisa'i*, p. 151).

54. Ibn Kathir, *Qisas*, vol. I, p. 200.

55. Ibn Kathir, *Qisas*, vol. I, p. 202.—This and similar traditions must be read as religious legitimization of female circumcision. The scripturalist context is important in that Abraham's circumcision, sign of God's covenant, plays a prominent role in the Islamic Hadith. For a contemporary reading, cf. the Azharite scholar Abd al-Wahhab al-Najjar who quotes both Genesis 17:1–14 (circumcision of Abraham) and "The Gospel of Barnabas" (circumcision of Adam) to confirm the religious significance of this act (*Qisas al-anbiya'* [Cairo: al-Halabi, 1966], p. 94). Here it may also be significant that female circumcision is said to have begun with the Egyptian woman Hagar, since this custom is mainly prevalent in the Nile regions.

56. Ibn Kathir, *Qisas*, vol. I, p. 200.

57. Ibid., pp. 202–203. According to al-Kisa'i, Ishmael was seven years old at the time of this banishment, i.e. the banishment had still occurred before Isaac's birth (Thackston, *al-Kisa'i*, p. 151).

58. According to some traditions, the Ka'ba had first been built by Adam but was then in a million pieces because of its destruction during the deluge; while it was covered with water, Noah's ark had floated over it in circles for forty days (Thackston, *al-Kisa'i*, p. 151; Ibn Kathir, *Qisas*, vol. I, p. 113).

59. "The Prophet said: 'This—i.e., Hagar's running—is why people run between the two of them' (during the pilgrimage)". Ibn Kathir, *Qisas*, vol. I, p. 204.

60. Newby, *Prophet*, p. 66.

61. Ibn Kathir, *Qisas*, vol. I, p. 204. Al-Kisa'i has Ishmael scratching the earth with his finger in the presence of the angel Gabriel (Thackston, *al-Kisa'i*, p. 152).

62. Ibn Kathir, *Qisas*, vol. I, p. 204–205; Thackston, *al-Kisa'i*, pp. 152–153. In the "Egyptiana" chapter of the *Akhbar al-zaman*, a book of marvels attributed to the historian al-Mas'udi (?) (cf. above), Hagar's Egyptian origins are used to "confirm" the existence of a sacred and also an historical link between Abraham and the Pharaoh, the Hijaz and Egypt. According to this source, it was Hagar who sent word from Mecca to her former master the Pharaoh Tutis that "she was in a barren place and needed water (or, help). The Pharaoh then ordered a river dug in the East of Egypt and had it channeled by the foot of the mountain until it reached the harbor on the Red Sea.

Wheat and various crops were brought to the ships and taken to Jeddah and from there on camelback to Mecca, and thereby the Hijaz was revived for a while." (*Akhbar*, p. 232). When Hagar informed the Pharaoh that she had had a child, he was glad and sent her gold and jewels with which she adorned her son and also the Ka'ba. "Indeed, it is said that all the adornment for the Ka'ba in that age was given to her by the ruler of Egypt." Tutis also prayed for Ishmael in Egypt, and Abraham informed him that his (Abraham's) descendants would rule over Egypt for all time to come (ibid.).

63. At his father's behest, Ishmael divorced this woman because she was boorish and inhospitable; then he married another from the same tribe who in his father's eyes was polite and hospitable, so that the choice received Abraham's approval (Ibn Kathir, *Qisas*, vol. I, pp. 205ff.)

64. Ibn Kathir, *Qisas*, vol. I, p. 205; Thackston, *al-Kisa'i*, pp. 152–153.

65. Ibn Kathir, *Qisas*, vol. I, p. 207.

66. Ibn Kathir, *Qisas*, vol. I, pp. 225ff.

67. Ibn Kathir, *Qisas*, vol. I, pp. 225ff. On other traditions relating to the building of the Ka'ba, cf. Thackston, *al-Kisa'i*, p. 154; Firestone, *Holy Lands*, pp. 80–93; Newby, *Prophet*, pp. 66–67, 74ff.

68. Ibn Kathir, *Qisas*, vol. I, pp. 207, 228.

69. Ibn Kathir, *Qisas*, vol. I, 229; *Shorter Encyclopedia of Islam*, p. 196.

70. Ibn Kathir, *Qisas*, vol. I, p. 196; *Shorter Encyclopedia of Islam*, pp.196–197.

71. Cf. Michael M. J. Fischer and Mehdi Abedi, *Debating Muslims* (Madison: The University of Wisconsin Press, 1990), pp. 157ff.

72. The literature is reviewed in detail in Firestone, *Holy Lands*, pp. 116–151.

73. Thackston, *al-Kisa'i*, pp. 160–163.

74. *Qisas*, vol. I, pp. 211–217, 292ff.

75. Ibid., p. 292.

76. Newby, *Prophet*, pp. 76ff. In Jewish legend, according to Ginzberg, *Legends*, pp. 276ff., Satan's temptation was addressed to Abraham, Isaac, and Sara. The medieval Islamic Hadith included both versions, that of Sara and that of Hagar (Firestone, *Holy Lands*, pp. 110ff.).

77. Fischer and Abedi, *Debating Muslims*, pp. 162–163, 166.

78. Firestone, *Holy Lands*, pp. 149–151.

Chapter 4

1. On Joseph son of Jacob and Rachel, cf. Gen. 35:24, and Gen. chs. 37, 39–45. On rabbinic parallels, see Newby, *Prophet*, pp. 102–103.

2. For example, the Damascene *tafsir* specialist Abdallah al-Alami (d. 1936), author of a two-volume exegesis of Sura 12 written in the form of a fictitious "congress of '*ulama'* and learned Muslim ladies held in the Aqsa mosque in Jerusalem" points out that Sura 12 "deals with many of the ethical and social problems we encounter today . . . it is filled with historical and psychological lessons . . . it speaks of human emotions and inclinations, the dreams of the young, the family order, relations among brothers, the nature of woman, the morals of kings, princes, and governors, the exaltedness of prophets" (*Mu'tamar tafsir surat Yusuf*, ed. Muhammad Bahja al-Baytar [Damascus: Dar al-fikr, 1962], p. 8). In his Qur'anic commentary, the Egyptian fundamentalist Sayyid Qutb (d. 1966) says much the same thing when he speaks of the sublime psychological, doctrinal, educational, and also merely stirring aspects of this superb story, which "does not omit a single human emotion . . . without stooping to that loathsome quagmire which in the *jahili* twentieth century is called 'realism' or 'naturalism.' . . ." (*Zilal*, vol. IV, pp. 1951–1952).

3. Exegesis understands *al-'aziz* not as a name but a title, in the meaning of "the notable." Cf. Gen. 39:1ff where Potiphar is identified as an officer of Pharaoh, captain of the guard.

4. Exegesis is divided on the speaker in these verses. Some classical interpreters attribute the words to Joseph speaking about his (former) master. Others, including the modern interpreters, attribute the words to the woman who is speaking about Joseph. Cf. below.

5. Cf., e.g., Bukhari, *Sahih* (Cairo: al-Halabi, n.d.), vol. 3, p. 243.

6. Muslim, *Sahih, kitab* 48 (*kitab al-dhikr wal-du'a*), 97–99; as listed in A. J. Wensinck, *A Handbook of Early Muhammadan Tradition* (Leiden: Brill, 1927), pp. XII and 78. The ideological construct of the female's irresistible and also inherently evil and destructive power is not part of the Qur'anic message; Qur'anic histories like the one here under consideration, however, have served to give it Qur'anic moorings.

7. The fact that Joseph is a slave and his mistress highborn figures as an important aspect of the impropriety of this relationship. On this point, cf. also Ibn Kathir, *Qisas*, vol. I, p. 323.

8. Ibn Ishaq (d. 767), one of Tabari's early sources, only records "they praised him" (Newby, *Prophet*, p. 106).

9. Baydawi identifies the Aziz's wife as Ra'il.

10. The Prophet Muhammad who saw Joseph during his night journey described him as "beautiful as the full moon." The women at the banquet, in turn, saw the radiance of his face reflected on the walls (Baydawi, *Anwar*, vol. I, p. 458).

11. Baydawi interprets the Qur'anic *akbarnahu* twice: once in the meaning of "they found him grand," "they praised and extolled him," and once again in the intransitive "they began to menstruate." The latter interpretation leaves the Qur'anic direct object pronoun suffix *-hu* unexplained.

12. Nizam al-Din al-Hasan ibn Muhammad ibn al-Husayn al-Qummi al-Nisaburi, *Ghara'ib al-Qur'an wa-ragha'ib al-furqan* (Cairo: al-Halabi, n.d.)

13. Nisaburi quotes "one of the *'ulama'* who said that he feared women more than Satan because, according to the Qur'an, Satan's cunning is weak (4:76) whereas women's cunning is enormous (12:28)." Nisaburi registers his disagreement with this *'alim* because "if women's cunning were enormous in comparison to men's cunning, then the women would triumph over the men and strip them of all their rational powers. This has clearly not happened. And since women are the snares of Satan, as indicated by the Prophet himself, then their powers, if they were enormous, would make Satan's powers enormous as well" (*Ghara'ib*, vol. 5, p. 101).

14. Some mystics and philosophers among the classical exegetes have identified the woman protagonist of this story with *al-nafs al-ammara bil-su'* (cf. Qur'an 12:53), "the soul" of physical or animal appetites "which commands evil" and the lowest of the three stages of development that the human soul may attain. (*Shorter Encyclopedia of Islam*, p. 433; cf. also Smith and Haddad, *Death and Resurrection*, p. 16).

15. Qutb stipulates that Joseph was twenty-five and the woman about forty at the time of the attempted seduction (*Zilal*, vol. IV, p. 1979).

16. Such as the spectre of his father, tablets bearing Qur'anic verses, finally even the angel Gabriel himself, knocking him on the chest (vol. IV, p. 1981). For these traditions in the medieval sources, cf. above.

17. *Jahiliyya*, "spiritual ignorance," is the Muslim name for the pre-Islamic Arabian period and its society and culture. The term appears in medieval and, especially, modern and contemporary religious literature to denote "un-Islamic practices" that corrode Muslim morality and righteousness.

18. An exception is the derisive characterization of Zulaykha as *al-mar'a al-jadida*, "the new woman" (an allusion to the title of Qasim Amin's promodern 'feminist' book first published in 1900) which is found in the Qur'anic *tafsir* of Sura 12 authored by the Damascene theologian Abdallah al-Alami. For this conservative interpreter, Zulaykha represents "the new woman . . . because she is arrogant, impudent, very highly educated, and rebellious against the laws of veiling and seclusion" (Alami, *Mu'tamar*, pp. 508–509 and 517–519).

19. E.g., Thackston, *al-Kisa'i*, pp. 172–180; and Ibn Kathir, *Qisas*, vol. I, pp. 318–337.

20. "Literary work rhyming in doublets."

21. Other famous versions are the romantic epic of Firdawsi (d. 1020) and the mystic epic of Attar (d. ca. 1230), both also written in Persian.

22. Cf. Knappert, *Islamic Legends*, pp. 92–104 (a Swahili version).

23. According to Genesis 41:45 and 50, and 46:20, Joseph's wife was Asenath daughter of Potipherah priest of On. Thackston stipulates that Islamic legend has combined Potiphar's wife and Asenath daughter of Potipherah in the figure of Zulaykha (*al-Kisa'i*, p. 351 n. 100).

24. Cf. Thackston, *al-Kisa'i*, pp. 178–180; and Ibn Kathir, *Qisas*, vol. I, p. 334.

25. An old tale of love of a Bedouin man for his cousin whom he was not permitted to marry; perhaps first given literary form in Umayyad times; later the theme of numerous epics in Persian, Turkish, Urdu, etc., but also celebrated in folksongs and popular tales. Cf. Reynold A. Nicholson, *A Literary History of the Arabs* (Cambridge: Cambridge University Press, 1962), pp. 237–238.

26. This is true even when her story is not provided with a "happy ending." A popular reader on women in the Qur'an speaks of Zulaykha's gladness at her exoneration of Joseph in front of the Pharaoh, which frees her of the heavy burden of guilt for having wronged him. "[T]hen the curtain came down on this woman's life. Some say she lived with her memories in sadness and despair. Others say that she travelled far away and all news of her was lost. In any case, her life . . . is interwoven with her love for Joseph" (al-Shal, *Qisas*, p. 62).

27. Yusuf Ali's explanatory notes to his translation of Sura 12 reflect some of this ambiguity. He repeats the tale that the Aziz was a eunuch, that Zulaykha was a princess, that their marriage was a marriage in name only. Zulaykha's desire to seduce Joseph, though sinful, represented only the lowest level of her love; during their separation, while Joseph was imprisoned, she then "learned the vanity of carnal love. . . . Joseph had taught her to question herself whether, in spite of all her sin, she could not yet be worthy of him . . . perhaps her husband was dead, and she was a widow . . . she must see whether she could understand love . . . (as) that pure surrender of self which has no earthly stain to it." (A. Yusuf Ali, transl., *The Holy Qur'an* [Washington: The Islamic Center, 1978], pp. 560, 570).

Chapter 5

1. On these figures and events in the life of Moses, cf. Exodus chs. 1–18. For biblical and rabbinic parallels, see Newby, *Prophet*, pp. 113ff.

2. *Tabut* is also used in Qur'an 2:248 in the meaning of "Ark of the Covenant," while Noah's "ark" in the Qur'an is *al-fulk*, "the ship"; cf. above.

3. These are the same words as those spoken by the Aziz to his wife after his purchase of Joseph (12:21).

4. These words are said to have been her last, spoken before her martyr's death.

5. Since this is also the Qur'anic designation of the father of the virgin Mary, there has been a Christian tradition of assuming a Qur'anic "confusion" of Mary (Maryam) the mother of Jesus with Miriam (Maryam) the sister of Moses and Aaron. This allegation has been strongly rejected by Muslims. (Cf. ch. 1, above, and ch. 7, below). Some interpretative works list more than one figure of Moses. On Ibn Ishaq's three figures by that name, cf. Newby, *Prophet*, pp. 114ff.

6. Thackston, *al-Kisa'i*, pp. 213–216; Ibn Kathir, *Qisas*, vol. II, pp. 5–6.

7. Thackston, *al-Kisa'i*, p. 215.

8. *Qisas*, vol. II, p. 7. To explain why Moses' older brother Aaron was not similarly threatened, Ibn Kathir reports that by Pharaonic decree the child murders occurred every other year, because the Israelites were also useful to the Egyptians. Aaron, said to have been three years older than Moses, was thus born during an "amnesty year" (ibid.).

9. Thackston, *al-Kisa'i*, pp. 215–216.

10. Ibn Kathir, "in accordance with al-Ash'ari and community consensus," places God's inspiration to Moses' mother into the category of "guidance," not "prophethood" (as claimed by Ibn Hazm "and other Mu'tazilites") (*Qisas*, vol. II, p. 8); on the question of women's prophethood, cf. ch. 7 below.

11. Al-Kisa'i here also reports that the ark drifted into a pool of Nile water in the Pharaoh's palace, which had been constructed to cure the seven royal daughters from disease. When the young women picked up the infant Moses, they were healed (Thackston, *al-Kisa'i*, pp. 216–217). Thackston sees alchemical elements in the story's fire, water, and healing components (ibid., p. 352, n. 100).

12. Either by Pharaoh's daughter (Thackston, *al-Kisa'i*, p. 217) or by Asya, Pharaoh's wife (Ibn Kathir, *Qisas*, vol. II, pp. 8–9).

13. Thackston, *al-Kisa'i*, p. 218. "Jochebed," Moses' mother, is here said to have nursed him in the palace for three years.

14. Ibn Kathir, *Qisas*, vol. II, p. 11. In concert with other medieval interpreters, Ibn Kathir here points out the magnitude of God's bounty, which reunited Moses' mother with her son, permitted her to care for him, and do all of this while deriving an income.

15. Ibn Kathir *Qisas*, vol. II, p. 8; Thackston, *al-Kisa'i*, p. 217. Thackston develops the identification of Asya with the Christian martyr St. Catherine of Alexandria, who was of royal lineage, and also with Esther, biblical royal consort and adversary of the king's favorite "minister" Haman (*al-Kisa'i*, pp. 351–352, n. 100).

16. Together with Mary mother of Jesus, the Prophet's wife Khadija bint Khuwaylid, and his daughter Fatima (Thackston, *al-Kisa'i*, p. 213). On the "ranking" of Asya, Mary, and women of the Prophet's family, cf. below.

17. Thackston, *al-Kisa'i*, p. 214.

18. This husband is often identified as Harbil and said to have been "the believer from among Pharaoh's family who concealed his faith" (Qur'an 40:28). For this and other identifications, cf. Thackston, ibid., p. 352–353 n. 101.

19. Ibid., pp. 218–219, 231–232.

20. *Qisas*, vol. II, pp. 381ff.

21. Some traditions include the Prophet's wife A'isha in this distinguished group (Ibn Kathir, *Qisas*, vol. II, pp. 375–380).

22. Cf. ch. 7, below.

23. For this combination of myth and history, Newby and others have used the term "mythomorphism" (Newby, *Prophet*, p. 17).

24. Cf. ch. 7, below.

25. Ibn Sa'd (d. 845), *Kitab al-tabaqat al-kabir*, vol. 8, ed. Carl Brockelmann (Leiden: Brill, 1904), p. 8.

26. To Abu Hala Hind ibn al Nabbash, and thereafter to Atiq ibn Abid ibn Abd Allah (ibid., p. 8).

27. Syed A. A. Razwy, *Khadija-tul-Kubra* (Elmhurst: Tahrike Tarsile Qur'an, Inc., 1990), pp. 13–14.

28. Cf. below, Part II.

29. al-Shal, *Qisas*, pp. 118-122.

30. al-Shal, *Qisas*, p. 117. This writer (p. 119) adds that Asya rejoiced in Moses' *da'wa* ("call to the cause of true monotheism"), and that she used to listen to Moses' exhortations from behind the *hijab* ("curtain separating believing womenfolk from male strangers"). On the *hijab* of Qur'an 33:53 and its interpretations, cf. Part II, below.

31. Al-Sha'rawi, *Qadaya*, pp. 10–11; and Stowasser, *Impulse*, p. 267.

32. There is no medieval consensus on whether this *shaykh* was the Madyanite prophet Shu'ayb. Majority opinion is that he was not, even though he is said to have been a relative of Shu'ayb (nephew, or first cousin); else, perhaps, a believer who belonged to Shu'ayb's community, or the *kahin* ("soothsayer") of the Madyanites (cf. Ibn Kathir, *Qisas*, vol. II, p. 19, where his name is given as Yathrun). The disagreement continues in modern popular literature; cf. Sha'rawi, *Qadaya*, p. 20, as opposed to al-Shal, *Qisas*, p. 114.

33. Thackston, *al-Kisa'i*, p. 222; cf. al-Shal, *Qisas*, pp. 113–114.

34. Because of her suggestion to hire Moses, medieval traditions have ranked this young woman among "the three most discerning people." She is said to share this honor with the Aziz of Egypt who, having purchased the prophet Joseph, instructed his wife to "make his stay honorable"; and also with the first caliph of Islam, Abu Bakr, who appointed Umar ibn al-Khattab as his successor (Ibn Kathir, *Qisas*, vol. II, p. 19). In modern popular interpretation, this young woman's strength by contrast is said to have emerged when she was lost with Moses in the Sinai . . . on a cold and rainy night, and about to begin labor in the birth of their child; then, as soon as God had called Moses and he returned from the sacred place, "a new stage began for this woman . . . she became her husband's spiritual ally and supporter" (al-Shal, *Qisas*, pp. 115–116).

35. Ibn Kathir, *Qisas*, vol. II, pp. 16–17. It was of a weight that only ten men could budge.

36. Ibn Kathir, *Qisas*, vol. II, p. 158.

37. Moses then was destitute. He was very hungry, and his sandals had fallen off his feet during his journey from Egypt to Madyan (Ibn Kathir, *Qisas*, vol. II, p. 17).

38. Ibn Kathir, *Qisas*, vol. II, p. 18; here meant are the modest stride and downcast eyes of the paradigmatic "free" (and by definition "respectable") Muslim woman as opposed to the expansive stride and roving eyes of the paradigmatic "slave woman." Female slaves were women born into slavery, or non-Muslims taken prisoners of war; traded at slave markets or sent as gifts to important men, they were poor and exploited or, in some cases, highly educated and/or powerful. While they represented a large and important segment of medieval Muslim societies, in legal rights and obligations, status and societal "expectation" slave women were a class apart from free women.

39. Thackston, *al-Kisa'i*, p. 222.

40. Ibn Kathir, *Qisas*, vol. II, pp. 19, 159; Thackston, *al-Kisa'i*, pp. 221–222. For a modern version, al-Shal, *Qisas*, p. 114. The Islamic institution of gender segregation has traditionally involved injunctions against any form of female "presence" in relation to strangers. Forbidden, then, were sight (hence, female segregation in the home and veiling when abroad); speech; the jiggling of hidden jewelry; and also scent. On issues of gender segregation, cf. Part II, below.

41. Paraphrase of al-Sha'rawi, *Qadaya*, p. 21.
42. Cf. Stowasser, *Impulse*, pp. 269–270.
43. al-Sha'rawi, *Qadaya*, pp. 23–26; cf. Stowasser, *Impulse*, pp. 269–270.
44. Al-Sha'rawi, *Qadaya*, p. 22.

Chapter 6

1. Cf. I Kings 1–11.
2. *Shorter Encyclopedia of Islam*, (p. 550) and Newby (*Prophet*, p. 162) here suggest a link with I Kings 4:33.
3. Cf. I Kings 10.
4. Ibn Ishaq (d. 767) reports that the queen and her people may have been Manichaeans (Newby, *Prophet*, p. 164). In the eighth century, Manichaeanism was widespread especially in Iraq and regions further east in the Islamic empire; it was then rigorously combatted by the Abbasids.
5. Exegesis commonly ascribes this sentence to Solomon.
6. Islamic legend has further magnified and elaborated upon Solomon's wisdom and powers. He is considered one of four great world rulers (together with Nimrod, Nebuchadnezzar, and Alexander the Great); he is also said to have excelled in divination and the occult sciences and was a renowned magician in possession of a talismanic ring and other such relics (magic mirror, miraculous pebble, magic carpet, and the like). Much of this material is said to be of rabbinic origin (Cf. *Shorter Encyclopedia of Islam*, pp. 549–551; also Newby, *Prophet*, pp. 161ff.) The saga of Solomon has also left its imprint in tales of The Thousand and One Nights as well as other Middle Eastern, African, and Asian folklore.
7. Cf., e.g., Ibn Kathir, *Tafsir*, vol. III, p. 360. On a number of different genealogies for Bilqis, cf. Tabari, *History*, vol. III, William M. Brinner, transl. (Albany: State University of New York Press, 1991), p. 156; also Thackston, *al-Kisa'i*, p. 354 n. 115.
8. Thackston, *al-Kisa'i*, pp. 310ff and Ibn Kathir, *Qisas*, vol. II, pp. 290–291. The medieval historian al-Mas'udi (d. 957) reports "the pretty story" that Bilqis, "daughter of al-Hadhad," had a jinni mother. During a hunt in the forest, her father saw two snakes, one white and one black. He was commanded to kill the black snake, which put him in touch with the local jinn. Their leader married him to his daughter but also imposed conditions, and when al-Hadhad broke the conditions, his fairy bride disappeared from him after having conceived Bilqis. Mas'udi adds that Bilqis later ruled the Yemen for a period of 120 years, while Solomon's rule over the Yemen lasted for 23 years (*Muruj al-dhahab*, vol. II, ed. Muhammad Muhyi al-Din Abd al-Hamid [Cairo: Dar al-raja', n.d], pp. 4–5).
9. This account is found in *al-Kisa'i*, Thackston, *al-Kisa'i*, pp. 310–313; cf. also Ibn Kathir, *Qisas*, vol. II, pp. 290–291.
10. This scribe who wrote the letter (27:30) is generally identified with "the one who had knowledge of the Scripture" (27:40); cf. below.
11. Thackston, *al-Kisa'i*, pp. 314–315; Ibn Kathir, *Qisas*, vol. II, pp. 292ff.; Ibn Kathir, *Tafsir*, vol. III, pp. 360–361.
12. Thackston, *al-Kisa'i*, p. 315; Ibn Kathir, *Tafsir*, vol. III, p. 362. An (unascribed) folk legend tells that Bilqis sent Solomon one thousand carpets woven with gold thread, also musk, precious woods, and ambergris. These were refused (or never offered), because at Solomon's behest the jinn wove a carpet the length of nine *farasang* (twenty-seven miles) along which they erected one golden wall and one made of silver, each guarded by devils, satans, and odd-looking animals. The queen's ambassadors were

distraught by the time that they arrived, after a long walk on the precious carpet, at the steps of the prophet's throne (Knappert, *Islamic Legends*, pp. 142ff).

13. According to Ibn Ishaq, the person who moved the throne ("he who had knowledge of the Scripture") was (also) Asaf ibn Barakhya. He was able to do so because he knew the Ineffable Name (Newby, *Prophet*, pp. 162, 166).

14. Ibn Kathir, *Tafsir*, vol. III, p. 364.

15. Ibid., p. 363.

16. Ibn Ishaq in Newby, *Prophet*, pp. 164–165; Ibn Kathir, *Qisas*, vol. II, p. 296.

17. Thackston, *al-Kisa'i*, p. 316. According to Ibn Kathir (*Qisas*, vol. II, p. 297 and *Tafsir*, vol. III, pp. 365–366) her legs were, indeed, hairy, "because she had no husband," and it was then that on Solomon's orders depilatories were first introduced (by the jinn or the satans) as an alternative to shaving one's legs with a razor.

18. Ibn Kathir, *Tafsir*, vol. III, pp. 360, 365; cf. Knappert, *al-Kisa'i*, pp. 144–145. Knappert (*Islamic Legends*, pp. 151–154) also records the related folk tale of "the queen of Abyssinia" who had a donkey's foot of which she was magically cured when she visited Solomon, whom she then also married; this story is said to be part of Near Eastern and African folklore (ibid., p. 151). Arab friends from North Africa, Egypt, and the Levant have told me that in their countries male villagers, when observing a veiled female walking by, are apt to scrutinize and discuss her feet as indicative of her character and, especially, hidden physical attributes and sexual and other powers. In the case of the queen of Sheba, a donkey's foot would have indicated not only her half-human, half-jinni nature but also that there was something dangerous, satanic, about her jinni half. In medieval Europe the cloven hoof was a sign of the Devil, and on a woman it was the sign of a witch.

19. Ibn Kathir, *Tafsir*, vol. III, pp. 365–366.

20. This son was named Rehoboam (Thackston, *al-Kisa'i*, p. 316). In Christian Abyssinian legend, the queen's name appears as Makeda and the Abyssinian ruling house is said to have descended from her union with Solomon (*Shorter Encyclopedia of Islam*, p. 63).

21. Ibn Kathir, *Qisas*, vol. II, p. 297 ; cf. Knappert, *al-Kisa'i*, p. 145.

22. Ibn Kathir, *Qisas*, vol. II, p. 297. Ibn Kathir's predecessor and source Ibn Ishaq here has Solomon instruct Bilqis that "in Islam, women must marry" (Newby, *Prophet*, pp. 161, 166–167). According to this source (p. 167) and also Tabari (*History*, vol. III, transl. Brinner, pp. 164–165) Bilqis' husband was made ruler over the Yemen; Solomon's jinn continued to carry out construction projects for the pair, and "*their* rule" went on until Solomon died.

23. Western scholarship has surmised that, to Muslims, the figure of the queen of Sheba "did not properly belong to Islam" (*Shorter Encyclopedia of Islam*, p. 63).

24. For example, Ibn Kathir, *Tafsir*, vol. III, pp. 363, 366 questions the credibility of traditions on the nature of the queen's presents for Solomon, details concerning her hairy legs, etc, calling them "fanciful tales imported from the Israelites which are of questionable authenticity"; this critical spirit is less pronounced in Ibn Kathir's much shorter *Qisas* rendition of the same story where detail is either omitted or introduced factually, but in shorthand fashion (cf. *Qisas*, vol. II, pp. 288ff).

25. Ibn Kathir, *Qisas*, vol. II, p. 291. Perhaps historical reasoning also had some influence on exegetic reasoning here. The *Surat al-Naml* records the political wisdom of Sheba's queen and also her decision to submit in Islam, and the Hadith then tells that a close relationship between this queen and God's prophet Solomon followed thereafter and no conquest of the Yemen ensued. Conversely, in the Persian case,

rejection of Muhammad's call to submission led to warfare and the overthrow of the Iranian dynasty during the Islamic-Arabian conquest of Iran.

26. Cairo: al-Halabi, n.d., vol. 4, p. 228.

27. Reading: Addison Wesley, 1991, pp. 49–61.

28. E.g., al-Shal, *Qisas*, pp. 74–81.

29. Vol. 5, p. 2640.

30. Ibid., pp. 2640–2643.

31. Ibid., p. 2643.

Chapter 7

1. 19:2–15 (Middle Meccan), 21:89–90 (Middle Meccan), and 3:38–41 (Medinan). In all cases, the story is immediately followed by verses on Mary's sinless conception of the prophet Jesus.

2. On the priest Zacharias, his wife Elisabeth (of the daughters of Aaron), and their son John, cf. Luke 1–3; on John also Matthew 3 and 14; Mark 1; John 3.

3. Temple niche, or a secluded cell or upstairs chamber in the house of worship; cf. below.

4. Cf. *Shorter Encyclopedia of Islam*, p. 328.

5. In Zacharia's figure in Islamic hagiography, Western biblical scholarship has seen "the conflation of Haggadic elements associated with Zechariah, the prophet and high priest in the time of King Joash, and Zachariah, the father of John the Baptist" (Newby, *Prophet*, p. 201, with further references).

6. Thackston, *al-Kisa'i*, pp. 326–327.

7. Ibn Kathir, *Qisas*, vol. II, pp. 388–389.

8. In the Qur'an, Jesus is "a word from God" (3:42) and "His word bestowed upon Mary" (4:171).

9. Ibn Kathir, *Qisas*, vol. II, pp. 388–389.

10. E.g., the *Qisas al-anbiya'* by the Azharite Shaykh Abd al-Wahhab al-Najjar (Cairo: al-Halabi, n.d.).

11. On Mary, cf. Matthew chs. 1 and 2, and Luke chs. 1 and 2. On Mary in the Gospels, the extracanonical gospels, and early Christian popular religiosity, cf. Gail Paterson Corrington, *Her Image of Salvation* (Louisville: Westminster/John Knox Press, 1992), pp. 145–195; and Marina Warner, *Alone of All Her Sex: The Myth and the Cult of the Virgin Mary* (New York: Random House, 1983), 339 pp.; esp. pp. 3–33.

12. Jane I. Smith and Yvonne Y. Haddad note that "there are 70 verses that refer to her, and she is named specifically in 34 of these (24 in relation to Jesus, son of Mary). . . ." ("The Virgin Mary in Islamic Tradition and Commentary," *The Muslim World*, vol. 79, [1989], p. 162).

13. In one instance, a Sura bears the name of a sage (31: Luqman). Sura 111 (*Lahab*, "Flame") refers to the fires of hell and not to the Prophet's uncle Abu Lahab. The latter was a zealous enemy of Islam and is said to have cursed Muhammad after the inception of his prophethood. This Sura depicts his and his wife's punishment in the hereafter.

14. Cf. *Shorter Encyclopedia of Islam*, p. 329.

15. According to Islamic exegesis, a secluded cell or upstairs chamber in the temple, or "mosque". In this, the temple's "most prestigious part," Mary was given the privilege of complete privacy in her devotions, since the door to this chamber was always locked and only Zacharia had the key (Tabari, *Tafsir*, vol. 6, pp. 353–358; Ibn Kathir, *Qisas*, vol. II, pp. 372, 385).

16. Middle Meccan: 19:16–35; 23:50; 21:91. In these Suras, the emphasis lies on the miracle of Mary's conceiving (of) the spirit while a virgin.

17. 3:33–37, 42–51, 59; 4:156,171–172; 66:11–12; 5:19, 75, 78, 119–120. In Suras 4 and 5 (and other related Medinan Suras) the thrust is toward the negation of divinity of Mary and, especially, Jesus. In addition to the verses here indicated, Mary's name appears frequently in the Qur'an as part of the formula "Jesus son of Mary." According to Islamic exegesis, this matronymic name derives from the fact that Jesus had no creaturely father and is, therefore, an honorific title (cf., e.g., Zamakhshari, *Kashshaf*, vol. I, p. 279; Razi, *Tafsir*, vol. VIII, p. 53). For the Western debate concerning this name, cf. Geoffrey Parrinder, *Jesus in the Qur'an* (London: Faber and Faber, 1965), pp. 22–29.

18. Exegesis has variously identified this *mashraqa*, "eastern place," as the easternmost chamber of Mary's house; or an area east of Jerusalem; or a place east of "the mosque" on Mount Zion, al-Aqsa mosque in Jerusalem (Tabari, *Tafsir*, vol. 16, p. 49; Zamakhshari, *Kashshaf*, vol. 3, p. 7; Razi, *Tafsir*, vol. 21, p. 196; Baydawi, vol. 1, p. 578; Ibn Kathir, *Qisas*, vol. II, 386).

19. *Li-ahaba laki*, "so that I give you."

20. Some interpreters appear to have identified this "remote place" (where Jesus was born) with the "eastern place" (where the annunciation took place). Additional proposed locations include: the remotest corner of Mary's house; the mountains surrounding Jerusalem; an area behind Mount Zion; various places in Palestine on the way from Nazareth to Bethlehem; a place in Damascus; a place on the way of Mary's and Joseph's journey to Egypt. Some prominence, however, is given to the town of Bethlehem in Palestine (Tabari, *Tafsir*, vol. 16, pp. 48, 50; Zamakhshari, *Kashshaf*, vol. 3, p. 8; Razi, *Tafsir*, vol. 21, pp. 196, 201–202; Ibn Kathir, *Qisas*, vol. II, pp. 390, 395, 411ff.)

21. (Or, perhaps, "from below the palmtree"). Islamic exegesis is divided on whether the speaker in this verse is the angel Gabriel (who is also said to have acted as midwife in Jesus's birth) or whether it is Jesus himself. If the latter, then the child spoke to his mother before, or right after, birth and his words preceded those which he addressed to her people while in the cradle (Tabari, *Tafsir*, vol. 16, pp. 52–53; Zamakhshari, *Kashshaf*, vol. 3, p. 9; Razi, *Tafsir*, vol. 21, p. 204; Baydawi, *Anwar*, vol. 1, p. 579; Ibn Kathir, *Qisas*, vol. II, pp. 390–391).

22. In Islamic exegesis, the "fast" here imposed upon Mary was to consist of her silence. The interpreters stipulate that "silence" was part of "the fasting ritual of the Jews," but they also emphasize that *sawm* (the Islamic fast) does not include the duty to remain silent. Furthermore, however, exegetes have also understood this directive as the divine command that Mary should leave the word, i.e. the defense of her innocence, to her son Jesus (Tabari, *Tafsir*, vol. 16, p. 57; Razi, *Tafsir*, vol. 21, p. 206; Ibn Kathir, *Qisas*, vol. II, p. 392). A contemporary source emphasizes that "(firstly) the word should be left to the better spokesman and (secondly) silence should be maintained in the presence of fools." (Muhammad al-Sayyid Tantawi, *Tafsir Surat Maryam*, part 16 of *al-Tafsir al-wasit lil-Qur'an al karim* [Cairo: Matba'at al-sa'ada, 1985], p. 36).

23. Mary's designation as "sister of Aaron" (and also "daughter of Amram") has led some non-Muslims to allege a Qur'anic "confusion" of Miriam (Maryam) the sister of Aaron and Moses with Mary (Maryam) the mother of Jesus. This controversy is very old (cf. ch. 1, above), and refutation of the allegation by Muslim authorities is well documented. According to the *tafsir*, Mary was addressed as "sister of Aaron" because the Qur'an is drawing a comparison, or because she did have a brother by that name (Tabari, *Tafsir*, vol. 16, pp. 58–59; Zamakhshari, *Kashshaf*, vol. 3, p. 11; Razi, *Tafsir*,

vol. 21, pp. 207–208; Baydawi, *Anwar*, vol. 1, p. 580; Ibn Kathir, *Qisas*, vol. II, pp. 393–394).

24. Exegesis here defines prayer and almsgiving, two of the five "pillars of religion," as the main means of individual religious purification: prayer because it purifies the soul, and almsgiving because it "purifies one's wealth" when it is spent on the needy, the guests, and in support of wives, slaves, and relatives (Ibn Kathir, *Qisas*, vol. II, p. 396). In Jesus's case, *zakat* (almsgiving) is understood as "purification of the body from defiling sin," since Jesus was known to have adhered to a canon of voluntary poverty. Although he had no material wealth to give, his *zakat* also included the *sadaqa* (freewill offering) of the powers with which he had been endowed (Tabari, *Tafsir*, vol. 16, p. 61).

25. To the Qur'anic interpreters, this statement of loyalty of Jesus toward his mother is both indication that Jesus had no father and also proof of the chastity of Mary, since God does not enjoin his sinless prophets to kindness toward fornicators (Tabari, *Tafsir*, vol. 16, p. 61; Razi, *Tafsir*, vol. 21, p. 215; Ibn Kathir, *Qisas*, vol. II, p. 396).

26. These words of Jesus are almost identical to God's words to, and about, John (19:14–15).

27. On the terminology employed in this verse (and elsewhere), cf. Parrinder, *Jesus*, pp. 127–128.

28. Smith and Haddad translate *qarar* as "a place of flocks" ("The Virgin Mary in Islamic Tradition," p. 171).

29. Parrinder suggests that the Qur'anic story of Jesus's birth was revealed twice because of "the different audiences in Mecca and Medina" (*Jesus*, p. 18). This argument would, of course, be unacceptable to most Muslims.

30. *Muharrar(a)*, "consecrated," has denoted "freedom to serve in the place of worship without worries about personal maintenance," . . . "worship of God beyond work for this world" (Smith and Haddad, "The Virgin Mary in Islamic Tradition," pp. 165–166).

31. In exegesis, the *mihrab* (technical term for the prayer niche) is generally thought of as an honored, or the most honored, space in the mosque, perhaps an upstairs chamber. This space is said to have provided Mary with complete privacy in worship, since only Zacharia had the key to its door and would lock Mary in when he was not around (Tabari, *Tafsir*, vol. 6, pp. 353–358; Ibn Kathir, *Qisas*, vol. II, p. 372, 385); cf. above.

32. Mary's story is here interrupted by the story of Zacharia's prayer for a good child; the angels' glad tidings of the birth of John, "a witness to the truth of a word from God"; Zacharia's question of how this might be; and God's "sign" of Zacharia's silence for the duration of three days (3:38–41).

33. Of either sex: *irka'i ma'a l-raki'in* (masculine plural).

34. Of either sex: *kanat min al-qanitin* (masculine plural).

35. *'ibada*, the service of the slave (*'abd*) to his master, and also human worship of God.

36. Many of the Hadith-recorded legends on Mary and the child Jesus agree with the apocryphal gospels (The Protevangelium of James; The Arabic Infancy Gospel; The Infancy Story of Thomas; The Pseudo-Matthew Gospel; The Nativity of Mary; The Transitus Mariae; and the History of the Blessed Virgin Mary). Although condemned as noncanonical by Bishop Gelasius at the Council of Rome of 494 A.D., these remained popular with Eastern Christians. On the apocryphal gospels and their spread and influence, see Thackston, *al-Kisa'i*, pp. 354–356, n. 119., and the works of Gail Paterson Corrington and Marina Warner, quoted above.

37. The following segment, while generally based on different sources, reflects the main points made by Jane I. Smith and Yvonne Y. Haddad in "The Virgin Mary in Islamic Tradition and Commentary" (*The Muslim World* vol. 79 [1989], pp. 161–187). Their article has been helpful in arranging the materials here considered over and above indicated direct quotations.

38. Ibn Ishaq, *Life of Muhammad*, p. 152.

39. While the Christian delegates are said to have accepted Muhammad's apostleship on this occasion, they clung to their faith and asked the Prophet to impose upon them the *jizya* (head-tax imposed upon the *ahl al-kitab*) (Ibn Ishaq, *Life of Muhammad*, pp. 270ff; Ibn Kathir, *Qisas*, vol. II, pp. 397–398).

40. This applies to all genres of *tafsir*, including the *qisas al-anbiya'*; cf., e.g., Ibn Kathir, *Qisas*, vol II, p. 367.

41. E.g., Sayyid Qutb, *Fi zilal al-Qur'an*, vol. 4, pp. 2298ff. Qutb and many other interpreters have here decried Muslim-Christian doctrinal differences. In his exegesis of the revelation on Mary, the nineteenth-century modernist Muhammad Abduh regretted that as a matter of course, Christian missionaries consider the Qur'anic dicta which agree with the Bible as "borrowed," and those that do not, as "incorrect." He adds that to Muslims, the Qur'an is truth, and where its teachings differ from those of the Bible they represent the divine rectification of the Bible's mistakes and omissions (*Manar*, vol. 3, p. 302).

42. Marina Warner, writing about the Christian tradition, has linked this name with Hannah, mother of Samuel. Prototypical affinity of Samuel and Jesus, and the geneological link between his mother Hannah and Mary, made for "a relationship so close that by the second century Mary's mother was believed to be called Anna, another form of the name Hannah." (*Alone of All her Sex* [New York: Vintage Books, 1983], p. 12).

43. Thackston, *al-Kisa'i*, p. 327.

44. Ibn Kathir, *Qisas*, vol. II, p. 369.

45. Thackston, *al-Kisa'i*, p. 327; Ibn Kathir, *Qisas*, vol. II, pp. 369–371, 461. As was well known to the scholars of Islam, women in Jewish tradition are unfit to serve in a place of worship. The exegetic debate on God's acceptance of Mary for service in His temple is important in that it elucidates Muslim reasoning for the traditional Islamic exclusion of women from religious and other public offices, because of the pollutant of menstruation. This issue is discussed below in relation to Mary's Qur'an-proclaimed quality of "purity" (*tahara*).

46. According to Tabari, Anna exclaimed after Mary's birth that she had borne a *gharia*, (slave) girl. With Zamakhshari, this generic exclamation became the "meaning" of the name Mary, "in their language"; Zamakhshari provides an exegetic synonym in *'abida*, "servant/slave (girl)." Baydawi adds that Mary's mother conveyed this name with the expectation that God would protect Mary until she became worthy of it. The Shi'ite exegete Tabarsi (d. 1153) equates *'abida*, "servant/slave girl" with *khadima*, connoting "most obedient servant (of God)." Suyuti (d. 1505), aware of this tradition of interpretations of the name, brings linguistics back to the social reality of his time when he stipulates that "a male may dedicate himself to the service of God, but the weaker sex may not, because of the frailties of her gender." (cf. below.) The preceding is quoted from Michael B. Schub, "The Male is not like the Female: An Eponymous Passage in the Qur'an" (*Zeitschrift für arabische Linguistik*, Heft 23 [1991], pp. 102–104). Schub adds that in Jewish legend the name Miriam is equated with "bitter" (in reference to the bondage in Egypt), an ad hoc folk etymology; Muslim exegetes disregarded this reading in favor of their own ad hoc solution. "However, both groups saw an

eponymous dimension in their respective texts, and felt the need for commentary." (ibid., p. 104).

47. Ibn Kathir, *Qisas*, vol. II, pp. 370–371, 461. This hadith is one of a cluster of prophetic traditions transmitted through several chains of distinguished authorities. Ibn Ishaq reports that after the Muslim conquest of Mecca (630 A.D.), the Prophet cleansed the Ka'ba of all objects of polytheistic worship. The Quraysh had put pictures in the Ka'ba including one of Jesus and one of Mary. The Prophet ordered the pictures erased except those of Jesus and Mary (*Life of Muhammad*, p. 552). According to Ibn Hisham, all pictures were erased (ibid., p. 774).

48. Ibn Ishaq reports that both parents, i.e., Amram and Anna, had died by this time (*Life of Muhammad*, p. 275).

49. Later, a grievous famine befell the children of Israel, and Zacharia was unable to support Mary. Lots were cast again, and Mary's maternal cousin George (Jurayj) the ascetic, a carpenter, became Mary's guardian (Ibn Ishaq, *Life of Muhammad*, p. 275). This cousin has also been identified as Joseph the carpenter (cf. *Shorter Encyclopedia of Islam*, pp. 329, 653). On this figure, fellow servant in the temple and main care-taker of Mary and her son Jesus, cf. below.

50. Tabari, *Tafsir*, vol. 6, pp. 402-403.

51. Ibid., pp. 353ff; Thackston, *al-Kisa'i*, p. 328; Ibn Kathir, *Qisas*, vol. II, pp. 373ff, 385. Modernist exegesis, given to the elimination of legendary materials, has sought the nature of Mary's sustenance from God in provisions gained by secondary means, such as the charity of visitors to the temple; else, the story has been understood as parable for God's provision of the means of livelihood for mankind at large (Baljon, *Modern Muslim Koran Interpretation*, pp. 22, 65–66, quoting the Pakistani exegete G. A. Parwez and the Egyptian Tantawi al-Jawhari).

52. Thackston, *al-Kisa'i*, p. 328; Ibn Kathir, *Qisas*, vol. II, p. 385.

53. On the Qur'anic prophet Joseph son of Jacob, cf. above, ch. 4.

54. According to Tabari, Mary and Joseph both served in "the mosque on Mount Zion." Joseph there took over Mary's share of the work when her pregnancy had weakened her (*Tafsir*, vol. 16, pp. 49–50); cf. Razi, *Tafsir*, vol. 21, p. 202; Ibn Kathir, *Qisas*, vol. II, pp. 388, 390.

55. On the identification of God's spirit with Gabriel, cf. below.

56. Tabari, *Tafsir*, vol. 6, p. 402.

57. Tabari, *Tafsir*, vol. 16, pp. 45–46; Zamakhshari, *Kashshaf*, vol. 3, p. 7; Razi, *Tafsir*, vol. 21, p. 196; Baydawi, *Anwar*, vol. 1, p. 578.

58. If Gabriel had appeared to Mary in his angelic form, he would have frightened her into fleeing (Zamakhshari, *Kashshaf*, vol. 3, p. 7; Razi, *Tafsir*, vol. 21, pp. 196–197; Baydawi, *Anwar*, vol. 1, p. 578; Ibn Kathir, *Qisas*, vol. II, p. 386). For Zamakhshari, the angel's beauty presented a test of Mary's chastity. Baydawi, on the other hand, speculates whether the angel's beauty was not also a means to arouse Mary's sexual desire "so that 'her semen' would drop down into her womb" (ready for fertilization). On the notion of 'female semen' (formed during sexual excitation) as argued by Hippocrates and Galen and developed by Muslim authorities such as Ibn Sina and Ibn Qayyim, cf. Basim F. Musallam, *Sex and Society in Islam* (Cambridge: Cambridge University Press, 1983), pp. 43–52.

59. Zamakhshari, *Kashshaf*, vol. 3, p. 7; Razi, *Tafsir*, vol. 21, p. 197.

60. For most exegetes, Mary's words "no human has touched me" are metonymic for sexual intercourse within lawful marriage (Zamakhshari, *Kashshaf*, vol. 3, p. 7; Razi, *Tafsir*, vol. 21, p. 199; Baydawi, *Anwar*, vol. 1, p. 578). According to Ibn Kathir, Mary was "an ascetic, not of the kind that marries" (*Qisas*, vol. II, p. 385). In any case, her

words to the angel are understood as indication of her chastity, not doubt of God's omnipotence. On this issue, cf. below.

61. Exegesis records a variant reading: "that He (God) give you a pure boy" (Tabari, *Tafsir*, vol. 16, p. 47; Razi, *Tafsir*, vol. 21, p. 198; Baydawi, *Anwar*, vol. 1, p. 578). This variant reading is attributed to Abu Amr ibn al-A'la.

62. Razi, *Tafsir*, vol. 21, p. 198.

63. Tabari, *Tafsir*, vol. 16, p. 48; Zamakhshari, *Kashshaf*, vol. 3, p. 8; Razi, *Tafsir*, vol. 21, p. 201; Baydawi, *Anwar*, vol. 1, pp. 578–579; Thackston, *al-Kisa'i*, p. 328; Ibn Kathir, *Qisas*, vol. II, p. 387–388. Emphasis is placed on the fact that no physical contact occurred between the angel and Mary, and that Mary was fully clothed (e.g., Ibn Kathir, *Qisas*, vol. II, p. 387).

64. Interpreters agree that Jesus' creation in Mary's womb was an instance of *kharq al-'ada* ("the violating of the the usual course of nature"). As to the physical process of "how" the spirit awakened life in Mary's womb, the medieval rationalist Razi considers "auto-generation." This, he says, is possible when the body's 'four humors' stand in a specific quantitative relationship to each other for a specific period of time; when this occurs, the *nafs* (life substance) is irresistibly drawn into that body. Razi goes on to say that some animals (mice, snakes, scorpions) have been observed to self-generate in this manner from inanimate matter. Razi further considers "auto-suggestion" ("mental imaginations"), when the mind's imaginings bring forth all sorts of unusual and involuntary physical behavior and functions (Razi, *Tafsir*, vol. 8, pp. 50– 52). The modernist Muhammad Abduh, once again following Razi, also speaks of "auto-generation" (*tawallud dhati*), and he reminds his readers that the transformation of inorganic into organic matter is of great concern to modern science. His preference, however, here lies with the notion of "auto-suggestion" when the mind, or strong emotions, overpower the body. Abduh reiterates Razi's claim that Mary's faith in the angels' message so affected her constitution (*mazaj*) that it generated the fertilization process in her womb. Like other modernists, Abduh was fascinated not only with rationalism but "natural causes," and so he adds that natural energy forces are often invisible, as is the case with electricity, and that the spirit that gave Mary her son may have been such a force, even though it (he) belonged to a higher order (*Manar*, vol. 3, p. 308). Contemporary conservative and fundamentalist interpreters have stated their distance from such "rationalist" interpretations by affirming that the "how" of Mary's pregnancy is one of God's mysteries beyond human understanding and, hence, is not of man's concern (Muhammad al-Bahi, *Tafsir Surat Maryam* [Cairo: Maktabat Wahba, n.d.], p. 14; Sayyid Qutb, *Fi zilal al-Qur'an*, vol. 1, pp. 396–397; vol. 4, p. 2307).

65. Razi, *Tafsir*, vol. 21, pp. 201–202; Thackston, *al-Kisa'i*, pp. 328–329; Ibn Kathir, *Qisas*, vol. II, p. 388. Zamakhshari reports that Joseph thought of killing Mary because he assumed that she had sinned. The angel Gabriel informed him that the child was from the holy spirit, and Joseph let her be (vol. 3, p. 8).

66. Tabari, *Tafsir*, vol. 16, pp. 48, 50; Razi, *Tafsir*, vol. 21, p. 201. Ibn Kathir adds that both children were conceived on the same day (*Qisas*, vol. II, pp. 388–389); else, they were born on the same day (Thackston, *al-Kisa'i*, p. 329).

67. Ibn Kathir, *Qisas*, vol. II, p. 389. Other instances of Jesus speaking before birth (such as 'studying the Torah aloud') are recorded in Smith and Haddad, "The Virgin Mary," p. 169.

68. Zamakhshari, *Kashshaf*, vol. 3, p. 8; Razi, *Tafsir*, vol. 21, p. 202; Ibn Kathir, *Qisas*, vol. II, p. 389. Even the eight months' pregnancy is regarded as miraculous in that, according to the interpreters, "no child other than Jesus born after eight months has lived."

69. E.g., Ibn Kathir, *Qisas*, vol. II, p. 390. On the geographical identification of Jesus' birthplace (the "remote place" of 19:22), cf. above.

70. Exegetes have explained these words in psychological terms both selfcentered (fear of accusations and loss of reputation) and also altruistic (fear that those who would malign her would thereby fall into sin). The words have not been understood as indication of disobedience or lack of faith. Cf. below.

71. Tabari, *Tafsir*, vol. 16, p. 54; Zamakhshari, *Kashshaf*, vol. 3, pp. 8–9; Razi, *Tafsir*, vol. 21, p. 203; Baydawi, *Anwar*, vol. 1, p. 579; Thackston, *al-Kisa'i*, p. 329; Ibn Kathir, *Qisas*, vol. II, pp. 391–392.

72. Ibn Kathir, *Qisas*, vol. II, p. 393. Some say that Joseph took Mary and her son to a cave and that they stayed there for forty days "until Mary was healed of childbirth" (Zamakhshari, *Kashshaf*, vol. 3, p. 11). In Islamic law, the *nifas* is the forty-day period of a woman's confinement, followed by the *ghusl* (major ablution). The traditions on Mary's forty days of isolation after Jesus' birth, then, stipulate that this was a normal birth with postpartem bleeding.

73. Zacharia and Joseph searched for Mary and found her and her child seated beneath a tree. Mary was silent, but Jesus spoke to Joseph and announced his prophethood. When the king heard of this, he ordered that Mary and her son be killed. Zacharia then commanded Joseph to take mother and child to Egypt, and the three of them departed together (Thackston, *al-Kisa'i*, pp. 329–33).

74. Ibn Kathir, *Qisas*, vol. II, p. 393.

75. On this transmitter of Biblical lore, cf. above.

76. Ibn Kathir, *Qisas*, vol. II, pp. 411–412.

77. E.g., Sayyid Qutb, *Fi zilal al-Qur'an*, vol. 4, p. 2305.

78. Tabari, *Tafsir*, vol. 16, p. 60; Ibn Kathir, *Qisas*, vol. II, pp. 395–396. According to Zamakhshari, they said: "her scorn is harder on us than her fornication," and they thought of stoning her to death (punishment for fornication in Islamic canonical law), but desisted when Jesus had spoken. Zamakhshari also reports that on this occasion the infant Jesus stopped nursing, propped himself up in the cradle, pointed at them with his index finger, and exonerated his mother against their slanderous accusations that she had been unchaste. Thereafter, he remained silent until he had reached normal speaking age (*Kashshaf*, vol. 3, p. 11).

79. Razi, *Tafsir*, vol. 21, p. 209.

80. This recalls Luke's Gospel: "the Holy Spirit shall come upon you" (Luke 1,35).

81. According to the Bible, "the Spirit (descended) like a dove" at Jesus' baptism, and Jesus performed his works "armed with the power of the Spirit" (Mark 1,10; Luke 4,14).

82. This recalls Genesis 2,7: "The Lord God . . . breathed into his nostrils the breath of life."

83. Fazlur Rahman here proposes that the spirit is "the highest form of the angelic nature and closest to God," but considers whether the spirit is not also "the actual content of revelation, or a power that develops in the prophet's heart and comes into actual revelatory operation when needed" (*Themes*, pp. 96–98).

84. Reasons given are that the Qur'an speaks of Gabriel as spirit (2:97); that Gabriel is a spirit-like creature, or created of spirit; that religion was "spirited" by Gabriel's conveyance of revelations; or because God metaphorically called Gabriel His spirit to convey His love for him, as one would call a lover "my spirit" (*ruhi*). (Razi, *Tafsir*, vol. 21, p. 196)

85. On 21:91, see Razi, *Tafsir*, vol. 22, p. 218, also vol. 21, pp. 200–201; on 66:12, see Razi, vol. 30, p. 50.

86. Cf. the Qur'anic interpretation of the Azharite shaykh Muhammad al-Sayyid al-Tantawi, *Tafsir surat Maryam* (Cairo: Matba'at al-Sa'ada, 1985) pp. 26 and 30, and the Qur'anic interpretation of the Egyptian fundamentalist Sayyid Qutb, *Fi zilal al-Qur'an*, vol. 4, p. 2306.

87. On The Word (Logos) as Christ's essence/name in John 1,1 and Revelations 19,13 (cf. Colossians, 1 and Hebrews, 1), and The Word as God's creative power in Genesis 1 and Psalms 33, 6, cf. Parrinder, *Jesus*, pp. 47–48.

88. *Tafsir*, vol. 8, pp. 49–50; some of Razi's arguments are already found with Tabari, *Tafsir*, vol. 6, p. 411.

89. *Manar*, vol. 3, pp. 304–305.

90. *Fi zilal al-Qur'an*, vol. 1, p. 397.

91. The distinction between *nabi* ("giver of news from God") and *rasul* ("God's messenger"), on the whole established in the Qur'anic text, was recognized and elaborated upon by mainstream orthodox theologians. *Nabi* to them generally meant a divine envoy without a revealed book, while *rasul* was an emissary with a law and a revealed book (cf. Rahman, *Themes*, pp. 81–82). These theologians, however, have always restricted both categories of envoys to males. Some Mu'tazilite interpreters even considered the angels' words to Mary as a miracle vouchsafed to Zacharia, the acknowledged prophet of that time, or as a miracle in preparation for the prophethood of Jesus (Zamakhshari, *Kashshaf*, vol. 1, p. 277; refuted by Razi, *Tafsir*, vol. 21, p. 206; cf. Baydawi, *Anwar*, vol. 1, p. 155).

92. Abu Muhammad Ali ibn Ahmad Ibn Hazm, *al-Fasl fi al-milal wal-ahwa' wal-nihal*, vol. 5, ed. Dr. Muhammad Ibrahim Nasr and Dr. Abd al-Rahman Umayra (Jeddah: Ukaz Publications, 1402/1982), pp. 119–120.

93. Ibid., p. 121. Ibn Hazm derives the notion of ranking from Sura 2:253.

94. In the Catholic faith, Mary's purity is enshrined in the dogma of her immaculate conception. Because of its preeminent importance to the Christian dogma of original sin, Mary's purity in Catholicism is doctrinally much more specific than is the Qur'anic notion, and the two cannot be equated (George Anawati, "Islam and the Immaculate Conception," in *The Dogma of the Immaculate Conception: History and Significance*, ed. E. D. O'Connor [Notre Dame, Indiana: University of Notre Dame, 1958], pp. 447–461; quoted in Smith and Haddad, "The Virgin Mary in Islamic Tradition," p. 172). It is noteworthy, however, that Muslim popular piety has affirmed the notion of immaculate conception in the case of the Prophet, his parents, and even his grandparents (Smith and Haddad, ibid., p. 174).

95. Tabari, *Tafsir*, vol. 16, pp. 45–46; Zamakhshari, *Kashshaf*, vol. 3, pp. 7–8; Razi, *Tafsir*, vol. 21, pp. 196, 201; Baydawi, *Anwar*, vol. 1, pp. 578–579; Thackston, *al-Kisa'i*, p. 328; Ibn Kathir, *Qisas*, vol. II, p. 385, cf. p. 457.

96. Zamakhshari, *Kashshaf*, vol. 3, p. 11; Ibn Kathir, *Qisas*, vol. II, p. 393.

97. E.g., Razi, *Tafsir*, vol. 8, p. 46; Baydawi, *Anwar*, vol. 1, p. 155.

98. He adds that the Prophet's daughter Fatima was equally pure, i.e., never defiled, and therefore given the honorific title of *al-Zahra'*, "the Radiant" (or, "Luminous") (*Manar*, vol. 3, p. 300). Cf. below.

99. (Some add that Mary was "purified" from Jewish slander concerning Jesus' birth). Tabari, *Tafsir*, vol. 6, p. 400; Zamakhshari, *Kashshaf*, vol. 1, p. 277; Razi, *Tafsir*, vol. 8, p. 46; Baydawi, *Anwar*, vol. 1, p. 155; Ibn Kathir, *Qisas*, vol. II, p. 374; Abduh and Rida, *Manar*, vol. 3, p. 300. While these theologians clearly define Mary's purity in terms of *'isma*, "sinlessness," which is also the quality Islamic dogma ascribes to God's prophets, the scholars fail to reconsider the issue of Mary's prophethood in this context. The reason, of course, lies with the doctrine of Mary's physical nature as that of ordinary women.

100. Ibn Kathir, *Qisas*, vol. II, pp. 370–371. Ibn Kathir (ibid., p. 461) adds that Satan came to prick Jesus but pricked the *hijab* with which Mary had curtained herself from her people (Sura 19:17).

101. Muhammad Jamal al-Din al-Qasimi, *Tafsir al-Qasimi* (Cairo, 1914) vol. 4, p. 841; and Isma'il Haqqi, (here in reference to Mary, Khadija, Fatima, and Asya), *Tafsir* (n.pl., n.d.) p. 447; both as quoted in Smith and Haddad, "The Virgin Mary in Islamic Tradition," pp. 173 and 179. Farid al-Din al-Attar, famous biographer of Sufi saints, wrote that "attainment of purpose lies not in appearance but in [sincerity of] purpose. . . . Since a woman on the path of God becomes a man, she cannot be called a woman." (Quoted in Reuben Levy, *The Social Structure of Islam* [Cambridge: Cambridge University Press, 1969], p. 132.)

102. Smith and Haddad, "The Virgin Mary in Islamic Tradition," p. 173. To grant women (even holy women) the right to act as prayer leaders for male worshippers is a radical departure from Islamic law that excludes women from this, and other, public functions.

103. Zamakhshari, *Kashshaf*, vol. 1, p. 277; Baydawi, *Anwar*, vol. 1, p. 155; al-Suyuti (d. 1505) (Jalal al-Din Muhammad ibn Ahmad al-Mahalli and Jalal al-Din Abd al-Rahman ibn Abi Bakr al-Suyuti, *Tafsir al-Qur'an al-'azim* [Cairo: Matba'at al-istiqama, n.d.], p. 52). These interpretations must be understood as part of the ongoing medieval debate on whether women should have full access to the mosque for prayer. Razi's opinion may well represent the "liberal" stance in this debate when he interprets 3:43 to mean that "women's emulation of men (in public prayer practices), while being invisible to (screened off from) them, is better than the emulation of women (*sc.* in private prayer)." In other words, women's participation in public prayer was to be condoned as long as they were not visible to the male members of the congregation (*Tafsir*, vol. 8, p. 47).

104. This title does not appear in the Qur'an, but pious Muslims often use it in reference to Mary. Smith and Haddad document that in popular Muslim piety this title is also applied to the Prophet's daughter Fatima ("The Virgin Mary in Islamic Tradition," pp. 179–180).

105. Mary's purification "from the touch of men" (e.g., Razi, *Tafsir*, vol. 8, p. 46) could imply perpetual virginity, but the matter is not fully discussed. Some modern interpreters appear to deny that Mary retained her virginity beyond Jesus' birth (cf. al-Bahi, *Tafsir Surat Maryam*, p. 14).

106. Baljon, *Modern Muslim Koran Interpretation*, pp. 69–70; Parrinder, *Jesus*, pp. 69ff. Smith and Haddad rightly place Sayyid Ahmad Khan's interpretation into the context of "intensive and aggressive Christian missionary activity in India which depicted Jesus as superior to Muhammad, even citing the Qur'an as proof. Thus the denial of virginity, although not in the tradition of Islam, may well be seen as part of the apologetic to defend the faith against its Christian detractors" ("The Virgin Mary in Islamic Tradition," p. 175).

107. Cf. Abduh and Rida, *Manar*, vol. 3, p. 300. Even the Indian Muslim modernist Abu al-Kalam Azad (d. 1958) stated in his *Tarjuman al-Qur'an* (1930) that "the Qur'an accepts the dogma" (of the virgin birth); cited in Baljon, *Modern Muslim Koran Interpretations*, p. 70.

108. Mary knew full well that God has the power to create a child outside of "customary natural processes" (*'ada*), since she knew that He had created Adam from inanimate matter (Razi, *Tafsir*, vol. 21, p. 199; Baydawi, *Anwar*, vol. 1, p. 156).

109. Razi (vol. 21, p. 203) records traditions attributing similar words to Abu Bakr, Umar, and Ali (first, second, and fourth caliphs of Islam), and to the Prophet's

first *mu'adhdhin* ("caller to prayer"), Bilal. It is noteworthy that the interpreters here fail to mention the very similar words of the Prophet's wife A'isha, which she is said to have uttered at the end of her life, i.e. after her involvement in public politics, for which she was much criticized (Cf. below, Part II).

110. Physical modesty, i.e., a sense of "shame at the birth-process" that involves "the uncovering of genitalia," is also reckoned among the factors of Mary's distress, as are the pains of childbirth. (Tabari, *Tafisr*, vol. 16, pp. 50–51; Zamakhshari, *Kashshaf*, vol. 3, p. 9; Razi, *Tafsir*, vol. 21, p. 202; Ibn Kathir, *Qisas*, vol. II, p. 390). The modern exegete Sayyid Qutb explains Mary's words by relating them to her "physical and psychological pain," the perplexion of the virgin who has no knowledge of physical matters, the young woman's fear to confront a censorious society (*Fi zilal al-Qur'an*, vol. 4, p. 2307).

111. Muhammad al-Sayyid Tantawi, *Tafsir Surat Maryam*, p. 35.

112. Zamakhshari, *Kashshaf*, vol. 1, p. 277; Razi, *Tafsir*, vol. 8, pp. 45–46; Baydawi, *Anwar*, vol. 1, 155.

113. Tabari, *Tafsir*, vol. 6, pp. 393–400; Razi, *Tafsir*, vol. 8, pp. 45–46; Ibn Kathir, *Qisas*, vol. II, pp. 375–381; *Manar*, vol. 3, p. 300.

114. Ibn Kathir, *Qisas*, vol. II, pp. 375–383. Moses' sister is here sometimes included among the members of the Prophet's celestial household.

115. The other three were Abraham's wife Sara, the Pharaoh's wife Asya, and Moses' sister. Jane McAuliffe, "Chosen of All Women: Mary and Fatima in Qur'anic Exegesis," *Islamochristiana* VII (1981), pp. 26–27.

116. Mahmoud Ayoub, *Redemptive Suffering in Islam: A Study of the Devotional Aspects of 'Ashura' in Twelver Shiism* (The Hague: Mouton, 1978), p. 50.

117. McAuliffe, "Chosen," pp. 22–23; Ayoub, *Redemptive Suffering*, pp. 70–72, 75. According to some Shi'i thinkers, the quality of virginity was common to both as well; and, indeed, popular piety refers to both Mary and Fatima as *al-batul*, "the Virgin." Since Fatima was married to a husband who fathered her children, virginity in her case has sometimes been defined as freedom from menstruation; McAuliffe (p. 23) quotes a tradition found in an early twelfth-century Shi'i exegesis according to which the Prophet defined virginity in these terms.

118. Ayoub, *Redemptive Suffering*, pp. 27, 30, 39, 48–50.

119. Ibid., p. 35.

120. Louis Massignon, "La notion du voeu," *Studia orientalistica* II, p. 111; and Seyyed Hossein Nasr, *Traditional Islam in the Modern World* (London: Routledge and Kegan Paul, 1987), p. 262; both as quoted in Smith and Haddad, "The Virgin Mary in Islamic Tradition," pp. 180–181.

121. McAuliffe, "Chosen," pp. 23–24, 26–27.

122. Parrinder links these and similar Qur'anic passages on Mary and Jesus with early Christian heresies and heretical practices, especially Adoptionism, Arianism, Patripassianism, and Mariolatry, whose tenets are "as heretical to Christianity as they are to Islam" (*Jesus*, pp. 62–63, 80, 126–141).

123. Ibn Kathir, *Qisas*, vol. II, p. 387.

124. Even though medieval traditions have attributed women's menstruation to Eve's disobedience (cf. above), the Tafsir here considered fails to link the notions of Mary's obedience and purity with Eve's disobedience and its punishment in the form of defilement. It is only in esoteric mysticism that the tetragram of Adam, Eve, Mary, and Jesus, placed into the context of God's selfrevelation, has been said to signify God's forgiveness for the sin of Eve through Mary (Smith and Haddad, "The Virgin Mary in Islamic Tradition," pp. 182–183).

125. Abd al-Mu'izz Khattab, *'Ishrun imra'a fi al-Qur'an al-karim* (Cairo: n.d.), p. 47; as quoted in Smith and Haddad, "The Virgin Mary in Islamic Tradition," p. 166.

126. Sayyid Qutb, *Fi zilal al-Qur'an*, vol. 4, pp. 2305–2306.

127. Qur'an 4:34. Smith and Haddad, "The Virgin Mary in Islamic Tradition," p. 187.

128. Nasr, *Traditional Islam in the Modern World*, p. 262, as quoted in Smith and Haddad, "The Virgin Mary in Islamic Tradition," p. 181.

129. Cf. Smith and Haddad, "The Virgin Mary in Islamic Tradition," p. 161.

130. In science, paradigms are "universally recognized scientific achievements that for a time provide model problems and solutions to a community of practitioners" (Thomas S. Kuhn, *The Structure of Scientific Revolutions* [Chicago: University of Chicago Press, 1962, 2nd ed., 1970], p. viii); paradigmatic adjustment, or paradigmatic shift, occurs when too many observed facts remain "anomalous" (ibid., pp. 52ff).

Chapter 8

1. The theme of their human weaknesses is fully developed in the Hadith; cf. below.

2. As indicated above, personal names occurring in the Qur'anic text are, on the whole, those of prophets; occasionally, figures of the far distant past are also mentioned. Mary the mother of Jesus is the only woman whose name appears in the Qur'an. From among Muhammad's contemporaries, the Qur'an mentions the names of Muhammad's uncle Abu Lahab (denounced together with his wife in Sura 111) and Zayd (ibn Haritha, Muhammad's adopted son, mentioned in 33:37).

3. Narrative source material used in the present segment is mainly culled from the *eighth volume* of the *Kitab al-tabaqat al-kabir* of Ibn Sa'd (d.845). The volume in question, entitled *Fi l-nisa'* ("On the Women") was edited by Carl Brockelmann (Leiden: Brill, 1904). Also consulted were the following works of medieval Qur'an exegesis: Abu Ja'far Muhammad ibn Jarir al-Tabari (d.923), *Jami' al-bayan 'an tafsir 'ay al-Quran*, ed. Mahmud Muhammad Shakir and Ahmad Muhammad Shakir (Cairo: Dar al-ma'arif, 1950s–1969), up to Qur'an 14:27; thereafter, *Jami' al-bayan fi tafsir al-Qur'an* (Beirut: Dar al-ma'rifa, 2d printing, 1972); Mahmud ibn Umar al-Zamakhshari (d.1144), *Kashshaf 'an haqa'iq ghawamid al-tanzil*, ed. Mustafa Husayn Ahmad, (Cairo: Matba'at al-istiqama, 1953); Abdallah ibn Umar al-Baydawi (d.1286?), *Anwar al-tanzil fi asrar al-ta'wil*, ed. H. O. Fleischer; phototypical reproduction, (Osnabrück: Biblio Verlag, 1968); Isma'il ibn Umar Ibn Kathir (d. 1373), *Tafsir al-Qur'an al-'azim*, (Cairo: Dar ihya' al-kutub al-'arabiyya, n.d.). It should here be noted that, in addition to information on the Prophet's wives, the classical Hadith and *tafsir* also contain much material on the Prophet's daughters: Zaynab, Ruqayya, Umm Kulthum, and Fatima. It is Fatima who emerges most prominently in these sources. This is not surprising in view of her status as wife of Ali ibn Abi Talib, mother of Hasan and Husayn, and member of the "holy family" (*ahl al-bayt, al al-bayt*) of, especially, Shi'i and Sufi piety and doctrine. While Fatima's role in Sunni Hadith and *tafsir* is important, it is even greater in Shi'i literature, which interprets a sizeable number of Qur'anic verses as revealed on account of, and specifically concerning, Fatima.

4. Cf. below.

5. Cf. Ibn Sa'd, *Nisa'* pp. 156–159; Tabari, *Tafsir*, vol. 22, pp. 15–18; Zamakhshari, *Kashshaf*, vol. 3, pp. 434–436; Baydawi, *Anwar*, vol. 2, p. 132; Ibn Kathir, *Tafsir*, vol. 3, pp. 498–500.

6. Muhammad Husayn Haykal, *The Life of Muhammad*, translated from the eighth

edition by Isma'il R. al-Faruqi (Indianapolis: North American Trust Publications, 1976), p. 293.

7. Sura 4:3 is generally dated soon after the battle of Uhud (third year hijra), several years before revelation of Sura 33:50. In her historical analysis of Sura 4:3 as a piece of legislation to "regularize" the institution of marriage in Islam, Gertrude H. Stern conversely stipulates that the Prophet had four wives, and not more, at the time of the revelation of 4:3. He later added others to this number in order to provide support for widows of slain Muslim warriors, thereby also setting an example for his community (*Marriage in Early Islam* [London: The Royal Asiatic Society, 1939], pp. 78–81). In similar fashion, Rudi Paret has understood this verse not as limitation of polygamous unions at four but as a call to the men of the community to conclude additional marriages in order to provide for the young women in their care who were orphaned by the war (*Schriften zum Islam*, ed. Josef van Ess [Stuttgart: W. Kohlhammer, 1981], pp. 43–49).

8. E.g., Zamakhshari (*Kashshaf*, vol. 3, p. 430, in exegesis of 33:38) indicates that by God's "law," or "custom" (*sunnat Allah*) David had 100 wives and 300 concubines, while Solomon had 300 wives and 700 concubines.

9. The technical term for this form of marriage is *hiba*. On the women who "gave themselves to the Prophet," cf. Ibn Sa'd, *Nisa'* pp. 98, 100–113, 145, 158; Ibn Hisham's notes to Ibn Ishaq, in *The Life of Muhammad*, A. Guillaume, transl. (London: Oxford University Press, 1955), p. 794; Tabari, *Tafsir*, vol. 22, pp. 15–18; Zamakhshari, *Kashshaf*, vol. 3, pp. 434–436; Baydawi, *Anwar*, vol. 2, p. 132; Ibn Kathir, *Tafsir*, vol. 3, pp. 498–500. On the practice of *hiba*, cf. below.

10. (Emphasis added). Perhaps because of the late date of this revelation in the Prophet's life and, especially, in consideration of the fact that it was vouchsafed after Muhammad had married all of his wives, classical exegetes have found in this verse more than the divine directive on the Prophet's right to unrestricted polygamy. All classical interpreters emphasize that this verse also entails God's permission (exclusively for the Prophet) to marry "a believing woman who offered herself" to him. This verse and its interpretations are considered more fully below.

11. Cf. Ibn Sa'd, *Nisa'*, pp. 8–11, 35–100, 156–159; Ibn Hisham's "Notes" in Ibn Ishaq's *Life*, pp. 792–794; Tabari, *Tafsir*, vol. 21, p. 99 and vol. 22, p. 21; Zamakhshari, *Kashshaf*, vol. 3, pp. 436–437; Ibn Kathir, *Tafsir*, vol. 3, pp. 481, 499, 500. Also Nabia Abbott, *Aishah—The Beloved of Mohammad* (Chicago: University of Chicago Press, 1942; 2d ed. London: Al Saqi Books, 1985), pp. 3–81 in the 2d ed.; W. Montgomery Watt, *Muhammad at Medina* (Oxford: Clarendon, 1956, lithographical reprint Oxford: Oxford University Press, 1962), pp. 393–399; Sa'id Harun Ashur, *Nisa' al-nabi* (Cairo: Matba'at al-Qahira al-haditha, n.d.), pp.1–171 passim. According to Ibn Hisham (who does not consider Rayhana a wife) the Prophet married thirteen women: "there were six Quraysh women among the Prophet's wives, namely, Khadija, A'isha, Hafsa, Umm Habiba, Umm Salama, and Sawda; the Arab women and others were seven, namely Zaynab bint Jahsh, Maymuna, Zaynab bint Khuzayma, Juwayriyya, Asma', and Amra; the non-Arab woman was Safiyya bint Huyay" (Ibn Ishaq, *Life*, p. 794). When Rayhana is included, the number rises to fourteen. Three of them (Khadija, Zaynab bint Khuzayma, and Rayhana) died while the Prophet was alive; he separated from Asma' and Amra; he died while being married to nine (Ibn Sa'd, *Nisa'*, p. 159).

12. The Prophet married Khadija when he was about twenty-five years old and she was in her early forties. He lived with her in monogamous marriage until her death some twenty-five years later. Khadija bore the Prophet two sons (al-Qasim and Abdallah

al-Tahir al-Mutahhar, both of whom died in infancy) and four daughters (Zaynab, Ruqayya, Umm Kulthum, and Fatima). The Prophet had no children with his other wives, but had a son, Ibrahim, from his concubine Marya the Copt. Ibrahim died when he was two years old.

13. E.g., Ibn Sa'd, *Nisa'*, pp. 100–107; Ibn Hisham's "Notes" in Ibn Ishaq's *Life*, p. 794. Cf. Watt, *Muhammad*, pp. 397–399.

14. Ibn Sa'd, *Nisa'*, pp. 108–115. Cf. Watt, *Muhammad*, p. 399.

15. The women identified in the sources as having engaged in *hiba* to the Prophet, and to whom these words are said to refer, are: Umm Sharik al-Asadiyya, or Ghaziya bint Jabir (who may be one and the same) (Ibn Sa'd, *Nisa'*, pp. 110–111, and Ibn Hisham's "Notes" in Ibn Ishaq's *Life*, p. 794). Other traditions link the verse with Maymuna bint al-Harith (or, al-Harth), or Zaynab bint Jahsh (Ibn Hisham's "Notes" in Ibn Ishaq's *Life*, p. 794). Additional names put forth in Qur'anic exegesis are those of Zaynab bint Khuzayma "mother of the destitute (*umm al-masakin*)" and Khawla bint Hakim ibn al-Awqas of the Banu Sulaym (Tabari, *Tafsir*, vol. 22, p. 17; Zamakhshari, *Kashshaf*, vol. 3, pp. 434–435; Baydawi, *Anwar*, vol. 2, p. 132; Ibn Kathir, *Tafsir*, vol. 3, pp. 499–500. Cf. Watt, *Muhammad*, pp. 398–399).

16. According to Ibn Sa'd and Ibn Hisham, Marya came from Hafn in the province of Ansina (or Ansa), i.e., she hailed from a place located on the east bank of the Nile in Upper Egypt (Ibn Sa'd, *Nisa'*, pp. 153–156; Ibn Hisham's "Notes" in Ibn Ishaq's *Life*, p. 691). Ibn Sa'd reports that Marya was sent to the Prophet as a gift from al-Muqawqas, "ruler of Alexandria, together with her sister, one thousand *mithqal* of gold, twenty robes, a mule, a donkey, and an old eunuch who was her brother. This occurred in the year seven after the hijra" (p. 153). Al-Muqawqas is the Islamic name for Cyrus, last Byzantine patriarch and ruler of Egypt who surrendered to the Muslim troops led by Amr ibn al-As (Cf. Gustav Weil, *Geschichte der Chalifen*, vol. I [Mannheim: Bassermann, 1846], pp. 105, 109–111, 121; and Christopher S. Taylor, "Sacred History and the Cult of Muslim Saints," *The Muslim World*, vol. 80, no. 2 [1990], p. 77).

17. Ibn Sa'd, *Nisa'*, p. 71. Qur'anic exegesis sometimes links the revelation of Sura 33:36 ["No believing man nor believing woman, when God and His Apostle have decided upon a matter, has the right to choose in (this) their matter. Who disobeys God and His Apostle is in manifest error"] with Zaynab's opposition to this marriage to Zayd.

18. During the fifth year after the hijra.

19. Ibn Sa'd, *Nisa'*, pp. 71–72.

20. Tabari, *Tafsir*, vol. 22, pp. 10–11; also his *Tarikh al-rusul wal-muluk*, vol. 2, ed. Muhammad Abu al-Fadl Ibrahim (Cairo: Dar al-ma'arif, 1961), pp. 562–563.

21. Tabari, *Tafsir*, vol. 22, pp. 10–11; cf. also Zamakhshari, *Kashshaf*, vol. 3, pp. 427–430; Baydawi, *Anwar*, vol. 2, pp. 129–130.

22. Ibn Kathir, *Tafsir*, vol. 3, p. 491.

23. E.g., Ibn Sa'd, *Nisa'*, p. 72.

24. *Tafsir*, vol. 22, pp. 10–11.

25. *Kashshaf*, vol. 3, pp. 428–429.

26. I.e., the divine legislation on the status of adopted sons of Sura 33:37, cf. below.

27. *Tafsir*, vol. 3, p. 491.

28. Tabari, *Tafsir*, vol. 22, p. 10; Ibn Kathir, *Tafsir*, vol. 3, p. 491.

29. Ibn Sa'd, *Nisa'*, 73; Zamakhshari, *Kashshaf*, vol. 3, p. 427; Baydawi, *Anwar*, vol. 2, p. 130; Ibn Kathir, *Tafsir*, vol. 3, pp. 491 and 505.

30. E.g., Baydawi, *Anwar*, vol. 2, p. 130.

31. Ibn Sa'd, *Nisa'*, p. 73; Zamakhshari, *Kashshaf*, vol. 3, p. 427; Ibn Kathir, *Tafsir*, vol. 3, p. 491.

32. Ibn Sa'd, *Nisa'*, pp. 71–82; Tabari, *Tafsir*, vol. 21, pp. 74–76 and vol. 22, pp. 12–13; Zamakhshari, *Kashshaf*, vol. 3, pp. 411–412 and 430; Baydawi, *Anwar*, vol. 2, pp. 122 and 130; Ibn Kathir, *Tafsir*, vol. 3, pp. 465–466 and 492. While 33:40 thus established that "Muhammad is not the father of any of your men," 33:6 later proclaimed his wives as "the believers' mothers." Stipulated in these strikingly parallel but contrastive revelations are 1. the permission for the Prophet to marry Zaynab and 2. the prohibition of any later (re)-marriage for any of the Prophet's established wives (legislated in 33:53); cf. below.

33. *Tafsir*, vol. 3, p. 492.

34. Cf. Fatima Mernissi, *The Veil and the Male Elite*, Mary Jo Lakeland, transl. (Reading: Addison-Wesley, 1991), pp. 110ff. (Hereafter quoted as *Veil*.)

35. Cf. Qur'an 33:59–60.

36. Mernissi, *Veil*, pp. 105ff, 170ff.

37. The term *hijab* occurs seven times in the Qur'an. In chronological sequence of revelation, the verses are: 19:17; 38:32; 17:45; 41:5; 42:51; 7:46; 33:53. In three instances, the term has metaphorical meaning, twice the meaning of a concrete object of visual separation, and once, in an eschatological context, which has been interpreted as a mixture of the two. The concept of *hijab*, therefore, involves both the concrete and the metaphorical, whence it developed to connote both the concrete and also the abstract (Cf. Stern, *Marriage*, p. 118). In some instances, though not in all, later uses of the term *hijab* derive from these Qur'anic bases (*Encylopedia of Islam*, 2d. ed., vol. III, pp. 359–361). Shared semantic theme of most of the meanings of *hijab* is the concept of "separation", most commonly in the sense of a (desirable) protection or an (undesirable) obstacle, which are either concrete, metaphorical, or abstract. The dictionary gives examples of *hijab* as a concrete protective device in a number of membranes by that name in the body, such as *al-hijab al-hajiz* (or, *hijab al-jawf*), "diaphragm"; *al-hijab al-mustabtin*, "*pleura*" (Ibn Manzur, d. 1311/12 A.D., *Lisan al-'Arab* [Beirut: Dar Sadir, 15 vols., 1955–1956], vol. 1, pp. 289–290). A related meaning, even though involving the concrete as well as the abstract, inheres in the *hijab* as "a supra-terrestrial protection, in fact an amulet . . . which renders its wearer invulnerable and ensures success for his enterprises" (*Encylopedia of Islam*, 2d. ed.,vol. III, p. 361). At the same time, the *hijab* in a metaphorical sense can be an obstacle to union, communion, indeed, comprehension of and participation in the truth. In the language of the mystics, the *hijab* is that painful barrier between man and God which, rooted in man's sensual or mental passion, conceals the truth and impedes man's progress toward God (Ibid., vol III, p. 361). Lastly, the *hijab* is both the concrete means to segregate an individual or a group of individuals from society at large, and also the abstract institution of such segregation. In medieval royal circles, the *hijab* was the curtain behind which the ruler was hidden from the eyes of courtiers and commoners alike. This practice, first documented for the Umayyads and Abbasids, later became part of an elaborate system of court ceremonials of, especially, the Fatimids (Ibid., vol. III, pp. 360–361). While the custom of screening-off was unknown among the Prophet and his four rightly guided (*rashidun*) successors, it is here divinely legislated for the female elite of the first Medinan community, the Prophet's wives.

38. Ibn Sa'd, *Nisa'*, pp. 74–75, 81–82, 124–125; Tabari, *Tafsir*, vol. 22, p. 26; Zamakhshari, *Kashshaf*, vol. 3, p. 437; Ibn Kathir, *Tafsir*, vol. 3, pp. 503–504; also Abbott, *Aishah*, pp. 20–24, and Mernissi, *Veil*, pp. 85ff.

39. Ibn Sa'd, *Nisa'*, p. 74.

40. Ibid., p. 126; also Tabari, *Tafsir*, vol. 22, p. 28; Zamakhshari, *Kashshaf*, vol. 3, p. 439; Baydawi, *Anwar*, vol. 2, 134; Ibn Kathir, *Tafsir*, vol. 3, p. 505.

41. Tabari, *Tafsir*, vol. 22, pp. 27–28; Zamakhshari, *Kashshaf*, vol. 3, pp. 438–439; Baydawi, *Anwar*, vol. 2, p. 134; Ibn Kathir, *Tafsir*, vol. 3, pp. 503 and 505.

42. Tabari, *Tafsir*, vol. 22, p. 28; Zamakhshari, *Kashshaf*, vol. 3, pp. 438–439; Baydawi, *Anwar*, vol. 2, p. 134.

43. Baydawi, *Anwar*, vol. 2, p. 134; Ibn Kathir, *Tafsir*, vol. 3, p. 503.

44. While the revelation of the bulk of the *hijab* verse is generally dated in the fifth year after the hijra, its last sentence containing the prohibition of marriage with Muhammad's wives "after him" is said to have been revealed in the ninth year after the hijra, i.e., toward the end of the Prophet's life. Cf. Abbott, *Aishah*, pp. 20–21, 57; also cf. below.

45. Paternal and maternal uncles do not belong in this "exempt" group. Traditionists agree that the term "their women" refers to free believing (Muslim) women and implies the permission to show *zina* ("embellishment," i.e., the head, including the hair, also hands and feet) in their presence, but nothing more (Tabari, *Tafsir*, vol. 22, pp. 30–31; Baydawi, *Anwar*, vol. 2, p. 134; Ibn Kathir, *Tafsir*, vol. 3, p. 506). They differ on the meaning of "what their right hands possess (slaves)." For some, female and male slaves alike are included here (Tabari, *Tafsir*, vol. 22, p. 31; Baydawi, *Anwar*, vol. 2, p. 134; Ibn Kathir, *Tafsir*, vol. 3, p. 506), while others apply the term to female slaves only (Ibn Kathir, *Tafsir*, vol 3, p. 506). Rudi Paret quotes Dirk Bakker's interpretation of "their women" as female slaves (*Man in the Qur'an*, [Amsterdam, 1965], p. 80 n. 89), and "their slaves" as male slaves (*Der Koran: Kommentar und Konkordanz* [Stuttgart: W. Kohlhammer, 2d printing, 1981] p. 401). It is noteworthy that, unlike Sura 24:31 addressed to "the female believers" in general (cf. below), 33:55 does not mention "husband, husband's father, and husband's sons" among the exempt categories. This textual feature of 33:55, according to some Muslim modernists, proves that the *hijab* verse and its exemptions were addressed to, and made obligatory for, only the Prophet's household in that Muhammad's father and his sons had died, and Muhammad himself, the husband, "was already mentioned" in this revelation. (Aftab Hussain, *Status of Women in Islam* [Lahore: Law Publishing Co., 1987], p. 151).

46. E.g., Ibn Sa'd, *Nisa'*, pp. 84, 91, 93.

47. *Veil*, pp. 85ff, 162ff. Conservative and fundamentalist Muslims will here reject Mernissi's historicist interpretation and also her conclusion that his women's segregation was merely the sacrifice Muhammad had to offer to the opposition in order to save the community of Islam. Modernists will agree with Mernissi's approach that segregation (and veiling, and other Qur'anic social laws) were decreed for the Medinan community and are now open for reinterpretation; but unlike Mernissi, Muslim modernists do emphasize the divine origin and nature of the Qur'an whose verses, then, are much more than mere records of historical political necessity. Cf. below.

48. Ibn Sa'd, *Nisa'*, p. 126.

49. This Qur'anic verse indicates both that the veil as head cover was known in Arabian society, and also that its wearing was the mark of women of social stature. Its imposition upon the Prophet's wives, daughters, and "the women of the believers" thus marks them as members of the new elite.

50. On these items, cf. R. P. A. Dozy, *Dictionnaire détaillé des noms de vêtements ches les Arabes* (Beirut: Librairie du Liban, 1969; photomechanical reproduction of Amsterdam: Jean Muller, 1845); *s.v.*

51. Cf. Ahmed, *Women and Gender in Islam* (New Haven: Yale University Press, 1992), pp. 79–101.

52. Ibn Ishaq, *Life*, pp. 310–311.

53. Darwish Mustafa Hasan, *Fasl al-khitab fi mas'alat al-hijab wal-niqab* (Cairo: Dar al-i'tisam, 1987), p. 51.

54. E.g., Tabari, *Tafsir*, vol. 18, pp. 93ff.

55. Tabari founded his own, short-lived *madhhab* called *Ja'fari*. Tabari opposed Ahmad ibn Hanbal in the capacity of jurist, i.e., as authority on *fiqh*, but recognized him as a traditionist, i.e., authority on hadith. Consequently, his relations with the supporters of Ahmad ibn Hanbal were strained.

56. Cf. Tabari, *Tafsir*, vol. 18, pp. 92–98, in exegesis of Qur'an 24:31.

57. Baydawi, *Anwar*, vol. 2, p. 20, in exegesis of Qur'an 24:31.

58. Ahmad ibn Muhammad al-Khafaji, *Hashiyat al-Shihab al-musamma bi-Inayat al-qadi wa-kifayat al-radi 'ala tafsir al-Baydawi* (Beirut: Dar Sadir, 1974), vol. 6, pp. 371–373.

59. For greater detail on this medieval exegetic debate, cf. Barbara Freyer Stowasser, "The Status of Women in Early Islam," in: *Muslim Women*, ed. Freda Hussain (London: Croom Helm, 1984), pp. 25–28.

60. Ibn Sa'd, *Nisa'*, pp. 11, 39–42, 44–45, 52–54. The betrothal occurred in the same year as Khadija's death. The Prophet first married Sawda, with whom he consummated the marriage while still in Mecca; he asked for A'isha's hand one month after the marriage with Sawda. A'isha is said to have been fifty years younger than the Prophet. She was eighteen years old when he died. Her death is said to have occurred in 678/9 A.D. at age sixty-six.

61. This detail is generally taken as proof that the "affair of the lie" occurred after the revelation of 33:53 had made the *hijab* obligatory for the Prophet's wives.

62. Ibn Ishaq, *Life*, pp. 493–499. Ibn Ishaq indicates that his account is based on various reports originating with A'isha and later assembled by al-Zuhri. These traditions also appear in Tabari, *Tafsir*, vol. 18, pp. 68–84; Zamakhshari, *Kashshaf*, vol. 3, pp. 171–177; Baydawi, *Anwar*, vol. 2, pp. 16–19; Ibn Kathir, *Tafsir*, vol. 3, pp. 268–278. (It is curious that these events are not related by Ibn Sa'd in his chapter on A'isha). Cf. also Abbott, *Aishah*, pp. 29–38. Among additional details reported by Ibn Ishaq is a hadith on the authority of A'isha that "the people found Ibn al-Mu'attal impotent . . . he never touched women . . . he was killed as a martyr after this" (p. 499). Ibn Sa'd relates that at the end of her life A'isha deeply regretted her role in this affair and also in the Battle of the Camel (during which she exhorted the forces opposing Ali ibn Abi Talib to fight, while the battle surged around her camel). A'isha is reported to have passed her last days in selfrecrimination (Ibn Sa'd, *Nisa'*, pp. 51–52). On both occurrences in relation to the classical Islamic doctrine of A'isha's model status, cf. below.

63. *Veil*, p. 163.

64. Canon law cases with unalterable punishments.

65. On the negative connotation of the term *zina* ("finery", "adornment") in the Qur'an, cf. Paret, *Der Koran: Kommentar*, pp. 44–45.

66. Theodor Nöldeke dates these verses into the end of the fifth year after the hijra (*Geschichte des Qorans* [Dritter reprographischer Nachdruck der 2. Auflage, Leipzig 1909–1938; Hildesheim: Georg Olms Verlag, 1981], vol. I, p. 207). The same dating is proposed by Stern who associates the "crisis" with the newly restrictive lifestyle imposed upon the Prophet's consorts by way of the *hijab* (33:53) (*Marriage*, p. 114ff.) Abbott places the revelation between years seven and nine after the hijra, mainly in consideration of the fact that the Coptic concubine Marya is said to have joined the Prophet's household in the seventh year after the hijra, and also because the tradi-

tions pertaining to the "crisis" mention the threat of a Ghassanid invasion (which, in turn, led to the Prophet's expedition to Tabuk in the ninth year after the hijra) (*Aishah*, p. 51). Classical Muslim exegesis here provides ample background materials of the "occasion for revelation" genre, but does not suggest a date for the revelations; cf. Ibn Sa'd, *Nisa'*, pp. 123–124, 129–39; Tabari, *Tafsir*, vol. 21, pp. 99–101; Zamakhshari, *Kashshaf*, vol. 3, pp. 422–423; Baydawi, *Anwar*, vol. 2, p. 127; Ibn Kathir, *Tafsir*, vol. 3, pp. 480–481 and vol. 4, pp. 385–390.

67. Cf. below under 66:1–5.

68. Ibn Sa'd, *Nisa'*, pp. 117, 123–124, 129–139. Cf. also Abbott, *Aishah*, pp. 48–56.

69. Beating of (potentially) rebellious wives was sanctioned in Qur'an 4:34, a later revelation but one which the Prophet is said to never have heeded.

70. Ibn Sa'd, *Nisa'*, pp. 129, 137; Tabari, *Tafsir*, vol. 21, p. 99.

71. Ibn Sa'd, *Nisa'*, p. 132; Ibn Kathir, *Tafsir*, vol. 3, p. 481.

72. One tribal woman reportedly left the prophet at this time (Ibn Sa'd, *Nisa'*, pp. 100–102, 137). Tabari (*Tafsir*, vol. 21, p. 100) only identifies her as "a Bedouin woman". Cf. Watt, *Muhammad*, p. 367. Abbot (*Aishah*, p. 52) observes that this woman, "with whom Mohammed was contracting a marriage supposedly in the Year 8, elected to leave him at the time of 'the choice.' Unfortunately, however, . . . the . . . traditions can be questioned, . . . because (one) is a singleton tradition and the (other) because of some uncertainty as to the identity of the woman in question and as to the real motive of her separation from Mohammed."

73. Tabari, *Tafsir*, vol. 21, pp. 100–101; Zamakhshari, *Kashshaf*, vol. 3, p. 422; Baydawi, *Anwar*, vol. 2, p. 127; Ibn Kathir, *Tafsir*, vol. 3, pp. 480–481.

74. Late in year five after the hijra according to Nöldeke (*Geschichte*, vol. I, p. 207), or during year seven, eight, or nine after the hijra according to Abbott (*Aishah*, pp. 56–57).

75. For the exegesis of these verses, cf. Tabari, *Tafsir*, vol. 21, p. 101, and vol. 22, pp. 203; Zamakhshari, *Kashshaf*, vol. 3, pp. 423–424; Baydawi, *Anwar*, vol. 2, p. 127; Ibn Kathir, *Tafsir*, vol. 3, pp. 481–482. All commentators agree that such punishment and reward will be meted out in the hereafter. They disagree on what would constitute for these women "clear abomination/manifest immoral behavior." Tabari (*Tafsir*, vol. 21, p. 101) identifies it as "a clear [or: proven] act of fornication." The Mu'tazilite Zamakhshari (*Kashshaf*, vol. 3, pp. 423–424) interprets the term as involving "all of their major sins" (*kaba'ir*), and also (specifically) their acts of ingratitude and rebellion against the Prophet, including their demands for the wealth which he was not able to provide. Thus, Zamakhshari opts against the meaning of "fornication" . . . "because God exempted the Prophet from this" (i.e., by providing him with virtuous and blameless wives). Ibn Kathir (vol. 3, p. 481) proposes "rebellion" (*nushuz*, cf. Sura 4:34) and "bad-temperedness," but is careful to point out that such behavior was contrary to these women's natures. On the other hand, the exegetes agree that the "working of righteousness" mentioned in 33:31 must be understood to mean: the women's efforts to create marital harmony and contentment, including frugality on their part.

76. Legal and theological doctrine decreed the application to all Muslim women of all but one of the Qur'anic restrictions imposed upon the Prophet's wives (the exception being prohibition of remarriage after the husband's death). Inspite of the specific wording of 33:32, then, interpreters have agreed that by this verse all Muslim women have been forbidden to use that "soft, effeminate [manner of] speech of the prostitutes" (or else, "that mellow tone of voice reserved only for the husband"); cf. Tabari, *Tafsir*, vol. 22, p. 3; Zamakhshari, *Kashshaf*, vol. 3, p. 424; Baydawi, *Anwar*, vol. 2, p. 128; Ibn Kathir, *Tafsir*, vol. 3, p. 482.

77. I.e., their textual location immediately subsequent to 33:30–32 (three verses explicitly addressed to "the Prophet's women").

78. Here it is only the *ahl al-bayt* clause of 33:33 that has consistently presented a problem for (especially the Sunni) Qur'anic interpreters, because of the large number of available trustworthy traditions according to which the Prophet is said to have excluded his wives from the *ahl al-bayt*; cf. below.

79. *wa-qarna fi buyutikunna*, "and stay in your houses": The exegesis indicates that the established reading of the second person feminine plural *wa-qarna* presents a grammatical problem, because the correct imperative form of *qarra/yaqarru* or *qarra/yaqirru* ("stay put in a place") would be *wa-qrarna* or *wa-qrirna*. Therefore, interpreters have proposed that the verb here employed may be *waqara/yaqiru* ("to behave with dignity/stay quietly, sedately in a place"); even so, the feminine plural imperative form would then be *wa-qirna*. In the end, however, the classical interpreters' lengthy grammatical explanations do not affect or override scholarly consensus 1. that the meaning of this imperative is "stay, remain," and 2. that it applies to all Muslim women (Tabari, *Tafsir*, vol. 22, pp. 3–4; Zamakhshari, *Kashshaf*, vol. 3, p. 425; Baydawi, *Anwar*, vol. 2, p. 12). Modernists attempting to prove that the Qur'an did *not* legislate the duty of female seclusion in the home *even* for the Prophet's wives have, on occasion, proposed to understand the *wa-qarna* as derived from *qara/yaqaru* ("to walk noiselessly on the toes, or the sides of the feet—so as to avoid the seductive jingle of anklets"), a reading already suggested by Baydawi (*Anwar*, vol. 2, p. 128) and which would be the only grammatically correct one. Cf. Nazira Zayn al-Din, *al-Sufur wal-hijab: muhadarat wa-nazarat* (Beirut: n.p., 1345/1928), pp. 180ff. The question remains, however, why women would be commanded "to creep around in their own homes" (Afaf Marsot's comment on this interpretation as quoted in my manuscript).

80. On *tabarruj*, see also Qur'an 24:60.

81. *al-jahiliyya al-ula*, the "former," or "first," or "foremost" *jahiliyya*. Exegesis here stipulates that this term has a contrastive meaning, i.e., that it must imply the existence of a "latter," or "second," *jahiliyya*. Some traditions place both periods into the pre-Muhammadan past (e.g., the "first" between Adam and Noah, or David and Solomon, etc., the "second" between Jesus and Muhammad). Preferred, however, is the interpretation of "the former *jahiliyya*" as the period of sinfulness before the rise of Islam, while its equivalent, "the latter *jahiliyya*," is believed to refer to the superstitions, pagan customs, iniquity and immorality that have crept into Islam since its foundation. (Tabari, *Tafsir*, vol. 22, pp. 4–5; Zamakhshari, *Kashshaf*, vol. 3, p. 425; Baydawi, *Anwar*, vol. 2, p. 128; Ibn Kathir, *Tafsir*, vol. 3, p. 438) As pointed out above, it is in this latter meaning that the concept of *jahiliyya* is used by contemporary Muslim thinkers, especially the fundamentalists among them.

82. As indicated above, the "you" here is in the second form masculine plural. Shi'i interpretation, also Sufi teaching and piety understand under *ahl al-bayt* (33:33, also 11:73) the "people of the mantle," that is, the Prophet, Ali, Fatima, Hasan, and Husayn; especially in Shi'ite belief, the latters' descendents are also included. The "purification" mentioned in 33:33 is thus often understood to mean that God purified Ali, Fatima, and their descendents, so that they share in the Prophet's *'isma* (immunity from sin) and thus are "more entitled" (*ahaqqu*), i.e., to guide and rule the Muslim community. The majority of traditions quoted by the classical Qur'an interpreters here considered *exclude* the Prophet's wives from membership in the *ahl al-bayt*. Nevertheless, the interpreters themselves (all of them Sunnis) either *opine* to include the wives, together with the Prophet's bloodrelatives, or even state their individual *opinion* that the term *ahl al-bayt* was directed exclusively at the Prophet's wives, "as established by the con-

text of the revelation" (Tabari, *Tafsir,* vol. 22, pp. 5–8; Zamakhshari, *Kashshaf,* vol. 3, p. 425; Baydawi, *Anwar,* vol. 2, p. 128; Ibn Kathir, *Tafsir,* vol. 3, pp. 483–486). A. Yusuf Ali follows the middle course when he says that "the statement in this clause is now more general, including (besides the Consorts) the whole family, namely, Hadhrat Fatima the daughter, Hadhrat Ali the son-in-law, and their sons Hasan and Husain, the beloved grandsons of the Prophet. . . ." (*The Holy Qur'an: Text, Translation and Commentary* [Washington D.C.: The Islamic Center, 1978], pp. 1115–1116). Rudi Paret interprets along similar lines, but also adds another, more original and also more inclusive reading of the *ahl al-bayt* clause when he says: "Mit den 'Leuten des Hauses' sind entweder die Angehörigen der Familie Mohammeds gemeint, oder die 'Leute des Gotteshauses', d.h. die Anhänger des in der Ka'ba symbolisierten Gottesglaubens" (*Der Koran: Übersetzung* [Stuttgart: W. Kohlhammer, 3d printing, 1983], p.295); cf. his exegesis of *ahl al-bayt* in Sura 11:73 in *Der Koran: Kommentar,* pp. 239–240.

83. *hikma,* "wisdom": Zamakhshari (*Kashshaf,* vol. 3, p. 425) identifies *hikma* as "the sciences and laws (of religion)," Baydawi (*Anwar,* vol. 2, p. 128) as "the content of the Qur'an;" cf. Paret's definition of *hikma* as "content of the revelation" (*Der Koran: Kommentar,* p. 68). Tabari (*Tafsir,* vol. 22, p. 8) and Ibn Kathir (*Tafsir,* vol. 3, p. 486) aptly sum up medieval legal theory when they identify *ayat* with the Qur'an, and *hikma* with "*the* (prophetic) *sunna.*"

84. Tabari, *Tafsir,* vol. 22, p. 4; Zamakhshari, *Kashshaf,* vol. 3, p. 425; Baydawi, *Anwar,* vol. 2, p. 128; Ibn Kathir, *Tafsir,* vol. 3, pp. 482–483.

85. Ibn Kathir, *Tafsir,* vol. 3, pp. 482–483.

86. Ni'mat Sidqi, *al-Tabarruj* (Cairo: Dar al-I'tisam, 1975), pp. 1–62 passim. This small treatise is very popular in Islamist circles and is available in a large number of editions.

87. Cf., e.g., Tabari, *Tafsir,* vol. 22, pp. 3–4; Zamakhshari, *Kashshaf,* vol. 3, p. 425; Baydawi, *Anwar,* vol. 2, p. 12.

88. E.g., Ibn Kathir, *Tafsir,* vol. 3, p. 482.

89. Some classical Qur'anic exegetes opine that the "verse of choice" (33:28–29) represented the option of divorce by the Prophet and remarriage with another man for those of the Prophet's wives who would have chosen "the world and its adornment" (Baydawi, *Anwar,* vol. 2, p. 127; Ibn Kathir, *Tafsir,* vol. 3, pp. 480–481). Therefore, revelation of 33:6 and the last sentence of 33:53 is said to have occured later than the revelation of 33:28–29. Abbott argues likewise when she notes that "in connection with the harem crisis (i.e., the Prophet's month-long separation from his wives), Mohammed's wives are referred to generally as his 'wives' or his 'women' and not as the 'Mothers of the Believers.' It is highly improbable that they had before then acquired that title and dignity and, as most commentators believe, the consequent prohibition of remarriage even after Mohammed's death. . . . The 'Verse of Choice' means nothing at all if it does not mean that those who 'desired the world and its adornment' were free to marry again after being divorced from Mohammed. The title and the prohibition were most probably more closely associated with the harem crisis than with the earlier occasion of the institution of the *hijab,* or seclusion. . . ." (*Aishah,* p. 57).

90. The Hadith reflects debate on this point when it reports that A'isha refused to be addressed as "mother" by a woman, saying: "I am not your mother, I am the mother of your menfolk" (Ibn Sa'd, *Nisa',* p. 46), while Umm Salama is reported to have said: "I am the mother of the men among you and also the women" (Ibn Sa'd, *Nisa',* p. 128). According to scholarly consensus expressed in Qur'anic exegesis on the "nature of motherhood" of the Prophet's wives, this honorific title means that: (1) their group must be exalted and honored by both male and also female Muslims,

"as mothers are," and (2) marriage with them is forbidden. In all other respects, they are like nonrelatives, and the injunction against marriage does not extend to their sisters or their daughters (Tabari, *Tafsir*, vol. 21, p. 77; Zamakhshari, *Kashshaf*, vol. 3, p. 414; Baydawi, *Anwar*, vol. 2, p. 123; Ibn Kathir, *Tafsir*, vol. 3, pp. 468–469).

91. Ibn Sa'd, *Nisa'*, p. 145. As it was, Talha ibn Ubaydallah eventually married A'isha's younger half-sister whose hand A'isha had previously refused to Umar ibn al-Khattab "because of his well-known severity toward the women, his own wives included" (Abbott, *Aishah*, pp. 59–60).

92. *Veil*, pp. 170–171.

93. Tabari, *Tafsir*, vol. 22, pp. 29–30; Zamakhshari, *Kashshaf*, vol. 3, p. 439; Baydawi, *Anwar*, vol. 2, p. 134; Ibn Kathir, *Tafsir*, vol. 3, p. 506.

94. Nöldeke places the events connected with 66:1–5 "before Ibrahim's birth" (which reportedly occcurred in the eighth year after the hijra) (*Geschichte*, vol. I, p. 208); Abbott's dates for this revelation are year seven, eight, or nine after the hijra (*Aishah*, pp. 59–60). Richard Bell has suggested that 66:5 ("threat of divorce and enumeration of wifely virtues") originally had the place of 33:35 ("enumeration of Islamic virtues in men and women, and their reward"), and vice versa (*The Moslem World*, vol. 29 (1939), p. 55, as quoted in Paret, *Der Koran: Kommentar*, pp. 400 and 482). That location would put the "threat of divorce" of 66:5 into close proximity with the "restriction" verses presented above. As indicated above, some medieval traditionists and exegetes have identified the events addressed in 66:1–5 with the "crisis" that led to the "verse of choice" of 33:28–29 (Cf. Ibn Sa'd, *Nisa'*, pp. 129–139; Tabari, *Tafsir*, vol. 28, pp. 100–106; Zamakhshari, *Kashshaf*, vol. 4, pp. 450–451; Ibn Kathir, *Tafsir*, vol. 4, pp. 385–390).

95. The form of address here is in the second person masculine plural.

96. Second person feminine plural.

97. Ibn Sa'd, *Nisa'*, p. 145; Tabari, *Tafsir*, vol. 28, pp. 100–102; Zamakhshari, *Kashshaf*, vol. 4, pp. 450–451; Baydawi, *Anwar*, vol. 2, pp. 340–341; Ibn Kathir, *Tafsir*, vol. 4, p. 386.

98. Tabari, *Tafsir*, vol. 28, p. 102; Zamakhshari, *Kashshaf*, vol. 4, p. 451; Ibn Kathir, *Tafsir*, vol. 4, p. 387.

99. Baydawi, *Anwar*, vol. 2, p. 340; Ibn Kathir, *Tafsir*, vol. 4, p. 387. On this story so popular in the Hadith literature, cf. Abbott (*Aishah*, pp. 44–45) and also below.

100. Zamakhshari, *Kashshaf*, vol. 4, p. 453; Baydawi, *Anwar*, vol. 2, p. 341; Ibn Kathir, *Tafsir*, vol. 4, p. 389.

101. Tabari, *Tafsir*, vol. 28, pp. 105–106; Ibn Kathir, *Tafsir*, vol. 4, p. 389.

102. Quoted at the beginning of this section.

103. Exegesis of the verse is found in Tabari, *Tafsir*, vol. 22, pp. 15–18; Zamakhshari, *Kashshaf*, vol. 3, pp. 434–436; Baydawi, *Anwar*, vol. 2, p. 132; Ibn Kathir, *Tafsir*, vol. 3, pp. 498–500. Abbott (*Aishah*, p. 60) places 33:50–52 into a "somewhat later period" than 66:1–5.

104. In this verse, the word "uncle" is used twice in the singular, and the word "aunt" twice in the plural. Ibn Kathir explains that "the males are here used in the singular because of their high rank, and the females in the plural because of their inferiority" (*Tafsir*, vol. 3, p. 499). Ibn Kathir also contrasts the merit of the marriage system here revealed with the deficiencies of Christian and Jewish marriage patterns; he says that "this verse establishes the sound median between 'going too far' and 'not far enough': Christians only marry women from whom they are removed by seven grandfathers or more, while Jews marry daughters of a sister or brother, a horrible custom" (ibid, vol. 3, p. 499).

105. According to Zamakhshari (*Kashshaf*, vol. 3, p. 430), David had 100 wives and 300 concubines, while Solomon had 300 wives and 700 concubines. Ibn Sa'd reports a number of traditions that decry Jewish criticism of the size of the Prophet's polygamous household: "the Jews said when they saw the Prophet of God marrying women: 'look at him who does not satisfy his appetite with food, by God, he has no ambition except for women', and they envied him the large number of his women, and they found fault in him because of it . . . (saying) 'if he were a prophet, he would have no desire for women' . . . But God showed them to be liars and informed them of God's favor and largesse" (i.e., to the Abrahamic line of prophets, which involved "a thousand consorts for Solomon and a hundred for David") (*Nisa'*, pp. 146–147).

106. Exegetes concur that all of the women to whom the Prophet was married at the time of this revelation belonged into one, or several, of the "categories" declared as "lawful" in 33:50, but that no *hiba* type marriage had been concluded with any of Muhammad's established wives (a few isolated traditions on Zaynab bint Jahsh, Zaynab bint Khuzayma, or Maymuna bint al-Harith [or, al-Harth] notwithstanding).

107. Ibn Sa'd, *Nisa'*, pp. 98, 100–113, 145, 158; Tabari, *Tafsir*, vol. 22, pp. 16–18; Zamakhshari, *Kashshaf*, vol. 3, pp. 434–436; Baydawi, *Anwar*, vol. 2, p. 132; Ibn Kathir, *Tafsir*, vol. 3, p. 499. The *hiba*-type marriage is here presented as a special prerogative of the Prophet.

108. Ibn Sa'd, *Nisa'*, pp. 111–112; Tabari, *Tafsir*, vol. 22, p. 19; Zamakhshari, *Kashshaf*, vol. 3, pp. 435–436; Ibn Kathir, *Tafsir*, vol. 3, pp. 500–501. Stern (*Marriage*, pp. 75–76, 151–157) considers *hiba* not an early Islamic innovation instituted in deference to the Prophet but a custom that survived from pre-Islamic times. Stern stipulates that *hiba* may have been "commonly practiced in earlier times, when a matrilinear society flourished in Arabia but . . . was less frequent at the time of the rise of Islam, when a patrilinear system had been established. . . . It also may be that its real significance was unknown to Ibn Sa'd, but that he was aware of the fact that it did not conform with the more usual type of marriage practiced by Muhammad at al-Madinah. . . ." (*Marriage*, p. 154) The *hiba*-type marriages documented in the Hadith mainly appear to have involved Arabian tribal women, and to have been of a "looser" type than those involving the Prophet's "established wives." It is possible that the Prophet considered, or else concluded, *hiba* linkages in order to gain the support of Arabian tribesmen. On *hiba* as remnant of pre-Islamic female selfdetermination, cf. Mernissi, *Beyond the Veil* (New York: John Wiley and Sons, 1975), pp. 19–21; on *hiba* as a category in proto-Islamic law, cf. David S. Powers, *Studies in Qur'an and Hadith: The Formation of the Islamic Law of Inheritance* (Berkeley: University of California Press, 1986), p.81. Regarding some curious traditions on how the Prophet's wives thwarted several of his intended marriages with Arabian tribal women (which may have included some cases of *hiba*), cf. below.

109. Ibn Sa'd, *Nisa'*, p. 145. Medieval exegetes, in turn, emphasized that *hiba* type marriages were lawful for the Prophet *only*, "as a sign of honoring his prophethood" (Tabari, *Tafsir*, vol. 22, pp. 16–18; Zamakhshari, *Kashshaf*, vol. 3, p. 435; Baydawi, *Anwar*, vol. 2, p. 135; Ibn Kathir, *Tafsir*, vol. 3, pp. 499–500).

110. Ibn Sa'd, *Nisa'*, p. 140; Tabari, *Tafsir*, vol. 22, pp. 19–20; Baydawi, *Anwar*, vol. 2, p. 132; Zamakhshari, *Kashshaf*, vol. 3, p. 436; Ibn Kathir, *Tafsir*, vol. 3, p. 501. These exegetes here mainly link 33:51 with the *hiba* clause of 33:50.

111. With reference to 33:52, cf. below.

112. Ibn Sa'd, *Nisa'*, pp. 121, 124, 141; Tabari, *Tafsir*, vol. 22, pp. 18–21; Zamakhshari, *Kashshaf*, vol. 3, p. 436; Baydawi, *Anwar*, vol. 2, pp. 132–133; Ibn Kathir, *Tafsir*, vol. 3, p. 501. The exegetes favor this second interpretation of 33:51.

113. Conversely, Nöldeke isolates 33:52 and dates this verse into "the last years of the Prophet's life" (*Geschichte*, vol. I, p. 208).

114. Tabari, *Tafsir*, vol. 22, p. 23; Zamakhshari, *Kahshshaf*, vol. 3, p. 436; Baydawi, *Anwar*, vol. 2, p. 127; Ibn Kathir, *Tafsir*, vol. 3, p. 501.

115. Ibn Sa'd, *Nisa'*, pp. 109, 142, 145; Tabari, *Tafsir*, vol. 22, pp. 21–24; Zamakhshari, *Kashshaf*, vol. 3, pp. 436–437; Baydawi, *Anwar*, vol. 2, p. 133; Ibn Kathir, *Tafsir*, vol. 3, pp. 501–503. Cf. Abbott, *Aishah*, pp. 60–61. In fact, the Prophet did not marry a new spouse after the seventh year of the hijra, i.e., his last marriage (to Maymuna bint al-Harith, or, al-Harth) was concluded long before this verse was revealed (Ibn Sa'd, *Nisa'*, pp. 94ff).

116. Tabari, *Tafsir*, vol. 22, p. 24; Zamakhshari, *Kashshaf*, vol. 3, p. 437; Baydawi, *Anwar*, vol. 2, p. 133; Ibn Kathir, *Tafsir*, vol. 3, pp. 501–502.

117. On *naskh* as an early Islamic legal-theological institution, cf., for instance, John Burton's introductory essay to Abu Ubayd al-Qasim ibn Sallam, *Kitab al-nasikh wal-mansukh*, ed. John Burton (Bury St. Edmunds: St. Edmundsbury Press, 1987), pp. 1–45; and David S. Powers, "The Exegetical Genre *nasikh al-Qur'an wa-mansukhuhu*," in *Approaches to the History of the Interpretation of the Qur'an*, ed. Andrew Rippin (Oxford: Clarendon Press, 1988), pp. 117–138.

118. This fundamental truth is central to Qur'anic sociopolitical legislation.

119. Izutsu remarks that "the ethico-religious system of the Qur'an is, very broadly speaking, based on the concept of eschatology. In other words, the ethics of the present world is not simply there as a self-sufficing system; on the contrary, its structure is most profoundly determined by the ultimate (eschatological) end to which the present world (*al-dunya*) is destined. In the Islamic system the thought—or rather the vivid image—of the Hereafter should behave as the highest moral principle of conduct" (*Ethico-Religious Concepts in the Quran*, p. 108).

Chapter 9

1. The Qur'an enjoins obedience to the Prophet (e.g., 24:52) and also calls him "the beautiful model" (33:21), "of noble nature" (68:4), blessed by God and His angels (33:56), sent "as a mercy for [or, to] the worlds" (21:107).

2. The Prophet's cosmic significance and concomitant role of savior of his community later came to be essential aspects of Sufi doctrine and piety. Cf. Annemarie Schimmel, *And Muhammad is His Messenger: The Veneration of the Prophet in Islamic Piety* (Chapel Hill: University of North Carolina Press, 1985), esp. pp. 24–175; also Seyyed Hossein Nasr, "Shiism and Sufism," in *Shiism: Doctrines, Thought, and Spirituality*, ed. Seyyed Hossein Nasr, Hamid Dabashi, and Seyyed Vali Reza Nasr (Albany: State University of New York Press, 1988) pp. 100–108. On similar doctrines concerning the innate nature of the Prophet and his descendants in Shiism, cf. Nasr, *Shiism*, pp. 127–187.

3. Tarif Khalidi, *Classical Arab Islam* (Princeton: The Darwin Press, 1985), p. 36.

4. Cf. ibid., pp. 36–37.

5. Gordon D. Newby, *The Making of the Last Prophet* (Columbia: University of South Carolina Press, 1989), pp. 1–32.

6. N. J. Coulson, *A History of Islamic Law* (Edinburgh: Edinburgh University Press, 1964), pp. 55ff; and Gordon D. Newby, "Tafsir Isra'iliyyat," *Journal of the American Academy of Religion*, vol. 47, no. 4S (1979), pp. 694–695.

7. Newby, "Isra'iliyyat," p. 695.

8. The other four compilers of *Sahih* collections are: Abu Da'ud (d. 888), al-Tirmidhi (d. 892), Ibn Maja (d. 896), and al-Nisa'i (d. 915).

9. Abu Abdallah Muhammad ibn Isma'il al-Bukhari, *al-Sahih,* ed. with "marginal commentary" by al-Sindi (Cairo: Dar ihya' al-kutub al-'arabiyya, n.d.) vol. 1, p. 1.

10. For additional samples of traditions taken from Ibn Sa'd's *Tabaqat,* cf. the exegetic materials quoted in the first segment of this chapter. This source is identified as Ibn Sa'd, *Nisa'* in the following narrative text and in its footnotes. Ibn Sa'd's Hadith collection was chosen here because of the fact that that author's interest lay mainly with writing biographical history, not a text for legal or theological purposes. He thus strove to give all points of view, contradictory though they often were, which in turn gives access to a greater number of early Muslim opinions than would be provided in a law-oriented Hadith collection.

11. For example, Mernissi's feminist "deconstruction" of several classical mysogynist traditions transmitted by the Prophet's contemporaries Abu Bakra and Abu Hurayra (*Veil,* pp. 49–81).

12. Many of these "household traditions" might, therefore, be read in relation to larger, as well as later, sociopolitical communal developments. This applies, for instance, to the many traditions that elevate A'isha (Muhammad's wife and Abu Bakr's daughter) at the expense of Fatima (Muhammad's daughter and Ali ibn Abi Talib's wife), or Fatima at the expense of A'isha. Similar valuation/devaluation traditions exist on several other individuals of the Prophet's household.

13. An example of this genre of medieval "reformulation" may be found in the traditions transmitted on the institution of *hiba* ("marriage offered by a woman without participation of a guardian or expectation of a dower"); this institution, presented above under Qur'an 33:50, is further pursued by way of the Hadith in what follows. Another example is constituted by the traditions which indicate that the Prophet's wives showed a special kind of jealousy toward Muhammad's wives of Jewish origin, and also his Coptic concubine; cf. below.

14. The images of the Prophet's wives in modern and contemporary Muslim literature are discussed below in the final segment of this chapter.

15. Several traditions report that God favored His Prophet with sexual potency "the power of forty men" by sending Gabriel with a cooking pot that contained meat. The food enabled the Prophet to have sexual intercourse with his nine wives in a single night. He is said to have performed the ablution after each sexual act (Ibn Sa'd, *Nisa',* p. 140).

16. The latter is reported of Sawda, an early wife whom the Prophet later wished to divorce until she begged him to retain her and gave her share of his time to A'isha (Ibn Sa'd, *Nisa',* pp. 36–37, 43–44, 121–122). The Prophet is said to have prayed to God that He might accept such equitable sharing "regarding things over which I have control," and forgive partiality "in things which are under your control, not mine (i.e., the love of the heart)" (ibid, p. 121).

17. On the women's family affiliations, cf. the Qur'anic chapter of this segment, above.

18. Ibn Hisham's notes to Ibn Ishaq (Ibn Ishaq, *Life*) pp. 792–794. Cf. Abbott, *Aishah,* pp. 82–176, 219. Safiyya, Muhammad's wife of Jewish descent, is also said to have been involved in early Islamic politics, but she is said to have been on the side of (the third caliph) Uthman whom she reportedly supplied with food and water during the siege of his house (Ibn Sa'd, *Nisa',* p. 91; cf. Abbott, *A'ishah,* p. 122).

19. Intercommunal tensions were largely contained by the Prophet during his lifetime, but erupted in three civil wars after his death. The main protagonists in the first military confrontation following the Prophet's death were A'isha (in alliance with Talha and al-Zubayr) against Ali ibn Abi Talib (husband of Fatima). The second, larger,

civil war was a confrontation between Ali and the Umayyads. The third war involved the attempt of Abdallah ibn al-Zubayr (A'isha's "adopted son") to wrest the caliphate away from the Umayyads. His "countercaliphate" occurred after A'isha's death.

20. Stern, quoting Wellhausen, points out that the term *ghayra*, "jealousy," denotes "feelings of the woman's male relatives toward her intended husband" and other manifestations of pride and jealousy of one's honor and position; simultaneously, of course, *ghayra* can also mean sexual jealousy between a man and a woman (*Marriage*, pp. 76–77), or jealousy of a woman toward another. Though not always clear in these texts, Arabic differentiates between *ghayra min* ("jealousy of a rival") and *ghayra 'ala* ("jealousy of/toward a loved one") (Marsot's comment on this manuscript).

21. It is reported that she later repented and asked the Prophet to forgive this remark of hers which had been brought on by jealousy (Ibn Sa'd, *Nisa'*, p. 67).

22. The Prophet said: "Little blond one, what did you think of her?" She said: "I saw an ordinary Jewess." In another, similar tradition, the Prophet answers: "Do not say this, because she has become a good Muslim" (ibid., p. 90).

23. Conversely, Ibn Sa'd reports two curious traditions according to which Safiyya, after declaring her long-standing love and desire for Islam, converted with the words: "You (Muhammad) have made me choose between *kufr* ["unbelief," here used to indicate Judaism] and Islam; God and His Apostle are more beloved to me than freedom (from slavery), or that I should return to my people" (Ibn Sa'd, *Nisa'*, p. 88). These traditions reflect a strongly negative attitude toward Judaism which contradicts both the Qur'an and also the shari'a.

24. Kalb, Kilab, Kinda, and Layth.

25. Stern points out that marriages to women from distant tribes were not the norm in the Prophet's time. In his own case such betrothals, whether proposed by himself or the women's relatives or the women in question (*hiba*), motivated though they may have been by the desire for political alliances, reportedly did not lead to marriages (*Marriage*, pp. 151–152)

26. *Nisa'*, pp. 100–104, 106.

27. One tradition reports that he also ordered "that she be given compensation" (*wa-matti'ha*) (Ibn Sa'd, *Nisa'*, p. 104). (On this term in the Qur'an, cf. 2:236 and 33:28). The term *mut'a* is used in medieval Qur'anic exegesis in the meaning of a "severance fee" paid to a wife with whom marriage had not been consummated. Payable in money or in kind, it should not exceed one half of the woman's dower, "but not be less than five dirhams, because the smallest (permissible) dower is ten dirhams" (Zamakhshari, *Kashshaf*, vol. 3, p. 423). Stern likewise argues against inferring from this term that this and similar marriages were of the *mut'a* (i.e., "temporary") type (*Marriage*, pp. 155–156).

28. *Beyond the Veil* (Cambridge, Mass.: Schenkman, 1975) pp. 19–20.

29. Mernissi is undoubtedly right when she says (ibid., pp. 19–20) that these episodes do not mean what they appear to mean on the surface. Later Muslim inability to imagine that the Prophet was "repudiated" and also, one would assume, the fact that the practice itself was no longer known demanded a different explanation of the events that was then found in the formulaic jealousy theme of Muhammad's wives.

30. Ibn Sa'd, *Nisa'*, p. 104.

31. Ibid, p. 104; this is said to have occurred in the ninth year after the hijra.

32. Ibid., p. 103; Ibn Hisham in his notes to Ibn Ishaq (Ibn Ishaq, *Life*, p. 794) says that the Prophet "married (Asma' bint al-Nu'man al-Kindiyya) and found (her) to be suffering from leprosy and so returned her to her people with a suitable gift."

33. The material on Marya is taken from Ibn Sa'd, *Nisa'*, pp. 153–156; on Marya also cf. above.

34. It was Islamic practice to manumit a female slave who had given birth to her master's child, especially if the child was a son.

35. Cf. above.

36. The Prophet's two sons by Khadija, al-Qasim and Abdallah, had both died in early childhood, so he was without a male heir until Ibrahim's birth. As it was, Ibrahim also died in infancy.

37. The origins of "miracle-relating traditions" are generally ascribed to the *qussas*, early Islamic story-tellers (e.g., Stern, *Marriage*, p. 13). Juynboll traces the beginnings of their profession into the period of the second caliph, Umar ibn al-Khattab (634–644). The edifying material they spread was, according to Juynboll, the 'proto-hadith' in that it was devoid of shari'a-related information on the *halal* (lawful) and *haram* (forbidden). Cf. *Muslim Tradition* (Cambridge: Cambridge University Press, 1983), pp. 11–17. On hagiographic and legal Hadith, cf. above.

38. Ibn Ishaq, *Life*, pp. 82–83. In popular legend, Khadija's miraculous experiences are more numerous. Jan Knappert quotes a Swahili poem describing Khadija's dream prior to her first meeting with Muhammad in which she saw the full moon falling into her lap whence its light shone out across all the countries of the world. The learned monk Bahira interpreted the dream as symbolizing her upcoming marriage with the future Prophet. Khadija also witnessed "the sign" of Muhammad's protection against the hot desert sun by means of a cloud that was, in reality, an angel's wings; she perceived this while sitting on the roof of her three-story house on the Northern outskirts of Mecca and watching her caravan's return. When Khadija had proposed marriage to Muhammad who was too poor to provide her with a *mahr* (bridegift), the angel Gabriel brought precious gems from heaven for her *mahr*. Khadija's *kafan* (burial shroud) was woven by angels and she received it from the hands of Gabriel. Before Khadija died, the Prophet told her where she would find him on judgment day, and he assured her that she would be with him in paradise (*Islamic Legends*, vol. I [Leiden: Brill, 1985], pp. 192–197).

39. *Wati'a 'ala 'unqiha*; the verb *wati'a* when transitive means "to have intercourse" (with a woman).

40. The old name of Medina.

41. In a Swahili folk version, A'isha's picture is painted by the angels, then Gabriel gives it to the Prophet with the words: "God tells you that she shall be your future wife" (Knappert, *Legends*, p. 199).

42. In some lengthy traditions, A'isha herself gives an account of miraculous and other special events that distinguished her life and signified her "superiority over the (other) wives of the Prophet." They were: "that the Prophet was married to no other virgin but me; that only my parents both made the hijra; that God revealed my innocence [after 'the affair of the lie,' see above]; that Gabriel brought him my picture from heaven and said: 'marry her, she is your woman;' that he and I did our ablutions in the same vessel, which he did with no other wife but me; that he used to pray while I lay stretched out in front of him, which he did with no other wife but me; that he used to receive revelations while in my company, which did not occur in the presence of another wife but me; that he died while lying between my lungs and my throat; that he died during the night in which he was wont to make his rounds to me; and that he was buried in my house" (Ibn Sa'd, *Nisa'*, pp 43–44).

43. Muslim popular piety has continued to embrace, and embellish upon, this hagiographic mode.

44. The term here used in Ibn Sa'd (*Nisa'*, p. 40) for an article, or a manner, of clothing is *hijab*. As presented above, traditional exegesis has understood the term *hijab*

(Qur'an 33:53) as a "curtain" to ensure the segregation of the Prophet's wives from strangers. The term may also have denoted the concept of segregation and other instruments to achieve it. Its use to signify articles of women's clothing, most notably the veil, is not Qur'anic but documented in the Hadith. Cf. below.

45. Obligatory seclusion/invisibility (subsumed under *hijab*) emerges as the primary Hadith criterion to distinguish the Prophet's wives from his concubines. To this is added "the sharing," the women's right to a share of the Prophet's time on an established and regular basis and/or their right to an established share of annual provisions, mainly dates from Khaybar. Occasionally, the criterion of "the choosing," i.e., the women's choice of God and His Prophet over the world and its adornment (33:28–29) is also included (Ibn Sa'd, *Nisa'*, pp. 91–93).

46. This story is noteworthy for two reasons: 1. Safiyya's "invisibility" is here clearly used as proof of her wifely status, and 2. the *hijab* concept of 33:53 (domestic seclusion) has been extended to include "concealment" when outside of the house. A similar legal point is made in the traditions that maintain that Hafsa bint Umar wore the *jilbab* ("mantle") in the presence of her maternal uncles (Ibn Sa'd, *Nisa'*, p. 48). As indicated in Qur'an 33:55, paternal and maternal uncles were not included among the blood relatives given the right to deal with the Prophet's consorts face-to-face rather than from behind a partition (*hijab*). Traditions such as these, then, are further examples of the merging of the *hijab* verses of 33:53 and 33:55 with clothing restrictions, here the *jilbab* ("mantle") verse of 33:59.

47. Similar (clearly normative) traditions exist on other wives of the Prophet (cf., e.g., Ibn Sa'd, *Nisa'*, pp. 98–99). The Hadith is here silent on whether A'isha performed her prayers with the community or in private (as Islamic law especially of the Hanbali school later "preferred" for Muslim women). A tradition indicating the Prophet's wives' participation in communal prayers is found in Ibn Sa'd, *Nisa'*, p. 37) where it is reported that Muhammad's wife Sawda, a tall and large woman, complained to the Prophet about the speed with which he performed the *rak'as* (ritual prayer movements) and said that she was afraid it would give her a nose bleed; the Prophet is reported to have been very amused.

48. Abu Hanifa and Malik ibn Anas considered this seclusion supererogatory, since they reckoned a husband's grandsons among the *dhawu mahram* (individuals to whom marriage is forbidden, hence seclusion not necessary) (Ibn Sa'd, *Nisa'*, p. 50; cf. p. 127).

49. According to some other traditions, it was the Prophet who commanded his wives to remain behind the *hijab* in the blind man's presence (Ibn Sa'd, *Nisa'*, pp. 8, 126, 128; also cf. Stern, *Marriage*, pp. 118–119).

50. Cf. Qur'an 33:30; 4:19; 65:1.

51. It is not certain that these conditions formed part of the Prophet's Farewell Address. The Hadith, however, reports that the second caliph Umar ibn al-Khattab forbade the Prophet's wives to perform the *hajj* until year 23 after the hijra, at which time he is said to have given in to their pleas. "He ordered their equipment and they were carried in litters covered in green, accompanied by Abd al-Rahman ibn Auf and Uthman ibn Affan, the latter riding in front of them and the former behind, so that the women were inaccessible. At night they camped with Umar at all stops" (Ibn Sa'd, *Nisa'*, p. 150). This pattern of concealing the women from the glances of all onlookers continued during Uthman's caliphate (ibid. pp. 150–153). In light of extensive traditions "advising against" women's participation in public prayer, the traditions on the Prophet's wives' righteous immobility after the Fairwell Pilgrimage may perhaps signify an early Islamic, but post-Muhammadan, attempt to exclude women from partici-

pation in the pilgrimage. Injunctions of this kind, however, were not carried by consensus and were not included in shari'a legislation.

52. This battle, instigated in part by A'isha bint Abi Bakr and fought against Ali ibn Abi Talib, centered and surged around A'isha's camel. It occurred in 656 A.D.

53. These traditions of repentance, as it were, salvage A'isha's status as *sunna*-providing model in the face of historical evidence that would otherwise cast a shadow on her qualifications for this role *as formulated by medieval Islamic legal-theological consensus.*

54. Other traditions report that A'isha used perfume (ibn Sa'd, *Nisā'*, p. 50), henna dye (p. 50), wore silk and leather (pp. 48–49), a number of red garments, both chemises and also cloaks (pp. 48–50), and had gold rings (p. 48). She forbade the use of fake hair but was in favor of hair dyes to darken the color (p. 357). These and many other, equally diverging traditions reflect the elevation of the Prophet's wives to sources of *sunna* as indicated above. They also show the proliferation of categories of *halal* (lawful) and *haram* (forbidden) behavior debated in early Islamic law.

55. Another wife, Zaynab bint Khuzayma, who died eight months after the marriage with the Prophet, was known as "mother of the poor" (Ibn Sa'd, *Nisā'*, p. 82); the Hadith may have confused the two Zaynabs.

56. Surely it was this theme of avoidance of the temptations of wealth that Muslim piety heralded as a note of warning in the newly money-rich Islamic community of the wars of conquest, and also during Islam's imperial phase.

57. Here in the general meaning of "the religious duties," not the specific meaning of "distributive shares" (Islamic estate law).

Chapter 10

1. Here used in the English translation by Isma'il Ragi A. al Faruqi (Indianapolis: North American Trust Publications, 1976).

2. Especially *Abqariyyat Muhammad* ("The Genius of Muhammad") (Beirut: Dar al-kitab al-lubnani, 1974).

3. Beirut: Dar al-kitab al-arabi, 1984. This book is a collection of the author's previous publications during the 1960s on The Prophet's Mother; The Prophet's Wives (1965); The Prophet's Daughters; The Lady Zaynab, Daughter of the Imam Ali; and The Lady Sukayna, Daughter of the Imam Husayn.

4. Cf. Charles D. Smith, *Islam and the Search for Social Order in Modern Egypt: A Biography of Muhammad Husayn Haykal* (Albany: State University of New York Press, 1983), pp. 89–157.

5. *Life*, pp. XLVIIff, XCIff.; Antonie Wessels, *A Modern Arabic Biography of Muhammad: A Critical Study of Muhammad Husayn Haykal's Hayat Muhammad* (Leiden: Brill, 1972), pp. 43, 241ff; Charles Smith, *Islam*, pp. 109–130.

6. Wessels, *Modern*, pp. 41ff, 194–241. The fact that the prominent theologian al-Maghari, then Rector of the Azhar, wrote a preface to Haykal's book on its first appearance (1935) may have contributed to its eventual acceptance by conservative Muslims (cf. Wessels, *Modern*, p. 40).

7. Therefore, Haykal's ideogram here is sui generis. On women's issues, Haykal does not question the medievals' extension of Qur'an 33:53 (*hijab* as "means of domestic seclusion of Muhammad's wives") to include "the veil" (as obligatory garment for all Muslim women), an issue much supported by the conservatives. On the other hand, like many modernists, Haykal speaks out in support of monogamy in Islam when he argues by the power of Muhammad's example that monogamy is the preferred form

of marriage for Muslims during "normal life" but not in times of war and other crises, when polygamy presents a solution to economic and social problems (cf. Wessels, *Modern*, pp. 108–109, 141–144).

8. Cairo: Dar al-ma'arif, 1962, 1966, 1968.

9. J. J. G. Jansen, *The Interpretation of the Koran in Modern Egypt* (Leiden:Brill, 1974), pp. 68ff.

10. Many other modern literary works on the Prophet do not at present appear influential in religious circles, because of the secularist leanings of their authors; cf. e.g., Taha Husayn's three-volume work *'Ala hamish al-sira* (Cairo 1933, 1937, 1946); Tawfiq al-Hakim's play *Muhammad* (Cairo 1936); Abd al-Rahman al-Sharqawi's *Muhammad rasul al-hurriyya* (Cairo 1962); and Naguib Mahfuz's controversial novel *Awlad haritna* (Beirut 1967).

11. The "age of spiritual ignorance" before the rise of Islam.

12. Haykal, *Life*, pp. 318ff; al-Aqqad, *Abqariyyat Muhammad*, pp. 99ff; Bint al Shati', *Tarajim*, pp. 206ff, 257; cf. Ma'mun Gharib, *Nisa' fi hayat al-anbiya'* ("Women in the lives of the prophets") (Cairo: Maktabat Gharib, 1977) pp. 114ff, 122ff.

13. Haykal, *Life*, p. 298; al-Aqqad, *Muhammad*, pp. 102ff; Bint al-Shati', *Tarajim*, pp. 208ff; Gharib, *Nisa'*, pp. 121ff.

14. Elimination of miraculous traditions applies even to Bint al-Shati's entirely Hadith-based work.

15. Muhammad Abduh, *al-Islam wal-mar'a fi ra'y al-imam Muhammad Abduh*, ed. Muhammad Amara (Cairo: n.d.) pp. 117–118. Some later modernist thinkers were less revolutionary. Mahmud Shaltut (d. 1963), Rector of the Azhar and outspoken champion of *ijtihad* (independent legal interpretation of Qur'an and Hadith), who supported women's rights to education and political participation, nevertheless argued in favor of polygamy as "part of Islam, and sanctioned by the shari'a" (*al-Islam 'aqida wa-shari'a* [Cairo: Dar al-shuruq, 1983], pp. 223ff). The modernist Muhammad Ahmad Khalafallah (cf. Part I, Ch. 1 above) takes a middle position when he stipulates that this Islamic practice may be necessary from time to time, so that Muslim society must legislate whether polygamy is in the public interest at any given time or not (*Dirasat fi al-nuzum wal-tashri'at al-islamiyya* [Cairo: Maktabat al-anglo al-misriyya, 1977], pp. 200–206).

16. Here, as on other social issues, debate as well as legislative proposals and measures have found legitimation within the inner-Qur'anic context. Modernists have argued that the Qur'an is "in essence opposed to" polygamy by joining Qur'an 4:3 with Qur'an 4:129 as proof that, justice among cowives being impossible, monogamy is the righteous form of marriage (cf., e.g., Jansen, *Interpretation*, pp. 92).

17. E.g. al-Aqqad, *Muhammad*, p. 119ff.

18. Ibid., p. 119.

19. Ibid., p. 119; Bint al-Shati', *Tarajim*, p. 206.

20. Haykal was acquainted with Orientalist literature through the work of Washington Irving, Thomas Carlyle, Emile Dermenghem, and William Muir (Wessels, *Modern*, pp. 205–241). From among these, he had some thorough knowledge of the writings of Dermenghem and Muir (cf. Isa Boullata, Review of *A Modern Arabic Biography of Muhammad: A Critical Study of Muhammad Husayn Haykal's Hayat Muhammad* by Antonie Wessels [Leiden: E. J. Brill, 1972] in *The Muslim World* vol. 64, 1974, p. 51). On the general stance of modern Muslim religious literature toward Orientalism, cf. Yvonne Y. Haddad, *Contemporary Islam and the Challenge of History* (Albany: State University of New York Press, 1982) pp. 125–133.

21. Cf. ch. 8, above.

22. While Haykal's premise is the Prophet's infallibility in the prophetic mission, as separate from his perfected humanity in all other areas of life, Bint al-Shati' speaks of the fusion of prophethood and manhood in Muhammad (cf. Bint al-Shati', *Tarajim*, pp. 199ff, 209ff, 246).

23. Bint al-Shati' links this fact with the fullness of life experienced by the Prophet (ibid., p. 204). al-Aqqad indicates that Muhammad's full manhood—which included his enjoyment of women—enhances rather than diminishes his stature. "We do not describe the Lord Messiah as 'undersexed' because he never married, nor must we describe Muhammad as 'oversexed' because he had nine wives simultaneously. There is nothing wrong if a great man loves and enjoys women, because this pertains to sound original nature, and there is nothing wrong with sound original nature" (*Muhammad*, p. 110).

24. al-Aqqad, *Muhammad*, pp. 110–111; Gharib, *Nisa'*, pp. 122ff.

25. al-Aqqad, *Muhammad*, p. 117.

26. Ibid., pp. 112–113, 118. Also Gharib, *Nisa'*, p. 122; the latter, mainly a popularizer of conservative ideas, quotes al-Aqqad throughout much of his chapter on the Prophet's wives, but in simplified fashion. Like many other popularizers, he is not comfortable dealing with complex issues (such as Muhammad's physical nature) and therefore here merely states that "Muhammad's public and also private life was entirely taken up by the struggle in the way of God (*al-jihad fi sabil Allah*). He worshiped God all night long until his feet were swollen from the standing and the bowing of his prayers (p. 120); he expected the same spirit of self-sacrifice from his wives whose requests for material wealth he rejected because he did not want them to live like kings and playboys" (p. 135).

27. al-Aqqad, *Muhammad*, pp. 113ff. Gharib spells this out when he says that the Prophet "controlled his sexual drive until his twenty-fifth year, in a hot country . . . where young men reach sexual maturity quickly, and their feelings are hot, and their desires unruly. . . ." (*Nisa'*, p. 121; cf. pp. 109–110).

28. On Khadija as the ideal of wifehood in contemporary Muslim interpretation, cf. below.

29. Muhammad's mother, Amina, had died when Muhammad was six years old.

30. Bint al-Shati', *Tarajim*, p. 223; Gharib, *Nisa'*, p. 119.

31. al-Aqqad attributes all of the Prophet's later marriages to his service of the common weal, or his generosity and sense of honor (*Muhammad*, pp. 116–118). Gharib states that "all of Muhammad's marriages were concluded by divine inspiration in the way of service to his mission" (*Nisa'*, p. 127).

32. Bint al-Shati', *Tarajim*, pp. 233ff, 240–241, 254, 272ff. Concerning the age difference of some forty-six or forty-seven years between the Prophet and A'isha, Bint al-Shati' remarks that this "was a very normal thing in early Muslim society, just as it was and continues to be in the Arabian Peninsula, the Egyptian countryside, parts of Eastern and Southern Europe, and the remote mountain regions of the United States" (p. 257).

33. al-Aqqad, *Muhammad*, pp. 115–117; Bint al-Shati', *Tarajim*, pp. 242ff, 304ff, 319ff, 355ff, 377ff, 382ff, 387ff.

34. Kenneth Cragg, *The Event of the Qur'an: Islam in its Scripture* (London: George Allen and Unwin, 1971), p. 17.

35. Medieval exegesis, fond of *asbab al-nuzul* literature, does not betray such qualms. In Cragg's words, the medieval approach to historical context was a tacit and "sustained reluctance to allow the contextuality its full implications" (*Event*, p. 114).

36. Haykal, *Life*, p. 295–297; al-Aqqad, *Muhammad*, p. 116; Bint al-Shati', *Tara-*

jim, p. 345; Gharib, *Nisa'*, pp. 127ff. Yusuf al-Qaradawi (*The Lawful and the Prohibited in Islam*, K. El-Helbawy, M. Moinuddin Siddiqui, Syed Shukry, transl. [Indianapolis: American Trust Publications, n.d.], pp. 223–226) follows the same line of argumentation but places greater emphasis on the inherent flaws of the custom of adoption as practiced in the Jahiliyya, which he describes as very similar to current Western adoption laws. He also stresses that the Prophet's mission to eradicate this custom constituted a true hardship; "although he knew through divine revelation that Zaid would divorce Zainab and that he would afterward marry her himself, human weakness occasionally overcame him, and he was afraid of facing the people" (p. 225).

37. Haykal, *Life*, pp. 294–295. Haykal's synopsis of these "fictitious elements and tales" is scathing: "[they allege that the Prophet] passed by her house in the absence of her husband and was struck by her beauty; that he opened the door of her house and, as the breezes played with the curtains of her room, he saw her stretched (*sic*) in her nightgown like a real Madame Recamier. . . ." (p. 295).

38. The paragraph continues in a more general vein: "Even if, though impossible, their claims were true, we would still refute them with the simple argument that the great stand above the law; that Moses, Jesus, Jonah, and others before Muhammad have likewise risen above the laws of nature as well as of society, some in their birth, others in their lives. None of this has affected their greatness. Muhammad, morever, legislated for man and society by means of his Lord's revelation. He executed those laws equally by his Lord's command. His life constitutes the highest ideal, the perfect example, and the concrete instance of his Lord's command. Would those missionaries have Muhammad divorce his wives in order not to exceed the limit of four prescribed by Islamic law after Muhammad? Wouldn't they then subject him to more severe criticism? But Muhammad's treatment of his wives was just and noble. . . . Evidently, Muhammad not only honored woman more than did any other man, but he raised her to the status which truly belongs to her—an accomplishment of which Muhammad alone has so far been capable" (*Life*, p. 298).

39. I.e., the Prophet's sudden liking for Zaynab, etc. For the medieval materials, cf. ch. 8, above.

40. Cf. Wessels, *Modern*, pp. 144ff.

41. Bint al-Shati', *Tarajim*, p. 342.

42. Ibid., p. 344. She goes on to say that Muhammad overcame desire in nobility and chastity. He would have refrained from this marriage forever, even though the common weal and personal interest required it. It was (only) his dissimulation that brought on God's reprimand (of Qur'an 33:37), because God commands that conscience and behavior be one, even if that involves struggle (ibid., p. 345). This argument already appears with al-Zamakhshari (*Kashshaf*, vol. 3, pp. 428–429; cf. above).

43. Haykal, *Life*, pp. 334–339; al-Aqqad, *Muhammad*, pp. 106–108; Bint al-Shati', *Tarajim*, pp. 283–292; Gharib, *Nisa'*, pp. 130–133.

44. al-Aqqad, *Muhammad*, p. 109.

45. Gharib here reiterates the classical argument of woman's lower nature and her power to wreak social anarchy (*fitna*): "When Islam protected woman's honor, it did not forget that the woman is by her very nature propelled toward fornication. . . . Islam does not forbid her to beautify herself, but disapproves of *tabarruj* ('public display') since she may only embellish herself for her husband, so that the instincts of all (other) males are not aroused" (*Nisa'*, p. 125).

46. Bint al-Shati', *Tarajim*, p. 293.

47. Ibid., pp. 278ff. On the medieval Hadith versions of this story, cf. ch. 9, above.

48. Ibid., p. 204; cf. al-Aqqad, *Muhammad*, p. 106. Bint al-Shati' attributes the

women's jealousy to their being females, "an emotional inheritance inclined toward Eve" (p. 293), but indicates that "their weak feminity awakened the Prophet's compassion" (p. 306). On the image of Eve in the Qur'an and its interpretations, cf. Part I, Ch. 2, above.

49. Bint al-Shati', *Tarajim*, pp. 208–209.

50. Ibid., p. 207.

51. This indicates the Prophet's station above ordinary males, since the husband has the right to physical punishment of a rebellious wife (Qur'an 4:34). According to al-Aqqad (some of whose mysogynist ideas have been introduced above in Part I, Ch. 2), this punishment was more effective than any other because "the woman knows that she is weak compared to the man. But she does not mind this as long as she knows that she . . . can overcome him by way of seducing him, and make up for her weakness through the desire she kindles in him. When he shuns her, he deprives her of this power. This, then, is psychological, not physical punishment. It is the struggle in which the female is stripped of all weapons and withdraws into humble defeat" (*Muhammad*, p. 124).

52. As shown above, the medieval sources placed far greater emphasis on A'isha, the young and willful wife who came to the Prophet as his virgin bride. By comparison to A'isha's, the classical Hadith material on Khadija is scanty.

53. Syed A. A. Razwy, *Khadija-tul-Kubra* (Elmhurst: Tahrike Tarsile Qur'an, 1990) pp. 146–147. This author also emphasizes Khadija's motherly care for the believers at large. "She found fulfillment in giving . . . she was always solicitous of the feelings of even the humblest and poorest women, and distressed by the distress of others" (pp. 136, 141). By contrast, A'isha is presented as a jealous selfcentered young woman given to tantrums (pp. 165–167).

54. She bore him his children, created a haven of security and serenity for him at home, was the first woman to believe in her husband's prophethood, and supported his mission both spiritually and also materially (Bint al-Shati', *Tarajim*, pp. 233–235; al-Aqqad, *Muhammad*, pp. 113–115, 118; Gharib, *Nisa'*, pp. 118ff).

55. Bint al-Shati', *Tarajim*, pp. 233–235.

56. Ibid., p. 204. This author describes A'isha's feelings during the month when the Prophet had withdrawn from all of his wives during a domestic crisis (cf. Qur'an 33:28–29). A'isha's heart then was torn with sadness and remorse "when she thought that he was all alone in his loft without a soft hand to wipe the sweat from his pure brow, remove the dust of battle, . . . that he was alone without a spouse to give him rest and relaxation" (p. 281).

57. Ibid., p. 204.

58. Ibid., pp. 311–312, 388.

59. Ibid, pp. 317–318, 352.

60. Ibid., p. 271.

61. Ibid., p. 323.

62. Ibid., p. 365.

63. Ibid., pp. 322–323, 364, 368, 387.

64. Ibid., p. 297.

65. Ibid., p. 331.

66. Ibid., pp. 311, 332. A'isha's participation in public affairs, especially the Battle of the Camel, is at odds with the latter point. The issue is here either deemphasized or addressed by way of strong criticism on the part of the Prophet's other widows. Elsewhere, it is called a mistake which A'isha came to regret bitterly (Gharib, *Nisa'*, p. 135). Cf. the conservative reading of this incident in Muhammad Abd al-Fattah al-Inani,

(President of the Fatwa Committee of al-Azhar), "Hukm al-shari'a al-islamiyya fi ishtirak al-mar'a fil-intikhab lil-barlaman" in *al-Haraka al-nisa'iyya wa-silatuha bil-isti'mar*, ed. Atiyya Khamis (Cairo: Dar al-Ansar, 1978), pp. 115ff, 124.

67. Gharib, *Nisa'*, p. 122, cf. p. 136.

68. On this concept, cf. Clifford Geertz, *The Interpretation of Cultures* (New York: Basic Books, 1973), pp. 91ff., 123ff.; also, by the same author, *Islam Observed* (New Haven: Yale University Press, 1968), pp. 98ff.

69. *Tahrir al-mar'a* (1899), in *al-A'mal al-kamila li-Qasim Amin*, vol. II, ed. Muhammad Amara (Beirut: al-Mu'assasa al-'arabiyya lil-dirasat wal-nashr, 1976), pp. 20, 54ff.

70. Ibid., pp. 35–37, 54ff, 68.

71. Ibid., pp. 43ff.

72. Abu l-A'la al-Mawdudi published a series of articles, written in Urdu, on women's *purdah* in the *Terjuman al-Qur'an*, which he then edited in book form in 1939. The English translation of this volume was done by al-Ash'ari, *Purdah and The Status of Woman in Islam* (Lahore: Islamic Publications, 1972). By then, the book had been translated into Arabic; it was first published in Damascus in the early sixties under the title *al-Hijab*. This book is now widely available in the Arab world, from a variety of publishing houses. The Arabic translation accessible to me is in the form of a Saudi Arabian publication (Jeddah: al-Dar al-sa'udiyya lil-nashr wal-tawzi', 1985). All following quotations are from the 1972 English translation.

73. Ibid., pp. 39–72.

74. Ibid., pp. 135–216.

75. Ibid., pp. 149ff.

76. Ibid., pp. 183–204.

77. Ibid., pp. 198–203.

78. Ahmed, *Women and Gender in Islam*, pp. 144–168.

79. Ibid., p. 164.

80. Muhammad Mutawalli al-Sha'rawi, *Qadaya al-mar'a al-muslima* (Cairo: Dar al Muslim, 1982), pp. 18ff.

81. Muhammad Kamil al-Fiqi [Former Dean of the Faculty of Arabic and Islamic Studies, al-Azhar University], *La tazlamu al-mar'a* (Cairo: Maktabat Wahba, 1985), pp. 59–66.

82. Ibid., p. 34.

83. Some say that it is the duty of the State and/or of society at large to save the woman's morals and reputation by paying her one fourth of her salary as a "pension" in order to enable her to return to domestic life. Cf. Sha'rawi, *Qadaya*, pp. 18ff., and al-Fiqi, *La tazlamu*, pp. 57ff.

84. In Sha'rawi's booklet *Issues of the Muslim Woman* (*Qadaya*), for instance, remarks on the *hijab qua* "veil" are about four times longer than his treatment of women's rights, or women and work, and even surpass in length what he has to say about women and the family.

85. Sha'rawi, *Qadaya*, pp. 43–63.

86. Ibid., p. 49.

87. Andrea B. Rugh, *Reveal and Conceal: Dress in Contemporary Egypt* (Syracuse: Syracuse University Press, 1986), pp. 149ff.

88. Ibid., p. 155.

89. Barbara Freyer Stowasser, "Liberated Equal or Protected Dependent? Contemporary Religious Paradigms on Women's Status in Islam," *Arab Studies Quarterly*, vol. 9 (1987), pp. 263–269.

90. Malcolm H. Kerr, *Islamic Reform* (Berkeley and Los Angeles: University of California Press, 1966), pp. 189ff.

91. Fazlur Rahman, *Islam and Modernity* (Chicago: University of Chicago Press, 1982), pp. 1–11; by the same author, "Roots of Islamic Neo-Fundamentalism" in *Change and the Muslim World*, ed. Philip H. Stoddard, David C. Cuthall, Margaret W. Sullivan (Syracuse: Syracuse University Press, 1982), pp. 28ff.

92. Stowasser, *Impulse*, p. 294.

93. E.g., the now old-fashioned but still oft-quoted monograph by the young Druze writer Nazira Zayn al-Din, *al-Sufur wal-hijab* (Beirut: n.publ., 1346/1928); on this work, cf. Rudi Paret, *Schriften zum Islam*, pp. 136–163. On these issues, also cf. Abd al-Aziz al-Khayyat, *Mafhum al-ikhtilat wa-hukmuhu* (Amman: Ministry of Awqaf and Religious Affairs, 1972), pp. 13ff.

94. Transl. Mary Jo Lakeland (Reading: Addison-Wesley, 1991). This book was also published under the title *Women and Islam: An Historical and Theological Enquiry* (Oxford: Basil Blackwell, 1991).

95. *Veil*, pp. 8–9, 17, 46ff.

96. The very proximity of their houses to the mosque in Medina ensured their participation in the political process. (*Veil*, pp. 113–114).

97. Ibid., p. 104.

98. Ibid., pp. 118ff, 129ff.

99. Ibid., pp. 130ff.

100. Ibid., pp. 179ff.

101. Ibid., pp. 185ff.

102. Listed in Bukhari, *Sahih*, vol. 4, p. 228 (in the context of ascension to the Persian throne of Khosroe's daughter).

103. *Veil*, pp. 49–61.

104. A similar weighing of Islam's early (Meccan) message (tolerant and egalitarian) against its later message (seen at least in part as adaptation to the socioeconomic and political realities of the Medinan community) underlies Mahmoud Mohamed Taha's *The Second Message of Islam* (first published in 1967; published in an English translation and with an introduction by Abdullahi Ahmed An-Na'im, Syracuse: Syracuse University Press, 1987). Shaykh Mahmoud Mohamed Taha was founder of the Republican Brothers, a Sudanese movement advocating Islamic reform and liberation from "sectarian forces." He was executed in 1985 for his opposition to impose traditional Islamic law in the Sudan. His student Abdullahi Ahmed An-Na'im has since developed his mentor's general principles into a concrete analysis of their implications for Islamic public law in *Toward an Islamic Reformation: Civil Liberties, Human Rights, and International Law* (Syracuse: Syracuse University Press, 1990). The Republican Brothers, and An-Na'im in particular, have been described as "unorthodox, reformist . . . in contradiction to contemporary Islamic modernism, conservatism, and fundamentalism" (John O. Voll, Foreword to An-Na'im, ibid., pp. IX-XII).

105. Voll, ibid., p. XII.

References

Abbott, Nabia. *Aishah—The Beloved of Mohammad.* 2d ed. London: Al Saqi Books, 1985.

Abu Ubayd, al-Qasim ibn Sallam. *Kitab al-nasikh wal-mansukh.* Ed. John Burton. Bury St. Edmunds: St. Edmundsbury Press, 1987.

Abduh, Muhammad. *Al-Islam wal-mar'a fi ra'y al-imam Muhammad Abduh.* Ed. Muhammad Amara. Cairo, n.d.

———. *Tafsir al-Qur'an al-hakim, al-shahir bi-Tafsir al-Manar.* Cf. Rida, al-Sayyid Muhammad Rashid.

Ahmed, Leila. *Women and Gender in Islam.* New Haven: Yale. University Press, 1992.

al-Alami, Abdallah. *Mu'tamar tafsir surat Yusuf.* Ed. Muhammad Bahja al-Baytar. Damascus: Dar al-fikr, 1962.

Ali, A. Yusuf. *The Holy Qur'an: Text, Translation and Commentary.* Washington D.C.: The Islamic Center, 1978.

Amin, Qasim. *Tahrir al-mar'a.* In *al-A'mal al-kamila li-Qasim Amin.* Ed. Muhammad Amara. Vol. II. Beirut: al-Mu'assasa al-'arabiyya lil-dirasat wal-nashr, 1976.

Anawati, George. "Islam and the Immaculate Conception." In *The Dogma of the Immaculate Conception: History and Significance.* Ed. E. D. O'Connor. Notre Dame, Indiana: University of Notre Dame, 1958.

al-Aqqad, Abbas Mahmud. *Abqariyyat Muhammad.* Beirut: Dar al-kitab al-lubnani, 1974.

———. *al-Mar'a fi l-Qur'an.* Beirut: Dar al-kitab al-lubnani, 1975.

Ashur, Sa'id Harun. *Nisa' al-nabi.* Cairo: Matba'at al-Qahira al-haditha, n.d.

Ayoub, Mahmoud. *Redemptive Suffering in Islam: A Study of the Devotional Aspects of 'Ashura' in Twelver Shiism.* The Hague: Mouton, 1978.

al-Bahi, Muhammad. *Tafsir surat Maryam.* Cairo: Maktabat Wahba, 1978.

Baljon, J. M. S. *Modern Muslim Koran Interpretation (1880–1960).* Leiden: E. J. Brill, 1961.

Barnes, John Robert. *An Introduction to Religious Foundations in the Ottoman Empire.* Leiden: E. J. Brill, 1986.

al-Baydawi, Abdallah ibn Umar. *Anwar al-tanzil fi asrar al-ta'wil.* Ed. H. O. Fleischer. Osnabrück: Biblio-Verlag, 1968. *Reproductio phototypica editionis,* 1846–1848.

Bint al-Shati' [A'isha Abd al-Rahman]. *Tarajim sayyidat bayt al-nubuwwa.* Beirut: Dar al-kitab al-arabi, 1984.

————. al-Tafsir al-bayani lil-Qur'an al-karim. Cairo: Dar al-ma'arif, 1968.

Boullata, Isa. Review of A Modern Arabic Biography of Muhammad: A Critical Study of Muhammad Husayn Haykal's Hayat Muhammad, by Antonie Wessels. The Muslim World, vol. 64, p. 51, 1974.

Brinner, William M., transl. and annot. The History of al-Tabari. Vol. III: The Children Of Israel. Ed. Eshan Yar Shater. Albany: State University of New York Press, 1991.

al-Bukhari, Abu Abdallah Muhammad ibn Isma'il. al-Sahih. Ed. with "marginal commentary" by al-Sindi. 4 vols. Cairo: Dar ihya' al-kutub al-'arabiyya, n.d.

————. al-Sahih. 9 vols. Cairo: al-Halabi, n.d.

Corrington, Gail Paterson. Her Image of Salvation: Female Saviors and Formative Christianity. Louisville: Westminster/John Knox Press, 1992.

Coulson, N. J. A History of Islamic Law. Edinburgh: Edinburgh University Press, 1964.

Cragg, Kenneth. The Event of the Qur'an: Islam in its Scripture. London: George Allen and Unwin, 1971.

————. The Mind of the Qur'an. London: George Allen and Unwin, 1973.

Darr, Katherine Pfisterer. Far More Precious Than Jewels: Perspectives on Biblical Women. Lousiville: Westminster/John Knox Press, 1991.

Darwish, Mustafa Hasan. Fasl al-khitab fi mas'alat al-hijab wal-niqab. Cairo: Dar al-i'tisam, 1987.

al-Din, Nazira Zayn. al-Sufur wal-hijab. Beirut: n.publ., 1928.

Dozy, R. P. A. Dictionnaire détaillé des noms de vêtements ches les Arabes. Beirut: Librairie du Liban, 1969; photomechanical reproduction of Amsterdam: Jean Muller, 1845.

The Encyclopedia of Islam. 9 Vols. Leiden: E. J. Brill, 1913–1938.

————. 2d ed. 6 Vols. (to date). Leiden: E. J. Brill, 1960–present.

Esposito, John L. Islam: The Straight Path. New York: Oxford University Press, 1988.

al-Fiqi, Muhammad Kamil. La tazlamu al-mar'a. Cairo: Maktabat Wahba, 1985.

Firestone, Reuven. Journey in Holy Lands: The Evolution of the Abraham-Ishmael Legend in Islamic Exegesis. Albany: State University of New York Press, 1990.

————. "Sarah's Identity in Islamic Exegetical Tradition." The Muslim World, vol. 80, no. 2, pp. 65–71, 1990.

Fischer, Michael M. J. and Mehdi Abedi. Debating Muslims. Madison: The University of Wisconsin Press, 1990.

Gardet, Louis, and M.- M. Anawati. Introduction à la théologie musulmane: Essai de théologie comparée. Paris: Librairie philosophique J. Vrin, 1970.

Geertz, Clifford. The Interpretation of Cultures. New York: Basic Books, 1973.

————. Islam Observed. New Haven: Yale University Press, 1968.

————. "Religion as a Cultural System." Anthropological Approaches to the Study of Religion. Ed. Michael Banton. London and New York: Tavistock Publications, 1966.

Gharib, Ma'mun. Nisa' fi hayat al-anbiya'. Cairo: Maktabat Gharib, 1977.

Ginzberg, Louis. The Legends of the Jews. 7 vols. Transl. Henrietta Szold. Philadelphia: The Jewish Publication Society of America, 1909–1938.

Haddad, Yvonne Y. Contemporary Islam and the Challenge of History. Albany: State University of New York Press, 1982.

————. "Sayyid Qutb: Ideologue of Islamic Revival." In Voices of Resurgent Islam. Ed. John L. Esposito. New York: Oxford University Press, 1983.

Haddad, Yvonne Y. On three joint publications with Jane I. Smith. Cf. Smith, Jane I.

Haykal, Muhammad Husayn. The Life of Muhammad. Trans. Isma'il R. al-Faruqi. 8th ed., Indianapolis: North American Trust Publications, 1986.

Hussein, Aftab. *Status of Women in Islam.* Lahore: Law Publishing Company, 1987.

Ibn Hazm, Abu Muhammad Ali ibn Ahmad. *al-Fasl fi al-milal wal-ahwa' wal-nihal.* Vol. 5. Ed. Dr. Muhammad Ibrahim Nasr and Dr. Abd al-Rahman Umayra. Jeddah: Ukaz Publications, 1402/1982.

Ibn Ishaq. *The Life of Muhammad.* Transl. A. Guillaume. London: Oxford University Press, 1955.

Ibn Kathir, Isma'il ibn Umar Abu l-Fida. *Qisas al-anbiya'.* 2 vols. Ed. Mustafa Abd al-Wahid. Cairo: Dar al-kutub al-haditha, 1968.

———. *Tafsir al-Qur'an al-'azim.* 4 vols. Cairo: Dar ihya' al-kutub al-'arabiyya, n.d.

Ibn Manzur. *Lisan al-'Arab.* 15 vols. Beirut: Dar Sadir, 1955–1956.

Ibn Sa'd, Muhammad. *Fi l-nisa'.* Vol. 8. of *Kitab al-tabaqat al-kabir.* Ed. Carl Brockelmann. Leiden: Brill, 1904.

Ibn Sallam, Abu Ubayd al-Qasim. *Kitab al-nasikh wal-mansukh.* Ed. John Burton. St. Bury St. Edmunds: Edmundsbury Press, 1987.

al-Inani, Muhammad Abd al-Fattah. "Hukm al-shari'a al-islamiyya fi ishtirak al-mar'a fil-intikhab lil-barlaman." In: *al-Haraka al-nisa'iyya wa-silatuha bil-isti'mar.* Ed. Atiyya Khamis. Cairo: Dar al-Ansar, 1978.

Izutsu, Toshihiko. *Ethico-Religious Concepts in the Quran.* Montreal: McGill University Press, 1966.

Jansen, J. J. G. *The Interpretation of the Koran in Modern Egypt.* Leiden: Brill, 1974.

Jeffery, Arthur. "The Qur'an as Scripture." *The Muslim World,* vol. 40, pp. 41–55, 1950.

Jomier, J. "Quelques positions actuelles de l'exégèse coranique en Egypte: Révélées par une polémique récente (1947–1951)," in *Mélanges.* Vol. 1. Institut Dominicain d'Etudes Orientales du Caire, 1954: 39–72.

Juynboll, G. H. A. *Muslim Tradition.* Cambridge: Cambridge University Press, 1983.

Kerr, Malcolm H. *Islamic Reform.* Berkeley and Los Angeles: University of California Press, 1966.

al-Khafaji, Ahmad ibn Muhammad. *Hashiyat al-Shihab al-musamma bi-inayat al-qadi wa-kifayat al-radi 'ala tafsir al-Baydawi.* 8 vols. Beirut: Dar Sadir, 1974.

Khalafallah, Muhammad Ahmad. *Dirasat fi l-nuzum wal-tashri'at al-islamiyya.* Cairo: Maktabat al-anglo al-misriyya, 1977.

———. *al-Fann al-qasasi fi l-Qur'an.* 2d ed. Cairo: Maktabat al-nahda al-misriyya, 1958.

Khalidi, Tarif. *Classical Arab Islam.* Princeton: The Darwin Press, 1985.

al-Khayyat, Abd al-Aziz. *Mafhum al-ikhtilat wa-hukmuhu.* Amman: Ministry of Awqaf and Religious Affairs, 1972.

al-Kisa'i, *Qisas al-anbiya'.* Cf. Thackston, W. M.

Kister, M. J. "Legends in *tafsir* and *hadith* Literature: The Creation of Adam and Related Stories." In *Approaches to the History of the Interpretation of the Qur'an.* Ed. Andrew Rippin. Oxford: Clarendon Press, 1988.

Knappert, Jan. *Islamic Legends.* 2 vols. Leiden: Brill, 1985.

Kuhn, Thomas S. *The Structure of Scientific Revolutions,* 2d ed. Chicago: University of Chicago Press, 1970.

Levy, Reuben. *The Social Structure of Islam.* Cambridge: Cambridge University Press, 1969.

al-Maraghi, Ahmad Mustafa. *Tafsir al-Maraghi.* 10 vols. Cairo: al-Halabi, 1945.

Martin, Richard C. "Structural Analysis and the Qur'an: Newer Approaches to the Study of Islamic Texts." *Journal of the American Academy of Religion,* vol. 47, no. 4S, pp. 665–683, 1979.

al-Mas'udi (?) *Akhbar al-zaman.* Ed. Abdallah al-Sawi. Beirut: Dar al-Andalus, 1980.

————. *Muruj al-dhahab.* 4 vols. Ed. Muhammad Muhyi al-Din Abd al-Hamid. Cairo: Dar al-raja', n.d.

al-Mawdudi, Abu l-A'la. *al-Hijab.* Jeddah: al-Dar al-sa'udiyya lil-nashr wal-tawzi', 1985.

————. *Terjuman al-Qur'an.* 1939. Trans. al-Ash'ari under the title *Purdah and The Status of Woman in Islam.* Lahore: Islamic Publications, 1972.

McAuliffe, Jane Dammen. "Chosen of All Women: Mary and Fatima in Qur'anic Exegesis." *Islamochristiana,* vol. VII, pp. 26–27, 1981.

————. "Qur'anic Hermeneutics: The Views of al-Tabari and Ibn Kathir." In *Approaches to the History of the Interpretation of the Qur'an.* Ed. Andrew Rippin. Oxford: Clarendon Press, 1988.

McFague, Sallie. *Metaphorical Theology: Models of God in Religious Language.* Philadelphia: Fortress Press, 1981.

Mernissi, Fatima. *Beyond the Veil.* Cambridge, Massachusetts: Schenkman, 1975.

————. *The Veil and the Male Elite.* Trans. Mary Jo Lakeland, Reading: Addison-Wesley, 1991.

Minear, Paul. *Images of the Church in the New Testament.* Philadelphia: Westminster Press, 1966.

Musallam, Basim F. *Sex and Society in Islam.* Cambridge: Cambridge University Press, 1983.

Na'im, Abdullahi Ahmed. *Toward an Islamic Reformation: Civil Liberties, Human Rights, and International Law.* Syracuse: Syracuse University Press, 1990.

al-Najjar, Abd al-Wahhab. *Qisas al-anbiya'.* Cairo: al-Halabi, 1966.

Nasr, Seyyed Hossein. "Shiism and Sufism." In *Shiism: Doctrines, Thought, and Spirituality.* Eds. Seyyed Hossein Nasr, Hamid Dabashi, and Seyyed Vali Reza Nasr. Albany: State University of New York Press, 1988.

————. *Traditional Islam in the Modern World.* London: Routledge and Kegan Paul, 1987.

Newby, Gordon D. *The Making of the Last Prophet.* Columbia: University of South Carolina Press, 1989.

————. "Tafsir Isra'iliyyat." *Journal of the American Academy of Religion,* vol. 47, no. 4S, pp. 685–697, 1979.

————. Book review in *Middle East Studies Association Bulletin,* vol. 25, no. 2, Dec. 1991, pp. 212–213.

Nicholson, Reynold A. *A Literary History of the Arabs.* Cambridge: Cambridge University Press, 1962.

al-Nisaburi, Nizam al-Din al-Hasan ibn Muhammad ibn al-Husayn al-Qummi. *Ghara'ib al-Qur'an wa-ragha'ib al-furqan.* Vol 5. Cairo: al-Halabi, n.d.

Nöldeke, Theodor. *Geschichte des Qorans.* I. Hildesheim: Georg Olms Verlag, 1981. (Third reprographic reprinting of Leipzig: Dieterichsche Verlagsbuchhandlung, 1909).

Paret, Rudi. *Schriften zum Islam.* Ed. Josef van Ess. Stuttgart: W. Kohlhammer, 1991.

————. *Der Koran: Kommentar und Konkordanz.* 2d ed. Stuttgart: W. Kohlhammer, 1981.

————. *Der Koran: Übersetzung,* 3d ed. Stuttgart: W. Kohlhammer, 1983.

Parrinder, Geoffrey. *Jesus in the Qur'an.* London: Faber and Faber, 1965.

Powers, David S. *Studies in Qur'an and Hadith: The Formation of the Islamic Law of Inheritance.* Berkeley: University of California Press, 1986.

————. "The Exegetical Genre *nasikh al-Qur'an wa-mansukhuhu.*" In *Approaches to the History of the Interpretation of the Qur'an.* Ed. Andrew Rippin, Clarendon Press, 1988.

al-Qaradawi, Yusuf. *The Lawful and the Prohibited in Islam.* Transl. K. El-Helbawy,

M. Moinuddin Siddiqui, Syed Shukry. Indianapolis: American Trust Publications, 1976.

Qutb, Sayyid. *Fi Zilal al-Qur'an.* 6 Vols. Beirut: Dar al-Shuruq, 1982.

Rahman, Fazlur. *Islam and Modernity.* Chicago: University of Chicago Press, 1982.

———. *Major Themes of the Qur'an.* Minneapolis: Bibliotheca Islamica, 1982.

———. "Roots of Islamic Neo-Fundamentalism." In *Change and the Muslim World.* Eds. Philip H. Stoddard, David C. Cuthall, Margaret W. Sullivan. Syracuse: Syracuse University Press, 1982.

al-Razi, Muhammad ibn Umar Fakhr al-Din. *al-Tafsir al-kabir.* 32 vols. Cairo:al-Matba'a al-bahiyya al-misriyya, 1934–1962.

Razwy, Syed A. A. *Khadija-tul-Kubra.* Elmhurst: Tahrike Tarsile Qur'an, 1990.

Ricoeur, Paul. "Biblical Hermeneutics." *Semeia,* vol. 4, pp. 29–107, 1975.

Rida, al-Sayyid Muhammad Rashid. *Tafsir al-Qur'an al-hakim, al-shahir bi-Tafsir al-Manar.* 12 vols. Beirut: Dar al-ma'rifa, second printing, n.d.

Rosenthal, Franz, transl. and annot. *The History of al-Tabari. Vol. I: General Introduction and From the Creation to the Flood.* Ed. Ehsan Yar-Shater. Albany: State University of New York Press, 1989.

———. "The Influence of the Biblical Tradition on Muslim Historiography." In *Historians of the Middle East.* Ed. Bernard Lewis and P. M. Holt. London: Oxford University Press, 1962.

Rugh, Andrea B. *Reveal and Conceal: Dress in Contemporary Egypt.* Syracuse: Syracuse University Press, 1986.

Schimmel, Annemarie. *And Muhammad is His Messenger: The Veneration of the Prophet in Islamic Piety.* Chapel Hill: University of North Carolina Press, 1985.

Schub, Michael B. "The Male is not like the Female: An Eponymous Passage in the Qur'an." *Zeitschrift für arabische Linguistik,* Heft 23 pp. 102–104, 1991.

Sidqi, Ni'mat. *al-Tabarruj.* Cairo: Dar al-I'tisam, 1975.

al-Shal, Jabir. *Qisas al-nisa' fi l-Qur'an.* Beirut: Dar al-jil, 1985.

Shaltut, Mahmud. *al-Islam 'aqida wa-shari'a.* Cairo: Dar al-shuruq, 1983.

al-Sha'rawi, Muhammad Mutawalli. *Qadaya al-mar'a al-muslima.* Cairo: Dar al-Muslim, 1982.

Shorter Encyclopedia of Islam. Eds. H. A. R. Gibb and J. H. Kramers. Leiden: E. J. Brill. Photomechanical Reprint. Ithaca, N.Y.: Cornell University Press, 1965.

Smith, Charles D. *Islam and the Search for Social Order in Modern Egypt: A Biography of Muhammad Husayn Haykal.* Albany: State University of New York Press, 1983.

Smith, Jane Y. *An Historical and Semantic Study of the Term 'Islam' as seen in a Sequence of Qur'an Commentaries.* Missoula: Scholar's Press, 1975.

Smith, Jane I. and Yvonne Y. Haddad. "Eve: Islamic Image of Woman." In *Women and Islam.* Ed. Azizah al-Hibri. Oxford: Pergamon Press, vol. 5, no. 2 of *Women's Studies International Forum,* 1982, pp. 135–144.

———. *The Islamic Understanding of Death and Resurrection.* Albany: State University of New York Press, 1981.

———. "The Virgin Mary in Islamic Tradition and Commentary." *The Muslim World,* vol. 79, pp. 161–187, 1989.

Smith, W. C. "The True Meaning of Scripture: An Empirical Historian's Nonreductionist Interpretation of the Qur'an." *International Journal of Middle East Studies,* vol. 11, pp. 487–505, 1980.

Sperber, Dan. *Rethinking Symbolism.* Transl. Alice L. Morton. Cambridge: Cambridge University Press, 1977.

Stern, Gertrude S. *Marriage in Early Islam.* London: The Royal Asiatic Society, 1939.

Stowasser, Barbara Freyer. "The Status of Women in Early Islam." *Muslim Women.*
    Ed. Freda Hussain. London: Croom Helm, 1984.

————. Ed. *The Islamic Impulse.* London: Croom Helm, 1987. Reprint Washington,
    D.C.: Center for Contemporary Arab Studies, Georgetown University, 1989.

————. "Liberated Equal or Protected Dependent? Contemporary Religious Paradigms
    on Women's Status in Islam." *Arab Studies Quarterly,* vol. 9, pp. 260–283, 1987.

al-Suyuti, Jalal al-Din Abd al-Rahman ibn Abi Bakr and Jalal al-Din Muhammad ibn
    Ahmad al-Mahalli. *Tafsir al-Qur'an al-'azim.* Cairo: Matba'at al-istiqama, n.d.

al-Tabari, Abu Ja'far Muhammad ibn Jarir. *Jami' al-bayan 'an ta'wil ay al-Qur'an.* 16 vols.
    Eds. Mahmud Muhammad Shakir and Ahmad Muhammad Shakir. Cairo: Dar
    al-ma'arif, (1950s)–1969.

————. *Jami' al-bayan fi tafsir al-Qur'an.* 32 vols. Beirut: Dar al-ma'rifa, 1972.

————. *Tarikh al-rusul wal-muluk.* 8 vols. Ed. Muhammad Abu al-Fadl Ibrahim. Cairo:
    Dar al-ma'arif, 1960–69.

————. *The History of al-Tabari. Vol. I: General Introduction and From the Creation to the
    Flood.* Ed. Ehsan Yar-Shater. Trans. and annotated by Franz Rosenthal, Albany:
    State University of New York Press, 1989.

————. *The History of al-Tabari Vol. III: The Children of Israel.* Trans. and annotated
    by William M. Brinner. Albany: State University of New York Press, 1991.

Taha, Mahmoud Mohamed. *The Second Message of Islam.* Trans. and intro. by Abdullahi
    Ahmed An-Na'im. Syracuse: Syracuse University Press, 1987.

Tantawi, Muhammad al-Sayyid. *Tafsir surat Maryam.* Part 16 of *al-Tafsir al-wasit lil-
    Qur'an al karim.* Cairo: Matba'at al-sa'ada, 1985.

Taylor, Christopher S. "Sacred History and the Cult of Muslim Saints." In *The Muslim
    World,* vol. 80, no. 2, pp. 72–80, 1990.

Thackston, W. M., trans. *The Tales of the Prophets of al-Kisa'i.* Boston, Twayne Publish-
    ers, 1978.

Waldman, Marilyn Robinson. "New Approaches to 'Biblical' Materials in the Qur'an."
    The Muslim World, vol. 75, pp 1–16, 1985.

Warner, Marina. *Alone Of All Her Sex: The Myth and the Cult of the Virgin Mary.* New
    York: Random House, 1983.

Watt, W. Montgomery. *Muhammad at Medina.* Oxford: Oxford University Press, 1962.

————. Ed. (*Richard*) *Bell's Introduction to the Qur'an.* 2d ed. Edinburgh: University Press,
    1970.

Weil, Gustav. *Geschichte der Chalifen.* Vol. I. Mannheim: Bassermann, 1846.

Wensinck, A. J. *A Handbook of Early Muhammadan Tradition.* Leiden: Brill, 1927.

Wessels, Antonie. *A Modern Arabic Biography of Muhammad: A Critical Study of Muhammad
    Husayn Haykal's Hayat Muhammad.* Leiden: Brill, 1972.

al-Zamakhshari, Mahmud ibn 'Umar. *al-Kashshaf 'an haqa'iq ghawamid al-tanzil.* 4 vols.
    Ed. Mustafa Husayn Ahmad, Cairo: Matba'at al-istiqama, 1953.

Zwettler, Michael. "A Mantic Manifesto: The Sura of 'the Poets' and the Qur'anic
    Foundations of Prophetic Authority." In *Poetry and Prophesy: The Beginnings of a
    Literary Tradition.* Ed. James L. Kugel. Ithaca: Cornell University Press, 1990.

Glossary

ahl al-bayt the people of the house (the Prophet's family)

ahl al-kitab people of the Book, the adherents of a revealed religion

ahl al-'ilm professional theologians (in Islam)

asbab al-nuzul occasions for revelation

aya (pl. ayat) sign; Qur'anic verse

buhtan slander

da'wa call to Islam

dhawu mahram individuals in a degree of consanguinity precluding marriage

dhimma covenant of protection

dir' chemise

al-dunya this world (as opposed to the next); earthly things or concerns

fahm harfi literalist understanding

farida (pl. fara'id) religious duty

fatwa formal legal opinion

fiqh Islamic jurisprudence

fitna temptation; civil strife

fitra sound original nature

ghayra jealousy

hadd (pl. hudud) canon law cases with divinely defined punishments

hadith   Prophetic tradition, narrative relating deeds and utterances of the Prophet and his Companions

hajj   pilgrimage

hajiz   obstacle, barrier

halal   lawful, permissible

haqiqiyya adabiyya   literary truth

haqiqiyya 'aqliyya   rational truth

haraj   restraint, anguish

haram   forbidden, prohibited, unlawful

hiba   act by which a woman offers herself for marriage to a man without an intermediary (guardian) and without expecting a dower

hijra   the Prophet's migration from Mecca to Medina in 622 A.D.

hikma   wisdom

hijab   veil, partition, separation, screen

'awra   genitals, pudendum

'ibada   human worship of God, the service of the slave ('abd) to his master

'ibadat   religious observances

'idda   legally prescribed period of waiting during which a woman may not remarry after being widowed or divorced

'ifrit   demon

ifk   slander

ijtihad   independent interpretation of scripture; independent, scripture-based, judgment in a legal or theological question

i'jaz   the dogma of the Qur'an's Miraculous and Inimitable Nature

irba   natural force, cleverness

'isma   (prophetic) state of sinlessness, immunity from sin

isnad   record of authentication of a tradition

istishhad   supplementary attestation

i'tidad   full supportive force (of an argument)

izar   wrap

jahiliyya   period of paganism before the rise of Islam; superstitions, pagan customs that have crept into Islam since its foundation; spiritual ignorance

jihad fighting for a holy cause

al-jihad fi sabil Allah the struggle in the way of God

jilbab (pl. jalabib) mantle, cloak

kabira (pl. kaba'ir) mortal sin, major offense

kafan burial shroud

kahin soothsayer

khimar (pl. khumur) kerchief, veil

kunya honorific title

kufr unbelief

madhhab (pl. madhahib) orthodox rite (school) of Islamic jurisprudence (fiqh)

mahr dower, bridal money

mantiq 'aqli rational logic

mantiq nafsi psychological logic

masjid place of prayer, mosque

matn text

mihrab prayer niche

mu'adhdhin caller to prayer

mu'amalat human relations, conduct of people toward each other

muraja'a backtalk

munafiqun hypocrites

mut'a severance fee paid to a woman with whom marriage was concluded but not consumated

nabi prophet

nafs soul, life energy, nature, essence

naskh abrogation

niqab head veil

nushuz rebellion

qisas al-anbiya' tales of the prophets

qiwama guardianship

qass (pl. qussas) popular storyteller of religious lore

rak'a   specific movement(s) in ritual prayer

rasul   messenger, apostle; rasul Allah, the Messenger of God

al-rashidun   the rightly guided successors of the Prophet, the Orthodox Caliphs

rida'   cloak

ruh al-qudus   the holy spirit

sadaqa   freewill offering

sahih   sound, true, correct; a canonical tradition

al-salaf al-salih   the righteous forefathers

sanad   chain of authorities on which a tradition is based

satr   coveredness (by way of concealing garments)

sawm   fasting

saw'at   genitals

al-shari'a   the revealed, or canonical, law of Islam

sidq 'aqli   rational truth

sitr   curtain

su'   evil

sunbula   head of grain, ear of corn, wheat

sunna   custom, habitual practice, norm

al-sunna   (the Prophet's) sacred precedent, normative behavior; established as legally binding in Islamic law

tabarruj   public display; strutting about, swaggering, or displaying charms

tabut   ark

tafsir   exegesis, interpretation

tahara   purity

tawaf   circumambulation (of the Ka'ba)

ujur   dowers, remunerations, hires

umm (pl. ummahat)   mother

umm al-kitab   the source, original text of Scripture

umma   community, nation

'umra   lesser pilgrimage

wali   guardian

zakat   almsgiving, alms

zayy islami or shar'i   Islamic dress or apparel

zina   finery, adornment

Index

Surnames beginning with "al-" are alphabetized under the name that follows the al-.

DATE DUE

JAN 5 2002 APR 8 2002			
	DISCARDED		